D1328607

Changing Bodies in the Fiction of Octavia Butler

Changing Bodies in the Fiction of Octavia Butler

Slaves, Aliens, and Vampires

Gregory Jerome Hampton

LEXINGTON BOOKS
A division of
ROWMAN & LITTLEFIELD PUBLISHERS, INC.
Lanham • Boulder • New York • Toronto • Plymouth, UK

Published by Lexington Books
A wholly owned subsidiary of Rowman & Littlefield
4501 Forbes Boulevard, Suite 200, Lanham, Maryland 20706
www.rowman.com

10 Thornbury Road, Plymouth PL6 7PP, United Kingdom

Copyright © 2010 by Lexington Books
First paperback edition 2014

All rights reserved. No part of this book may be reproduced in any form or by any
electronic or mechanical means, including information storage and retrieval systems,
without written permission from the publisher, except by a reviewer who may quote
passages in a review.

British Library Cataloguing in Publication Information Available

Library of Congress Cataloging-in-Publication Data
The hardback edition of this book was previously cataloged by the Library of Congress as
follows:

Hampton, Gregory Jerome, 1968-
  Changing bodies in the fiction of Octavia Butler : slaves, aliens, and vampires /
Gregory Jerome Hampton
     p. cm.
  Includes bibliographical references and index.
  1. Butler, Octavia E.—Criticism and interpretation. I. Title.
  PS3552.U827Z69 2010
  813'.54—dc22
  2010026991

ISBN 978-0-7391-3787-1 (cloth : alk. paper)
ISBN 978-0-7391-9303-7 (pbk. : alk. paper)
ISBN 978-0-7391-3789-5 (electronic)

♾™ The paper used in this publication meets the minimum requirements of American
National Standard for Information Sciences—Permanence of Paper for Printed Library
Materials, ANSI/NISO Z39.48-1992.

Printed in the United States of America

For my family, Maria, Safi, and Hodari

/

Contents

Acknowledgments

I would like to thank Dr. Nahum Chandler for his support and encouragement during my years working on my doctorate degree. Without him, I would not have been brave enough to write this book. Thanks are also due to Drs. Doug Taylor, Dana Williams, and Greg Carr for their candid and insightful draft critiques and intellectual discussions. Dr. Wanda Brooks played an instrumental role in helping me get my manuscript in the right hands and for this I am eternally grateful. The students in my "Major Author" course at Howard University have been creatively influencing this project for the past seven years. Their heated discussions, never ending questions and raw passion for Butler's fiction has been inspirational.

My most heartfelt thanks are due to my wife Maria. Without her love and support I would not have possessed the time or sanity needed to produce this book.

Earlier versions of chapters 5 and 7 appeared in the *College Language Association Journal (CLAJ)* as *"Migration and Capital of the Body: Octavia Butler's* Parable of the Sower" http://cassell.founders.howard.edu:2109/citation.asp?tb=1&_ug=sid+AB6B7165%2D6208%2D4564%2DA153%2D2B319AA6D8E2%40sessionmgr6+dbs+aph+1A9E&_us=frn+1+hd+True+hs+True+cst+0%3B1%3B2+or+Date+ss+SO+sm+KS+sl+0+dstb+KS+mh+1+ri+KAAACB1C00056896+5022&_uso=hd+False+tg%5B0+%2D+st%5B0+%2Dhampton%2C++Gregory+db%5B0+%2Daph+op%5B0+%2D+mdb%5B0+%2Dimh+0513&fn=1&rn=1 *CLAJ* 49.1 (Sep2005): 56-73, and "Vampires and Utopia: Reading Racial and Gender Politics in the Fiction of Octavia Butler" *CLAJ* 52.1(Sep2008):74-91. I thank the editors of the *CLAJ* for permission to reprint this material.

Octavia Butler
and Science Fiction

The dominant thesis of this meditation is that the central fact of Octavia Butler's fiction is an ambiguous and elaborate configuration and reconfiguration of the body, human and otherwise. The body in Butler's fiction is indispensable in understanding how identity is formed and marshaled. To such a complicated negotiation, the question of just what constitutes a body, especially a human body, and its meanings is persuasively and profoundly raised, even if at times the terms and implications of such questioning remain enigmatic. This study is an inquiry into the shape and bearing of this problematic in early and contemporary texts spanning Butler's career.

One of the most fundamental insights that I have formulated in this interrogation of Butler's fiction has been that to acknowledge the problem of the body is to become conscious of the complexities surrounding the process of identifying the body, even if such an understanding might seem mundane. Throughout all of the complicated and fantastic narratives woven together by Butler's literary artistry the same question incessantly rises to the surface in her fiction, both novels and short-stories. How do we go about employing the differences that are constituted through our bodies? By assigning arbitrary symbols to ambiguous referents, society attempts to give order to the bodies that populate its existence. If understood simply as singular pronouns, race, sex, and gender are mystical processes of categorizing, but as a composite or somewhat unitary structure they help form the building blocks of the body's identity in society.[1] Butler's fiction presents unique ways to imagine and ultimately to understand the body and its plethora of identities. Her work allows the body to be thought outside of the traditional definitions of the term. In her fiction the body matters because it extends far beyond flesh and bone, the body becomes a boundless edifice for the articulation of difference.[2]

In *Changing Bodies in the Fiction of Octavia Butler: Slaves, Aliens, and Vampires*, I challenge the order and practicality of identifying the body by arbitrary signs and symbols. By examining Butler's societies and characters that are more historical and speculative than abstractly fictional or inventive, the notions of race, sex, and gender can be understood to have more potential for destruction, rather than for order in the play of social difference. The body as it is discussed in this meditation, is unbounded by time and space. It is a paradox that is talked about and imagined, but never clearly defined. This is made possible in part, by the genre in which Butler crafts her narratives.

To date, Butler is barely situated in the genre of Science Fiction (SF) by historical texts chronicling the genre. Despite the facts that she has won the appropriate awards (Hugo and Nebula)[3] and is widely anthologized, the scholarship engaging Butler's fiction has only recently begun to emerge in the form of academic journal essays and book chapters (see Haraway, Luckhurst, Melzer, Vint). Scholarship published in the 1980s and 90s on Butler's novels and short stories were too often cursory reviews or glances that overlooked the critical potential of the fiction. In my opinion, except for a few exceptions which I will engage in the chapters to follow, Butler's fiction has not been adequately situated or analyzed in the appropriate context. To be sure, interested scholars have been aware of her presence in the genre well before her death in February 2006. Oddly, those scholars have not saw fit to produce scholarship that focuses exclusively on the merits of Butler's fiction, until now. There are approximately sixty-six PhD dissertations and thirteen master theses written since 1993 that engage some aspect of Butler's fiction directly or at least mentions her writing in a significant manner in relation to other writers inside and outside of the SF genre. Again, despite this scholarly activity, there are sporadic and uneven readings given to Butler's work. Considering her contributions to the genre of SF and African American literature there is not yet a significant body of secondary literature that critically engages the value and content of Butler's fiction. It is my hope that this book will be one of the first to respond to Butler's fiction from a multifaceted perspective that does not exclude readers with esoteric jargon or essentialist genre hermeneutics. I would like to approach her fiction with a clarity and complexity that it deserves while maintaining the attention of thinkers inside and outside of the academy.

Butler's fiction is widely anthologized but is still treated as what Sheree Thomas refers to as "dark matter" or a "nonluminous form of matter which has not been observed but whose existence has been deduced by gravitational effect" (Introduction x). For those readers not invested in the genre of SF, Butler's fiction might never see the light of day. This is doubly tragic as the scope of Butler fiction transcends genre boundaries. Patricia Melzer asserts in *Alien Constructions* (2006), that "viewing Butler only in relation to SF limits the understanding of her work in terms of black women's imagination and cultural production" (37). One of Melzer's primary goals in her discussion of Butler's fiction is "to clarify feminist concepts by tracing them in thematic patterns in Butler's writing" (37). I would like to go a few steps beyond questions of feminism and gender to include questions of race, class, and power by presenting a broader and closer reading of Butler's fiction in terms of how identity is written upon the body.

Race matters a great deal in Butler's fiction and it is her employment of race that assists in setting her fiction on the borders of genre boundaries. In *Race Matters* (1994) Cornel West asserts that the common denominator of views about race imply the idea that black people are "problem people" (5). Sadly, West's DuBoisian reference holds true. According to Samuel Delany's article "Racism and Science Fiction," racism holds a significant presence in both the writing and culture of the science fiction genre (Thomas 383). Butler's fiction rejects the notion of a "problem people" and supports the idea that the problem is housed in the employment of the social construct of race as a variable of difference. "Butler's work refuses to clam one position based on a sexual, racial, and/or gender identity" (Melzer 42).[4] In *Playing in the Dark: Whiteness and Literary Imagination* (1992) Toni Morrison helps to explain Butler's state of dark matter in the genre of SF and the broader American literature.

> When matters of race are located and called attention to in American literature, critical response has tended to be on the order of humanistic nostrum— or a dismissal mandated by the label "political." Excising the political from the life of the mind is a sacrifice that has proven costly. I think of this erasure as a kind of trembling hypochondria always curing itself with unnecessary surgery. A criticism that needs to insist that literature is not only "universal" but also "race-free" risks lobotomizing that literature, and diminishes both the art and the artist. (12)

The point that I would like to emphasize here is not that race is everything in Butler's fiction but that race and other variables of difference have undoubtedly played a role in Butler's placement in the genre of SF. If Butler's fiction is to be read in the most rewarding fashion race can not to be placed in the margins of the reader's imagination. Butler's fiction is unique because it is openly racial, sexual, and ambiguous. "Her fiction reflects intersections of feminist theories, anti-colonial discourses, SF, and black women's writing, and correlate with what Mae Gwendolyn

Henderson[5] calls "simultaneity of discourses" (Melzer 38). Because of this simultaneity of discourse Butler's fiction is much easier to read than to analyze and to categorize.

SITUATING BUTLER INSIDE AND OUTSIDE

Writers like Butler function in a genre that is still being defined in part by their contributions. In Butler's case, she is transforming ideas surrounding bodies even as she has to assume or navigate an inherited ensemble of values and distinctions. It is this dynamic generic structure, in combination with her thematic attention to the question of the body that allows Butler to take up the subjects of the genesis and the possible apocalyptic decline of humanity in such a provocative fashion. The insights, juxtapositions, and revelations that are produced in Butler's fiction are due, in an important sense, to the flexibility of the genre of SF, especially to the willingness of the reader to consider what would be rejected as nonsensical in any other genre. The critic Brian Aldiss makes an insightful point about the quest of the SF genre and reader.

> The need to find a secret, an identity, a relationship, accompanied the questing traveler to other worlds or futures. Industrialization had assisted many sciences, including geology and astronomy. A new comprehension of the dynamism of the natural world (once regarded as a static stage of theological drama) was incorporated in Charles Darwin's theory of evolution, one of the great gloomy interventions of the nineteenth century which still colours our intellectual discourse . . . Here, it seemed, was the key to the most puzzling, most impressive question of identity of all—the identity of mankind (17).

Aldiss speaks to a point that I would like to echo throughout this meditation. SF is a literature very much invested in demystifying the identity of bodies. As industrialization created mechanical slaves the questions of humanity remained just as urgent as they were during Antebellum America. One of Butler's most significant interpretations of the genre has been to employ the future in a way that reminds her readers of historical questions of identity with narratives that may or may not be based on "historical fact" and reality, but are definitely valuable tools in seeing some aspects of reality in a clearer light. In other words, fantasy has always been viewed as an imaginative mirror reflecting pieces of reality. This fact does not evade the SF/fantasy works of Butler, despite the fact that her writing crosses so many blurred genre lines.

As a genre, SF is unique in its popular conception, but especially in its subject matter. With the appearance of the play *R.U.R* (Rossum's Universal Robots) in 1921 by Czech author and playwright, Karel Capek, SF was forever attached to the notion of servitude. Capek's *R.U.R.* told the story of a company that created synthetic men to be used as slaves. Eventually these synthetic men revolted and set out to destroy the humans who enslaved them (de Camp 19). Oddly enough Capek is credited for being the inventor of the word robot, or the mechanical male slave. It is Capek's contribution that almost invites the corollary placement of the African American body at the center of any discourse about robots or the extraterrestrial in general. This correlation is suggested by the status of slavery as a key American historical marker; a historical moment in which the African American body performs a pivotal role in the general social process. Since 1921 and Capek's contribution, SF has spoken directly to questions of the body through discourses of the master and the slave or the human and the "Other."[6] Thus, the genre of SF has been a primary site in which to examine the construction of otherness. Donna Haraway has continued the discussion of technology and marginalized bodies in ways that correlate what Capek and Butler might have been considering in their fiction. Where Capek speaks of a flesh and blood robot and Butler speaks of the American slave Haraway theorizes the cyborg (human/machine hybrid). Haraway's "A Cyborg Manifesto," "places questions of feminist cyborg subjectivity both in the context of Westernized concept of postmodernity and posthumanism dominated by technologies and institutions" (Melzer 26).

Much of the recent critical work on Butler has been inspired by connections Donna Haraway drew between feminist science fiction and feminist social theory in "A Cyborg Manifesto," and by her analysis of the Xenogenesis trilogy in the final chapter of her *Primate Visions.* (41)[7]

Traditional SF is largely grounded in the practice of creating unexplored territories or frontiers filled with "unfamiliar" and "unknown" bodies. Creatures from the deepest darkest corners of our imaginations have filled the pages of novels about the unknown and frightening. In turn, familiar and identifiably western heroes like Buck Rogers and Tarzan have been constructed to challenge and vanquish all who resist and all who are different. More modern versions of the same tradition (such as *Polymath* [Ace, 1963], *The Whole Man* [Ballantine, 1964], and *Long Result* [Faber and Faber, 1965], all by John Brunner; *Dangerous Visions* [Doubleday, 1967] by Harlan Ellison; and works by Felix Sultan) have made a space for writers such as Butler to revise, revitalize and re-imagine the past and the future of this genre. As Butler states in an interview with Joan Fry it was the craftsmanship and prolific nature of writers like Frank Herbert and John Brunner that supplied her with a fundamental understanding of the SF genre (Fry 58).

To escape the boredom of poverty Butler began writing at the age of ten years old. By the time she was twelve years old she became an avid reader of SF despite having been diagnosed with dyslexia. After seeing a SF film entitled *Devil Girl from Mars*, Butler decided to begin producing SF that did not avoid issues of race and gender. After studying at Pasadena City College, California State University, and UCLA, Butler participated in the Open Door Program of Screen Writers' Guild of America, West (1969–1970), and the Clarion Science Fiction Writers Workshop in 1970. Soon after her first short story "Crossover" was published in the Clarion's 1971 anthology, Butler began work on her first novel *Patternmaster* (1976).

Butler's emergence as a writer of SF, along with most other writers in the genre of SF/fantasy today, has followed paths first marked out in the work of three pioneers, John W. Campbell (1910–1971), Robert A. Heinlein (b. 1907) and Isaac Asimov (b. 1920). In the 1930s John Campbell was an engineering graduate student who had just about given up on his hopes of becoming a famous scientist. Writing SF literature took the place of experiments and graduate school as Campbell became the editor of *Analog* magazine, which was renamed *Astounding Stories* in 1937. Campbell took on the pseudonym "Don A. Stuart" and produced *Who Goes There* (1938), a story of a violent shape-shifter inhabiting the Antarctic, a persistent theme within SF.[8] Like the scientists who preceded her Butler has adroitly taken her experience as a black woman writer and woven it seamlessly together with influences of a dominantly white male SF tradition as well as a contemporary African American literary tradition to create something that is reflective of the past and the present.

In part three "Decade Studies" of his book *Science Fiction: Cultural History of Literature* Roger Luckhurst situates Butler's as a phenomenon of the 1980s. Luckhurst observes that during the 1980s

> a lot of writing about the increasing preponderance of virtual or cybernetic space has emphasized not only the interpenetration of human and machine, but also the potential decoupling of the self from the body. This can be seen as liberating, computer meditation allowing us "express multiple and often unexplored aspects of the self" unbound by physical limitations. (213)

Luckhurst's observation nicely includes several reoccurring themes in Butler's Patternist series which include the character Doro (a bodiless shape-shifting despot) from *Wildseed (1980)* and his progeny, discussed in *Mind of my Mind (1977)*. Ultimately, Lockhurst seems to believe that the body and "body horror" are essential when considering Butler's fiction during the period of the 1980s. Lockhurst acknowledges the importance of the body and hybridity in Butler's fiction and its influence on other strains of SF such as cyberpunk.

For a while, Octavia Butler became the exemplary feminist riposte to "masculinist" cyberpunk as well as the exemplary cyborg "woman of color" and postcolonial hybrid, having been claimed as Donna Haraway's "A Manifesto for Cyborgs." Yet Butler's concern with hybridity was never simply celebratory: it was bound up with violent history of African slavery and enforced miscegenation in America...Butler's bodies emerged from a more immediate context: the New Evolutionism of the 1980s. (217)

Despite the brevity of Luckhurst's mention of Butler's writing in his book, he does acknowledge a portion of her importance and contribution to the genre and names her work as "exemplary texts of the 1980s" (219). I will argue that Butler's work continues to present excellent examples of literature through the 1990s until Butler's death.

The History of Science Fiction[9] (2005) by Adam Roberts is another "historical" text that situates Butler primarily in the 1980s. However, unlike Luckhurst, Roberts does not attempt to locate Butler inside the genre per se. In fact Roberts unabashedly places Butler in a special margin called "non-genre writers." Butler does not fit inside of the genre of SF according to Roberts. Butler's "simultaneity of discourse" apparently disqualifies her work as traditional SF. It is unclear whether Roberts is complimenting Butler's works or short-changing it. Roberts notes that "the placement of a black woman at the core of this story (*Adulthood Rites*) inevitably brings us back to issues of racial difference, one of the topics to which Butler often returns in her fiction" (318). As race has not always been at the center of a great many SF narratives perhaps Roberts is attempting to suggest that Butler's fiction pulls what might be considered marginal in the genre of SF to the center.

According to Melzer, "Butler's work foregrounds the experiences of *female* characters and therefore can be understood as part of a feminist tradition in science fiction literature" (43). Sarah Lefanu places Butler squarely in the category of feminist science fiction writer. Lefanu honors Butler by situating her alongside feminist greats such as Joanna Russ, Margaret Atwood and Ursula Le Guin. Lefanu's *In the Chinks of the World Machine: Feminism & Science Fiction* (1988) is invested in discussing the "plasticity of science fiction" (9) and its ability to act as a genre unbounded for contemporary women writers. As such, Butler is only mentioned in passing and is described as a writer who employs "a traditional science fiction narrative framework" (88). Lefanu's text does not claim to be concerned with singular writers, however, Butler's sparse mention in such an important feminist text does give me inspiration to speak of Butler's very noteworthy feminist/womanist contributions.[10]

I was introduced to Butler's fiction as African American literature first and as SF much later. I began with *Kindred*; then to *Wildseed* and it was not until I began reading *Dawn* did I consider the genre of SF as a primary home for Butler's writing. This is all to say that I am perfectly comfortable locating Butler outside of the SF genre. However, because of the audience that I hope to reach with this book, excluding such a significant aspect of Butler's art would be neither fair nor wise. Butler's work foregrounds the experiences of *African Americans, females,* and the *generally marginalized body* and therefore can be understood as part of multiple literary traditions at once. Sandra Govan has often said that,

> Butler's growing body of work showed distinct ties to the African American literary canon, while maintaining and building upon its grounding in science fiction or fantasy, in speculative fiction. (14)

Timothy Spaulding's book *Re-Forming the Past (2005)* posits Butler's *Kindred* as a postmodern revisionary slave narrative.[11] Both Govan and Spaulding are specialists in the field of African American literature who would agree that Butler's work is born of and continues to respond to the African American literary tradition. It is my desire in this book to engage Butler's fiction in a fashion that locates it firmly in several traditions/genres so that it might receive readings which yield its greatest value.

CONTINUITIES IN SCIENCE FICTION

The decay and renaissance of empires on a national and global scale; secret societies that attempt to influence the course of history by manipulating biology and psychology; the opposition of free will and determinism; the interrelations of knowledge and action; and the confluence of powerful forces at particular points over the course of history are motifs common in the works of Asimov, Heinlein, and Butler. The most valuable connection among the three writers that I would like to emphasize at this juncture is their use of SF as a speculative literature. Don Riggs' essay "Future and 'Progress' in *Foundation* and *Dune*" illustrates several salient points of comparison:

> Narratives that take place in the future can be prophetic in intent and can use futuristic technologies to construct a contemporary plot with exotic elements, or can treat the future as a metaphor for the present by combining the two former alternatives to demonstrate the probable future that a continuation of current trends would create (116).

Asimov's, Heinlein's, and Butler's futures are of this last variety. Each author places humans in a future where they must find a way beyond weaknesses that would otherwise negate any hope for their survival. Greed, egomania, shortsightedness, sexism, racism, and xenophobia all plague humanity in the future(s). All envision the emergence of small, elite groups that develop methods of overcoming some of the evils that technological and biological advances by humanity have created. All three writers construct groups that assume the responsibility of guiding humanity towards versions of a better world:

> Asimov seems to indicate that this highest goal is in accord with the goals of the *Illuminati* or the *Philosophes* of the eighteenth century, who wished to see the actions of humanity synchronized with indices of an as yet imperfectly understood but benevolent reason . . . (116).

For Butler the highest goal for humanity is survival by any means necessary, but mainly by accepting difference and acknowledging the inevitability and omnipotence of change. The synchronization of humanity is not worthy of pursuit in Butler's narratives, primarily because "sameness" is not in Butler's definition of "better world." As her narratives seem to suggest, "sameness" or conformity does not ensure the survival of a species in a hostile environment. In fact the ability to change and adapt to nonconformity is often essential if a character wishes to survive any of Butler's narratives. Notwithstanding this latter fact, her work constructs communities dependent upon individuals and individuals dependent upon communities. Fredric Jameson speaks to the practicality of Butler's rejection of one type of utopianism and the embrace of another in *Archaeologies of the Future: The Desire Called Utopia and Other Science Fictions*, when he says,

> It has often been observed that we need to distinguish between the Utopian form and the Utopian wish: between the written text or genre and something like Utopian impulse detectable in daily life and its practices by a specialized hermeneutic or interpretative method. (1)

Butler's fiction consistently makes the distinction between what is possible and what is both impossible and impractical with regards to the bodies that her characters possess.

The elements of totalitarianism found in Butler's Patternist series, especially in *Patternmaster* (1976) and *Wildseed* (1980), are portrayed as restrictive and violent. The children of Doro claim to advocate peace and order for humans and Patternists yet systems of slavery and familial murder permeate their communities. In short, Butler's narratives render a view of social philosophies that are based on hierarchy and privilege. Asimov's *Foundation* embodies a very similar commentary on communal oriented philosophies through Dr. Hari Seldon, the psychohistorian, and his quest to prepare humanity for a cosmological "fall" that cannot be avoided, but can be shortened in its duration. Dr. Seldon predicts the future by examining the past and present and then mathematically calculating the probabilities of future occurrences. Asimov refers to this process as psycho-history, however it can also be viewed as an amalgamation of the past and present.

Notwithstanding the reference points and commonalties among Butler and older writers, the discussion of the body draws a distinct line between Butler's work and traditional SF written by white males. To introduce a protagonist who is black, female and bisexual (or at least not heterosexual) in canonical SF written for "weird youth interested in science and technology," (Harrison 34) would pose the threat of distracting the reader from the main plot; a plot that caters to a predominantly heterosexual adolescent white male audience. In an interview with Rosalie G. Harrison, Butler says that in the standard SF novel the "universe is either green or all white." In such literature the "extraterrestrial being" or "alien" is used as metaphor and literal embodiment of the other. Butler, on the other hand locates highly visual (race, sex, or species) and non-visual (gender and sexuality) identities at the center of her text and forces the reader to grapple with the notion of otherness as more than metaphor of allusion.

Although it is not my intention to discuss Butler's writing from a purely SF perspective, I do find it extremely useful to recognize her in a context that has both tradition and an understood definition in place. In an interview with Veronica Mixon, Butler speaks of the influence that white male writers as well as women writers such as Ursula K. Le Guin have had on her writing career. I think this point is pertinent to both the success and complexity of Butler's literature, not to mention her concern with increasing the number of African American readers of her texts and of SF as a genre. Butler employs both the architecture and themes from the genre of SF to discuss notions of identity that are of specific concern to women of color and other marginalized people. She employs the traditional tools that SF uses to influence young white adolescent males to (re)vision feminine slave narratives and possibly rethink the construction and locations of "Others" in literature and society.

In Marleen Barr's critical anthology, *Future Females* (1981), Eric Rabkin acknowledges the poor treatment of female characters and their bodies in the genre of science fiction. He suggests that "there is no denying that women characters have been exploited as sex objects by SF publishers and cover illustrators who seem to hold to the tantalizing credo that half a garment is better than none" (9). What Rabkin fails to mention in his article "Science Fiction Women Before Liberation" is that not only are the images of women poorly constructed in classic SF such as Robert Heinlein's *Puppet Masters* (1951) and H.G. Wells' *A Modern Utopia* (1905), but that the writing of women authors, until recently have been excluded from the SF canon. Rabkin goes on to point out the fact that despite the oversight of

SF, it has attempted to imagine women in alternative roles that have been bolder than any other literature.

The engagement of feminist notions is not at all unique to the works of Butler or the genre of SF. Joanna Russ, for example, was notorious for producing fiction that presented powerful heroines in a genre that often over looked the role of women. Her Nebula Award winning short story "When It Changed" (1972) and her novel *The Female Man* (1975), presented worlds where men were either extinct or obsolete and women fill all social roles. "It was to be expected that she [Russ] offended a great many of her male colleagues. She was called bitchy, strident, and propagandist" (Aldiss 363). Such harsh criticism also undoubtedly fell upon Ursula Le Guin as a result of her novel *Left Hand of Darkness* (1969). In Le Guin's ambisexual world of winter she attempted to write a race without gender, but only succeeded in creating a political battle field filled with female men. Where Russ and Le Guin speak of only gender, Butler speaks of gender and race as inextricable from each other, far more complicated than the racially homogeneous societies found in the works of her feminist predecessors.

In the *Left Hand of Darkness*, a world free of gender does not mean the end of all problems. War, slavery, and other blatant forms of oppression with which we are familiar might be absent, but Le Guin's assertion that rigid gender divisions are directly related to our largest social problems is a profound declaration that may be incomplete. What is lacking in Le Guin's line of questioning is how other identities complicate problems of the body in addition to gender. I contend that the fiction of Butler takes on such complicated questions and offers alternatives of survival in settings which are far from utopian or homogeneous. Butler helps further the alternative roles of women and their bodies in her narratives by refuting the normative construction of the body in general. For example, where some thinkers such as Michel Foucault would argue that the construction of the body is dependent upon markers like sex, where sex is a regulatory practice that produces the body it governs (Judith Butler 1), Octavia Butler's narratives imply that markers like sex can be non-defining and unnecessary coincidences with regards to the construction of a body. That is to say that the performance of sex or sexuality often has more meaning than an arbitrary marker connoting something little more than a physical difference. Butler does not fall victim to the temptation to identify the body as something purely physical or material. Cultural discourses in conjunction with the social and the personal play a large role in the construction of bodies in Butler's narratives. This type of approach to the body begins to disrupt many notions of binary intellectual thought because it places an emphasis on the fact that the body is and always has been constructed in multiple and contradictory ways.

Butler's work has been anthologized in several anthologies by SF writers as a writer who contributes to the eclectic nature of the genre. Isaac Asimov has praised Butler's writing highly in many of his books and articles criticizing the genre of SF and its contributors. Another African American writer established in the genre before Butler, Samuel Delany, has also been influenced by her work, if only indirectly. Delany's use of the "soft" sciences—biology, psychology, anthropology, and linguistic theory as opposed to the "hard" sciences—physics, astronomy, thermodynamics and computers—of the more traditional writers resembles, if not speaks, to the similar employment found in Butler's writing which did not come about until almost a decade after Delany's popularity in the genre. Delany's departure from formulaic space operas such as *The Ballad of Beta-2* (1965), *Babel-17* (1967), and *Nova* (1969) also seems to suggest that Butler's success with issues of race, gender and feminism, encouraged Delany to further engage issues of race, sexuality and queer theory as in his more recent *Return to Neveryon* series published from in 1979 to 1987. With notions of deconstruction and psychoanalysis at the center of Delany's novels and literary criticism, his work is definitely on a different linguistic plain than that of Butler's. However, one of the points that I will suggest in this meditation is that the theoretical gap between the two writers is beginning to close. The work of theoreticians such as Derrida[12] and Lacan[13] can be viewed as oblique augments of Butler's fiction.

A THEORETICAL FRAME FOR THE BODY

The theoretical framework for this book will not follow a single path. Just as Butler's fiction responds to several discourses at once, the hermeneutics involved in interpreting her fiction must also be varied. The feminist theory already mentioned by Lefanu and Melzer will be applied along with African American criticism and theory by Hazel Carby, Barbara Christian, and Angelyn Mitchell will also be employed throughout this text. Much of the theory addressing the discourse surrounding the body and the self will evolve from references to Foucault and Lacan. Sherryl Vint's *Bodies of Tomorrow* has been particularly useful in helping to frame the discussion of the body via the notion of "biopower."

In *Discipline and Punishment* and *The History of Sexuality*, volume 1, Foucault outlines his theory of biopower regarding the ways in which social control of the body can be used to produce a specific type of subjectivity within that body. What we learn from Foucault is that the body is integrally linked to the discourses that make it intelligible. Biopower, with its classifications of normal and abnormal, valid or invalid, produces bodies that fall outside of this field and hence cannot be seen. The radical insight of biopower and Foucault's notion of the disciplinary culture that deploys it is that we willingly participate in our own subjugation; we must in order to become subjects at all. (18)

Vint goes on to note that Judith Butler expands upon these ideas to arrive at her method of defining bodies that exist outside of normative discourses as beyond the material. A reoccurring theme that I will undertake throughout this book is how Butler consistently writes bodies beyond the normative/Western discourses with the result of encouraging readers of her fiction to rethink the body and the self.

Butler's fiction presents methods of imagining the body that allow us to understand how and why the body must be categorized. From this window readers of her work are better able to explore the meaning of various identities such as race, sex, and gender. These terms are seen for what they are, arbitrary markers designed to give stability to that which is unstable and ambiguous. SF is the window Butler uses to open the imagination of readers about the problematic of the body by painting the not-so-fantastic as the realistic.

Changing Bodies in the Fiction of Octavia Butler: Slaves, Aliens, and Vampires is an examination of the contradictory ways the body is legible in the fiction. The specific focus of this study is the question of figuration of the body in Butler's writing. The central argument of this study is that Butler's writing formulates and proposes an original figuration of the body that broadens the scope of how the body has been viewed traditionally. This is significant because Butler's construction of non-traditional bodies suggests that social values and practices are directly influenced by a society's understanding of the body. Butler's writing poses difficulties for the way we typically identify bodies. This difficulty arises because Butler's writing brings the structures we use to identify bodies as different and alike into critical awareness. Race, gender, and sex are posited in her narratives as functions of difference and likeness which demonstrate both the flaws and strengths in human behavior and methods of identification. Such a figuration amounts to a reconfiguration or reformation of the dominant conceptions of the body in contemporary thought. While the rationale behind the organization of this book may not be completely lucid to some, I would attempt to clarify my intentions by emphasizing the title of the book, *Changing Bodies in the Fiction of Octavia Butler: Slaves, Aliens, and Vampires*. Slaves, aliens, and vampires are the metaphors that Butler's fiction has used to highlight the construction and valuing of the marginalized body. The title reflects the chronology of my introduction to Butler's fiction and my topics of concern throughout the book.

In *Bodies of Tomorrow: Technology, Subjectivity, Science Fiction* (2007 by Sherryl Vint) she notes that,

> Butler's trilogy suggests that the body and its genetic code are part of subject, not just a base material house, but that an understanding of the body alone is not sufficient to understand human consciousness. The body, in Butler's work, is a cultural as well as natural product. (77)

Vint's observation applies to Butler's Xenogensis series (trilogy) as well as her Patternist series. The "self" and the "other" are notions that transcend simplistic discussions of material body and breaches discourses of cultural and spiritual histories.

In studying the problem of the body in Butler's narratives the most difficult and provocative questions are dependent on the boundaries of the body, i.e. its definitions and limitations. The body as a historical narrative is the focal point of the first chapter of this examination. In chapter one the body is considered as a text that can be reinvented through time and space and as a blank slate waiting to be inscribed with signs and symbols. *Kindred* is discussed as a postmodern text which anchors Butler's writing firmly in African American literary traditions while its SF elements necessitate a deconstruction of the notions of the African American body and American history.

As the bodies in Butler's fiction are often inscribed with narratives that complicate the identity of a particular body, chapter two addresses the terms and general discourse surrounding the notion of "bodily inscription." This chapter is invested in considering the weight of inscription upon a body and the ways the body is imaged because of inscribed identities. The *Wildseed* narrative and the characters of Doro and Anyanwu are central in understanding the formulation and employment of identities and performances of race, class, and gender. The two characters are shape-shifters who consciously change the narratives written upon their bodies and by doing so bring into question the value and stability of bodily inscriptions.

Butler's fist novel *Patternmaster* is the centerpiece of chapter three as it begins to outline the hierarchies of identity that are constructed in the Pattermaster series. In this chapter I consider distinctions between race and ethnicity and the role they both play in defining the body in a particular social structure. The Patternist race is written by Butler as an involuntary configuration of hierarchy that is both conceived and maintained in order to identify bodies that are hyper-marginalized. In the case of the *Patternist* series it is the hyper-marginalized race that is dominant and at the top of the social latter. As Butler's speculative narratives are varying according to historical time frame and social organization, race becomes a technology of identity.

Each chapter of this book is focused on the writing of the body in Butler's fiction. To this end, chapter four takes on the task of considering the ambiguity surrounding the African American body as it relates to the discourse of racial and gender ambiguity. Butler's Xenogenesis series is discussed as a location designed to re-figure the borders of identity and survival. W.E.B. Du Bois and Wole Soyinka are used as sources of racial and cultural theory that help explain how Butler's characters are able to employ elements of racial and gender ambiguity as survival mechanisms.

Another survival mechanism often located in Butler's fiction is religion or spiritual references. In chapter five I examine the ways Butler writes the body with religious markers in order to validate the struggle of her characters. Butler's consistent employment of black bodies and spiritual references in her *Parable of the Sower* and *Bloodchild and Other Stories*, appeals to an audience who identify with archetypes on the borders of the secular and the religious. In this chapter I examine the relationship between religion and SF and suggest that the two might be genres of folklore invested in policing the boundaries of the body.

Chapter six revisits the notion of hybridity mentioned in the fourth chapter. This chapter attempts to provide a more focused look at how Butler's writing is inextricable from the discourse of the hybrid. I use the novels *Parable of the Sower* and *Mind of My Mind* to demonstrate how the migration of marginalized bodies are valued by their ability to adapt or morph. The dominant argument in this chapter suggests that it is a body's hybridity that allows it to become valuable as a liberated subject as opposed to a subjugated object or mere capital in Butler's fiction. A primary goal of this chapter is to situate Butler's fiction in a discourse invested in the transformative possibilities of the body within literature.

Chapter seven focuses on the politics of the body and Butler's investment in the discourse of the political. By examining racial and gender politics in conjunction with the political value of dystopian elements present in Butler's *Parable* series, and her last novel, *Fledgling*, I attempt to begin quantifying the change that is evoked by complicated black female bodies. Vint makes an important comment about how the genre of SF can assist in addressing issues of sexual, racial, and cultural politics in Butler's fiction when she states that "SF is part of the field of ideology and such can work not only to comment on cultural politics of current moment but also intervene in and change this moment" (Vint 20). The richness of Butler's fiction is demonstrated by her texts' willingness to engage issues of global warming, economic and social disenfranchisement, or good old fashioned American racism.

The conclusions that are reached in this examination suggest that the configuration of the body is constantly varying and is dependent largely on circumstance and necessity. Furthermore, bodily inscriptions that have traditionally been used to distinguish bodies, such as biological differences, are in fact arbitrary differences that often transcend biology and reason. This texts accepts as a point of departure that the genre of SF, especially the fiction of Butler, is an ideal location for rethinking the process by which the body is constructed and identified. It is my intent to demonstrate that by reaching a better understanding of how the body is identified through narratives like Butler's, we can further our understanding of the power relations and identities attached to bodies that are seen as *other* or *different*.

The appendix includes two never before published interviews with Octavia Butler, and three of her African American colleagues, Nalo Hopkinson, Tananarive Due, and Steven Barnes. The first interview is a phone conversation that reveals some of Butler's thoughts on current events and a short story to be added to the new edition of *Bloodchild and Other Stories* (2005). The second interview takes the form of a panel discussion at the "New Frontier: Blacks in Science Fiction Conference" at Howard University in the Spring of 2003. My intentions with these two interviews are to reveal a side of Butler that may or may not have been revealed since her death and to provide evidence of how influential Butler was in the careers and lives of her colleagues and the shaping of the speculative fiction genre.[14]

NOTES

1. This process might be likened to the construction of a language (perhaps a language of the body, not to be mistaken with body language) as discussed in the *Course in General Linguistics* by the father of semiotics Ferdinand de Saussure.

2. I am suggesting that the body in Butler's fiction might be considered as a medium for a language; a vessel with the purpose of propagating information such as aesthetic and cultural values.

3. Butler has been awarded the Hugo in 1984 for Best Short Story "Speech Sounds" and 1984 for Best Novelette "Bloodchild." In 1984 Butler received the Nebula Award for Best Novelette "Bloodchild" and in 1999 for *Best Novel Parable of the Sower.*

4. Melzer makes this observation based on a quote taken from Jeffrey Allen Tucker's book on Samuel Delany entitled *A Sense of Wonder: Samuel R. Delany, Race, Identity, and Difference,* Wesleyan University Press, 2004.

5. Mae Gwendolyn Henderson's article "Speaking in Tongues: Dialogics, Dialectics, and the Black Woman Writer's Literary Tradition," can be found in *Feminist Theorize the Political.* Eds. Judith Butler and Joan W. Scott. New York: Routledge, 1992. 144–66.

6. Although Mary Shelley's *Frankenstein* (1818) precedes *R.U.R.*, Capek's dramatic situations more closely resemble the American Slave experience.

7. *Primative Visions: Gender, Race, and Nature in the World of Modern Science.* New York: Routledge, 1989, presents an excellent example of how Butler's fiction crosses genres and fields of study. Haraway is a Yale trained Biology professor. It is no surprise that a scientist would be interested in science fiction but Haraway's mention of Butler in the context of zoology is note worthy and as Melzer states, was inspirational.

8. Butler's Patternmaster series speaks of a rogue shape-shifter (Doro) of its own.

9. Despite his cursory mention of Butler's fiction Adam Roberts's *The History of Science Fiction* will be revisited in my chapter "Spiritual Sci-Fi." Roberts argument that the re-emergence of SF is correlative to the Protestant Reformation will be pertinent to several points made in that chapter.

10. I would like to suggest that Butler's fiction is "womanist" literature; writing that responds to the concerns of black feminists but also any person or group interested in seeking the end of oppression generally (racial, gender, sexual, etc.). I borrow my definition of "womanist" from Alice Walker but also from *The Black Woman Anthology* (1971) edited by Toni Cade Bambara.

11. Chapter one is partly an attempt to demonstrate how Butler's fiction responds to an African-American slave narrative tradition as well as time travel and quest narratives found in the genre of SF.

12. Where Derrida has been accused of questioning the rules of the dominant discourse through deconstruction, I feel Butler's works consistently questions the "rules" and values of dominant society with regard to placing value on the body. Butler's fiction demonstrates how a structure (body or identity) can only be understood by understanding its genesis. At the same time like Derrida, Butler's fiction suggests that for progress or forward movement to occur origin cannot be pure or simplistic, ambiguity and complexity is a requirement if any structure is to be understood.

13. Lacan's article "Mirror Stage" might be alluded to on several occasions in Butler's fiction. The idea of developing body image and a sense of self speak directly to two of Butler's characters, Doro and Lilith. The Patterist character Doro is very child-like from his introduction in *Wildseed* until his demise in *Mind of My Mind*. Despite this he has developed an Ego that can be identified by himself and all of his people despite the myriad of different bodies that he wears. Furthermore, the character Lilith is literally taken through the mirror stage that a child might go through during her awakening by the Oankali in *Dawn*. Lilith's narrative is largely a quest to define the boundaries that exist between Lacan's Other and self.

14. Further insight into Butler's character might be gained from Conseula Francis's book *Conversations with Octavia Butler (Literary Conversations Series),* University Press of Mississippi, 2009. This collection of interviews with Butler range from 1980–2006.

1

✛

Kindred: History, Revision, and (Re)memory of Bodies

The novel *Kindred* (1979) is easily one of Octavia Butler's most popular books. Its popularity is undoubtedly based on the fact that it lends itself to a very broad audience, as it blurs the boundaries of several genres (autobiography, slave narrative, science fiction/fantasy, contemporary African American fiction, etc.) within its first two chapters. Despite the novel's ability to blur genre borders, as far as the academy has been concerned, Butler is a Science Fiction (SF) writer. And because of this dubious fact, Butler's fiction has not been explored as critically as the works of other Black women writers of equal caliber until very recently. *Kindred* is both an important and accessible text because it is based on well researched historical fact and good story telling. What has been too often missed in readings of Butler's novels is that it crosses the slave narrative tradition with H.G. Well's time machine scenario not only to rewrite history (as has been stated by more than a few academic scholars), but to rewrite the body of the African American. *Kindred* is a "postmodern slave narrative that is invested in drawing parallels between two distinct time periods while interrogating how each time period informs the other in a mutual commentary" about marginalized bodies (Spaulding 27). The writing of bodies in Butler's text is largely dependent upon a narrative history and the memories that constitute the past and present. In other words, Butler's narrative allows us to imagine how the past can exist in the present and how the present can be manifested into the past by way of time travel. The novel *Kindred* tells of a twentieth century black woman who must (re)live certain aspects of the lives of her ancestors in order to insure her present existence. In this novel, slavery determines the value

1

of black and white bodies in nineteenth century antebellum America and continues to influence their value in the twentieth century.

The historical fact around which *Kindred* revolves is the American institution of slavery and its practice of treating African, black bodies, as chattel. To read of such a peculiar institution in a history book is far from experiencing its horrific reality. Even to remember slavery first-hand as a participant cannot compare to reliving the actual experience. Fortunately, the boundaries of time temporally separate our present world from that of the past. In *Kindred*, however, Butler disrupts such laws of time and physics. By taking Dana back to antebellum Maryland, the past and the present are bridged and the boundaries of physics and history are blurred. *Kindred* distorts the historical timeline of Edana (Dana) Franklin's past and present so that it is nonlinear. In Serryl Vint's "Only by Experience," she asserts that "*Kindred* is a key example of neo-slave narrative, an African American genre that investigates the history of slavery and reworks the nineteenth century slave narrative tradition" (241).

In the novel, this disruption happens in order that we and a protagonist, Dana, might do the impossible and seemingly undesirable: travel to a time in American history where black bodies were not recognized in law or general custom as possessed of value other than goods to be bought and sold. In Butler's "time machine" history is transformed, by way of the reader's imagination, into a present reality on numerous occasions so that we might see, through Dana's eyes, exactly how humans were magically turned into beasts. Such an experience exceeds memory obtained or produced in the reading of history books or second-hand slave narratives. Second-hand because the ex-slaves themselves have written their stories from memory formulated after their bondage. Thus, even the slave narrative would ostensibly be a second-hand experience or memory in addition to the description that ensues from it. Dana's mode of re-experiencing would, in the phenomenological sense, be even more radical than such a narrative because she is made to live an experience that happened before she existed.

By positioning Dana's story in this manner, Butler reformulates the laws of the written narrative. The narrative of *Kindred* is elevated to more than a tale told to an audience by a narrator. It becomes an experience which is shared by Dana and the reader. The reader, like Dana, becomes a passenger gaining access to a passage through time, beyond the formation of Dana's family history. Furthermore, according to Timothy Spaulding's *Re-Forming the Past* (2005), the novel *Kindred* "emphasizes the ideological foundations of American slavery that persist through time and cannot be isolated in one historical moment. Spaulding believes that such complex orientation toward time distinguishes postmodern slave narratives from traditional historical fiction" (27). In his article "Inventing History in Octavia Butler's Postmodern Slave Narrative," Marc Steinberg makes a similar point when he notes that

> Unlike other contemporary revisions of traditional slave narrative—most famously, Charles Johnson's *Middle Passage*, Sherley Anne Williams's *Dessa Rose*, and Toni Morrison's *Beloved*—Butler's narrative takes place in the relative present (though the neo-slave novel by convention imposes the past onto the present). The novel liberally borrows from very modern and post modern ideas concerning time continuity (Steinberg 467).

In this discussion I will take up the insights of both Spaulding and Steinberg along with other scholars who view Butler's work as both postmodern and reversionary with the aim to show how Butler's *Kindred* is unparalleled in its ability to deconstruct both "body" and "history" through its use of the genre of SF. Through the close textual analysis of content and form of the traditional masculine and feminine slave narrative, I discuss continuities and discontinuities with Butler's text to locate *Kindred* in the African American literary tradition. After establishing the conversation of the postmodern text with the traditional text the SF elements of *Kindred* are interrogated in order to see how Butler's fiction does what traditional and other postmodern texts are unable to achieve with regards to writing the body. My intent in this discussion is to suggest that Butler's employment of the SF genre in conjunction with postmodern literary traditions is an excellent laboratory for deconstructing African American identity and experience.

HISTORY OF A SLAVE NARRATIVE

The fact that written history is not necessarily equivalent to universal truth is far from controversial. Historians are constantly revising textbooks that were thought to be accurate for decades. The personal experience of one can seemingly become "the way it was" for many depending on countless variants. Steinberg reminds us that

> Butler points to ways in which past and present become interchangeable. She also writes of plausible historical actions and relationships, "filling in" possible gaps that may be evident in classic slave narratives. Butler assumes a non-Western conceptualization of history—one in which history is cyclical, not linear—in order to demonstrate ways in which certain forms of race and gender oppression continue late into the twentieth century and beyond. She incorporates postmodern fiction literary techniques to critique the notion that historical and psychological slavery can be overcome. (467)

Ultimately, the person or people with the resources to write and publish historical texts are the caretakers, or griots, of recorded memories. According to August Meier's *Negro Thought in America 1880–1915*, if we consider the attributes of the oral tradition, unwritten memories are often the location of the most accurate account of individual histories. It is what Dana does not remember about her past (and America's past) that fuels her adventure. Thus, it is Dana's unrecorded or unremembered memories that set in motion the making of her history and the construction of her body.

Despite that fact that *Kindred* takes place largely within the context of American slavery it is impossible to read the novel as merely a cousin or distant relative of the traditional slave narrative. The novel *Kindred* embraces and transcends many if not all of the slave narrative elements. Angelyn Mitchell writes:

> Butler certainly signifies on the nineteenth century female emancipatory narrative, especially Harriet Jacobs's *Incidents in the Life of a Slave Girl*. Examining the generic affinities between Butler's narrative and the emancipatory narratives, Sandra Y. Govan observes, "*Kindred* is so closely related to the experience disclosed in the slave narratives that its plot structure follows the classic patterns with only the requisite changes to flesh out character, story and action" [Homage to Tradition 89] (Mitchell 43).

Mitchell goes on to assert that Butler does much more that simply signify on the content and form of the slave narrative. According to Mitchell, Butler engages and revises the dominant themes of the nineteenth century slave Narrative. With the exception of Mitchell's treatment of *Kindred* as primarily a revised slave narrative, much of the scholarship that engages Butler's novel falls short of acknowledging its true complexity and ambiguity with regards to substance and structure.

The tradition of the slave narrative is one concerned to the identity of the Black person as human, intelligent, and deserving of freedom. The *Narrative of Frederick Douglass* (1845) begins with the words "I was born." By stating this obvious fact, the ex-slave/narrator writes him or herself into humanity. The ex-slave also moves a step closer to establishing the grounds of communication with sympathetic whites, especially abolitionists. Dana's experience on the other hand is one much less concerned with the notion of sympathy than the slave narrative. It is largely invested in the process of reliving the experience of slavery and better understanding the institution of slavery. It is through Dana's lived experience of slavery in the past that she can better understand the legacy of the institution of slavery in the present.

Other thematic moments in slave narratives, Douglass's, for example, such as the description of the physical brutality of slavery; the acquiring of literacy; the plot to escape; and the experience of freedom, all acted as the foundation of a literary recipe for the telling of the personal history / histories of the ex-slave. Subsequent writers similarly interested in exposing the injustice of slavery and reaffirming the humanity of the African American took up Douglass's recipe. In David Blight's introduction to the *Narrative of the Life of Frederick Douglass*, he attests to how Douglass's narrative fits many of the nineteenth century literary traditions such as the sentimental novel, the picaresque and captivity narratives. Blight is also careful to acknowledge Douglass's writing as historically influential to the American literary traditions that followed his own artful and self-conscious style of writing. Unfortunately, the narratives produced from this romantic rubric often constructed poor images of women and their varying experiences in slavery.

Characters such as Harriet Jacobs' Linda Brent, Frances Harper's Iola LeRoy, and Pauline Hopkins' Sappho serve as the best examples for the point I am making here. These three characters are so pious and chaste that they seem unreal and unbelievable in that they are absent of the flaws that would make them seem like flesh and bone women. In *The Changing Same: Black Women's Literature, Criticism, and Theory*, Deborah McDowell argues that such characters are "all trapped in an ideological schema that predetermined their characters," (McDowell 98). In other words, the narratives' attempt to avoid racial and gender stereotypes constructed during antebellum America often times got in the way of realistic portrayals of black women.

Hazel Carby's *Reconstructing Womanhood* (1987) is a feminist revision of the historical narrative of African American women writers. It contrasts the image of slave women as mere victims in narratives written by men to images of women as fully developed heroines, which are found in narratives written by women. Carby discusses the literary history of the emergence of Black women as novelists and suggests the forms in which Black women intellectuals made political as well as literary interventions in the social systems in which they lived.

The feminine slave narrative from the nineteenth century to the present continues to vary with regards to its formula and structure. This variation is largely due to nineteenth century moral ethics, which often prevented black women writers from creating "whole" heroines in character and experience. Such strict and constraining techniques were used by women of the era that Carby has described as "The Black Women's Renaissance" (1890–1930s) to create the model black woman character. Morally perfect and asexual characters like Iola in *Iola Leroy* (1892) by Frances E. W. Harper, Linda in *Incidents in the Life of a Slave Girl* (1861) by Harriet Jacobs, and Sappho from Pauline Hopkins's *Contending Forces* (1900) were limited in their character development.

These women were designed to be "race women," to uplift and re-define what it meant to be a black woman in America. These women characters were placed in opposition to the negative stereotypes that had been created during the antebellum and the Reconstruction eras. As such, they were present as always in a state of perfection. Unfortunately, these extremes excluded the articulation of the humanity and imperfections of each heroine's character. The Black Women's Renaissance constructed saints instead of black women:

> Iola Leroy, Harper's major character, does not attempt to understand either herself as an individual or black women as a group. Rather, Iola Leroy is a version of the "lady" Americans were expected to respect and honor, even though she is black. By creating a respectable ideal heroine, according to the norms of the time, Harper was addressing not herself, black women, or black people, but her (white) countrymen (Christian 334).

Thus, to a large extent this Black Women's Renaissance became homogenized and prevented the writers of the period from "discovering their unique voices" (McDowell 108). Of course, this phenomenon has to be considered along with the fact that during the same time period, the black middle-class upheld Victorian standards of gentility as a means of setting an example for other blacks and as a means of demonstrating equality (and moral superiority) to whites.

As a twentieth century novelist, Octavia Butler does not have to negotiate Victorian standards in order to construct her conception of an American black woman. Thus, *Kindred* is a narrative primarily concerned with Dana's experience within American slavery. In other words, Dana is the center of the narrative as opposed to the injustices of American slavery. Thus, the novel *Kindred* stands just outside of the traditional feminine slave narrative rubric largely because it is situated at the heart of such narratives. There are no political incentives to convince the readers of the narrative to end slavery. There is also no attempt to prove Dana's worthiness of acceptance by whites because both of these points have been accepted as fact long before the reader enters the narrative. In this way *Kindred* disrupts both the premise of traditional masculine slave narratives and Victorian notions of women.

Butler makes a departure from the traditionally masculine rubric by adding powerful female images to her already untraditional narrative. The feminine elements such as the heroine at the center of the text and the familial relationships are all analogous to those found in feminine slave narratives written by black women writers such as Harriet Jacobs, Harriet Wilson, and Pauline Hopkins. The practice of risking recapture in order to free a family member or spouse before or after one has successfully gained freedom is common in slave narratives. The heroine Linda, in

Incidents, illustrates an excellent example of such heroism. While in hiding from the authorities Linda risks recapture when she seeks to speak with her adolescent daughter Ellen despite the possibility that her daughter might reveal her secret location. Jacobs writes:

> I begged permission to pass the last night in one of the open chambers, with my little girl. They thought I was crazy to think of trusting such a young child with my perilous secret. I told them I had watched her character, and I felt sure she would not betray me; that I was determined to have an interview, and if they would not facilitate it, I would take my own way to obtain it (Jacobs 139).

The love and compassion that Linda Brent shows for her child is indicative of the way the black mother was written in the feminine slave narrative. Motherhood and its responsibilities were often just as if not more important to the black woman as was her own freedom. For Linda Brent, her children's freedom and the ability to maintain familial bonds with them were paramount. It is through Brent's family members and children that she is given the motivation and assistance needed to escape slavery. As a black woman also writing for the sympathy of white readers, her loyalty to her children and family act as excellent identifiable Victorian characteristics.

Likewise, the familial relationships Dana and her ancestors share were equally crucial for not only her freedom but the existence of her entire family. This similarity is one of several that marks *Kindred* as a revised, if not postmodern, feminine slave narrative. Just as Linda Brent used the threat on her children's lives as incentive to escape slavery, Dana uses a similar threat to motivate her entry into slavery and to negotiate for both her own life and the lives of her ancestors.

In Jacobs' narrative, Brent's character is written in such a way that she appears to be more concerned with the freedom of her children than her own. Brent would rather wait in her grandmother's cramped attic for seven years than to escape without the assurance that her children were both safe and free. Thus, according to the Victorian ethic, Brent's character becomes the paradigm of the "good" woman and mother. Dana is dependent on her ancestors in a very similar way, as Alice and Rufus are family members who need her assistance if she is to ever be born.

The question of choice becomes interesting when we consider that Dana had no choices and Linda Brent could have outwitted Dr. Flint long before seven years elapsed if her escape plans need not be influenced by her desire to ensure her children's freedom. Brent did not have the choice of a male slave such as Douglass to flee to freedom alone. Because of the Victorian ethic of the time and its influence within the literature and society, Jacobs did not have the option of being or presenting herself as a mother who would sacrifice her children to the horrors of slavery. It could be argued that since Octavia Butler does not write under the same constraints as Jacobs, Dana should have been able to resist the *Kindred* narrative. By resist, I mean that perhaps Dana could have combated her maternal instincts to rescue Rufus. Of course by doing such a thing, Dana would have probably ceased to exist or worse; remained in the past subject to permanent slavery. It is this utter dependency on the actions of her ancestors that eliminates Dana's options from doing anything but ensuring the birth of Hagar by any means necessary.

Dana is dependent on her familial relations in very much the same way that Linda Brent was dependent upon her family. Just as Linda's grandmother helped her escape from Dr. Flint, Alice helps Dana escape from Rufus by forfeiting her body and eventually her life. As Dana's ancestor Rufus is the key to the time portal that she enters and exits throughout the narrative. Rufus is also one of the necessary elements for the whole narrative. For example, without him the possession of unborn parents ceases to exist as well.

The similarities between *Kindred* and the traditional slave narrative are numerous, but the element of time travel makes obvious several important distinctions. According to Spaulding,

> Rather than merely imitating or revising the slave narrative form, the postmodern slave narrative critiques historical and fictional representations that rely on claims of verisimilitude. The novels call into question our tendency to regard realism as the ideal narrative mode for history and historical fiction; they implicitly assert that claims of authenticity, realism, and objectivity result, particularly in the discourse on slavery, in a potentially oppressive obfuscation of the past (Spaulding 5).

Ultimately, it is through Dana's familial relations that she is allowed to travel through time and space and from freedom to slavery. Crossing boundaries is thus at the core of the whole historical or narrative structure of the novel. And although Dana is dependent on her ancestors in many regards, the lives of her grandparents and parents will be decided on Dana's success or failure in a past that she helps to mold. The conceit of *Kindred* is that Dana sees how the bonds of the past become the very means to freedom from her legacy in the present; but not only is the past necessary to the present/future, but the present/future becomes the very way or means by which the past acquires its meaning in Dana's life.

KINDRED'S POSTMODERN ARCHITECTURE

Kindred begins with a prologue that immediately addresses the issue of the body. Dana's first words to the reader are, "I lost an arm on my trip home" (Butler 9). Before the narrative even begins, the question of the deconstruction and dismantling of a body has been established. The next sentence in the prologue situates another crucial issue at the center of the narrative. When Dana tells us, "And I lost about a year of my life and much of the comfort and security I had not valued until it was gone," (9) she does two very important things. The first is that she informs the reader that her tale will unfold around the notion of the displacement of the present as simply present, or as the only feature or heading of time. The second places a discussion of the loss of security in a position that is inextricable from issues of the body. A loss of security implies a loss of control over the environment surrounding an individual. If we consider the assessment of Olaudah Equiano (1745–1797) in his *Interesting Narrative*, we see that slavery entails the idea that a body, that of the slave, can be constantly vulnerable and subject to abuse. Thus, at the outset of the novel, its resolution depends on complicated questions of time, of travel, and of enslavement.

In *Kindred*, Dana is shifted into the antebellum South by Rufus's imagination (a metaphysical time-machine) where she loses her twentieth century ability to control the placement of her body. Dana, a twenty-six-year-old black woman, is pulled mysteriously back in time, from the year 1976 by a white, slave owning relative. I use the term "mysteriously" because it is not made entirely clear to the reader at this point, or indeed throughout the text, exactly how Dana's body is moved from one location in time and space to the next. What we do know is that Dana's great grandfather, Rufus Weylin, has somehow caused Dana to be transported through time and space back to antebellum Maryland, whenever his life is endangered. Not until Dana's life, that is her physical existence, in the past is threatened is she able to return to contemporary Los Angeles.

The physics involved in this seemingly magical transportation is left for Dana and the reader to figure out for themselves. What seems to be most important is that the system of transportation works and cannot be avoided. Although it may seem random, within the fabulous frame of this narrative, the existence of Dana and her family in the present are dependent on how well she copes with the very real results of the time traveling process of her reliving of the past. In a more practical sense Dana's method of transportation is important because it gives the reader a way of rethinking the relationship between the past and present.

In *Re-Forming the Past*, Timothy Spaulding juxtaposes *Kindred* with Ishmael Reed's *Flight to Canada*, with the intent to reveal how the two texts reject the boundaries of narrative realism in their retelling of slavery. Spaulding argues that the conflation of time in both novels acts as a critique of traditional history. As a result, both novels can be classified as postmodern slave narratives engaging in the dismantling of Enlightenment conceptions of history and identity and the narrative of Western cultural superiority

(Spaulding 3). I am in agreement with Spaulding's assessment of *Kindred's* postmodern activities but would like to emphasize its dismantling of the black body and its value in the past and the present as its most postmodern characteristic. The non-mimetic devices employed in *Kindred* such as time travel, simultaneously reinventing the past and the present, and teleportation via imagination, are all dependent on Butler's writing of the black body in what Spaulding calls a distinctly African American postmodernism—one influenced by postmodern thought but rooted in black history and informed by black identity politics (Spaulding 3).

Dana's movement through time in the narrative suggests that the past can exist in the present and that the present can exist in the past. If such a contradiction can occur, then the notion of memory becomes much more complicated than simply remembering something. If Rufus's imagination is Dana's primary method of transportation to the past, then her memory becomes her ticket back to the present. I use the term "memory" because in order for Dana to return to her present, she must first arrive in the past and then alter the past by at least saving Rufus's life. This altering necessitates a memory of the past in order to allow Dana to exist in the present.

Butler's fabulous fiction allows one to imagine the way the past fits into the present, beyond abstract thoughts, such that they become almost synonymous with each other. In this way Dana's method of time and space travel becomes a device that opens a space for re-figuring the "then" and "now" or memorization. If Rufus is the origin of Dana's experience in the past he must also be a central figure in her present. This is only possible if the past and the present are somehow inextricably connected outside any quantum understanding of time and space. And if this is indeed the case, Dana's method of traveling through time and space can be interpreted as rethinking the past and the present. Spaulding takes this notion further by suggesting that "[r]ather than drawing attention to the ways Dana's travel undermines the credibility of her slave experience, this element of the fantastic establishes her protagonist's truer, more complete understanding of slavery" (Spaulding 26). In other words, Dana's experience of freedom in her present is inextricable from her slave experience in the past.

In a much less fabulous manner, Dana's trip to the past can be compared to the middle passage experienced by slaves being transported from Africa to the Americas. Dana begins to feel dizzy and nauseated just before she is transported to a place outside of her home and away from her husband. The nausea that Dana experiences foreshadows her move to the past, but also can be considered analogous to the nausea and disorientation that captured Africans must have experienced as they were loaded onto slave ships headed for a new world at the end of a long middle passage.

On June 9, 1976, Dana and her husband Kevin (both writers) had just moved into their new home and were about to begin celebrating Dana's 26th birthday when her own private middle passage began. Dana recalls:

> The house, the books, everything vanished. Suddenly, I was outdoors kneeling on the ground beneath trees. Before me was a wide tranquil river, and near the middle of that river was a child splashing, screaming . . . Drowning! (Butler 13)

Dana rescues the child with the "ugly name" (Butler 14) from the river only to have her life threatened by the child's father. The shock of looking down the barrel of a rifle about to be fired ended Dana's first visit to the past as her nausea returned to take her back to her home in 1976 only a few moments later.

It is not until Dana's second trip to the past that an explanation of her excursion begins to be formulated. The little red headed child that Dana saved from drowning in the river is the same child she finds on her second trip setting fire to draperies at a window. Apparently the child is about to start a fire that will undoubtedly kill him and everyone else in the house. Dana puts out the fire and finds herself stranded with no money and no idea how to get home. The red headed child, Rufus, is four years older than he was during their last meeting, which for Dana was less than 24 hours ago in 1976. Rufus informs Dana that she is a long way from her home and her husband. By asking Rufus several questions, Dana deduces that somehow Rufus has set in motion the forces that have transported her body through time and space.

We also find out why Rufus's father was about to kill the person who had just saved his son's life. Because of Dana's clothing and dark skin, she was mistaken for a male slave attempting to harm Rufus and his mother. Rufus tells her, "You were wearing paints like a man—the way you are now. I thought you were a man" (Butler 22). "He [Daddy] thought you were a man too—and that you were trying to hurt Mama and me"(23). This moment of mistaken identity is the first sign that Dana's body has not only been moved through time and space but has also experienced a redefinition of social meaning. Black females in the antebellum South did not wear pants and certainly did not do so while saving little white boys from drowning. Therefore, at her moment of peril, Dana's body could have only been perceived as one thing in the mind of a slave owner with a rifle in his hands, a dangerous black *man*. In 1815, the year to which Dana is transported on her second trip, her body does not exist as it did in 1976. Dana's body has neither the security nor agency that it may have had in 1976. In 1815 the definition of Dana's body is reduced to property possessed by a white land owning male.

During Dana's second visit we find that from the temporal and histori-cal moment of 1976, Rufus Weylin is her great grandfather, and that she is on a plantation with thirty-eight slaves somewhere in Maryland during the year 1815. We also meet Dana's great grandmother, Alice Greenwood, who must give birth to Dana's grandmother Hagar Weylin to insure the 1976 existence of Dana. Rufus directs Dana to the home of the young Alice and her mother. We find that Alice's mother has a disturbing resemblance to Dana. When the three are visited by a group of slave patrollers Dana is mistaken for Alice's mother. "Apparently, I looked enough like Alice's mother to confuse him—briefly" (Butler 41). This encounter escalates into the life-threatening altercation that sends Dana back to 1976.

Dana is attacked by one of the Patrollers and is forced to knock him unconscious with a heavy stick. The fear of what would happen as a result of her act of self-defense was enough to render Dana unconscious. Despite the fact that Dana has obviously avoided a life-threatening situ-ation, at least temporarily, she still considers her life to be in danger. At this particular moment in the narrative, Dana is fully aware of the values placed on her body during the time period in which she is functioning. In other words, Dana knows that as a black person in the time and space that she is in, she is perceived as a powerless object, subject to physical abuse and loss of life. To slave patrollers, black bodies are sub-human and do not have the right to defend themselves from any abuse inflicted by white males. Such acts of defense are punishable by death. In the few hours that Dana spends in the world of Rufus and Alice she learns "first-hand" that the black female body is a location of presumed powerlessness and insecurity in 1815.

When Dana awakens we find that she has returned to her home and husband, Kevin, in 1976. Kevin Franklin, Dana's white, twentieth century husband, is a writer and is initially the antithesis of what the antebellum white male represents. In the third chapter entitled "The Fall," we learn that Kevin and Dana "fall" in love despite their racial difference and make a life together. Dana is able to love Kevin as an equal who happens to be white and male. By introducing such a relationship to an already com-plicated tale fully invested in a discussion of race relations in America, Butler seems to displace the possibility of reading Dana's fabulous experi-ences as simply black and white. Despite the fact that Dana is subjected to white racist antebellum slave patrollers, the narrative does not allow the obvious generalization that all white men are racist and thus evil. Kevin's presence in the narrative illustrates that racism is at least in part a func-tion of socio-historical time and place as well as individual personality.

The "racialization" and "gendering" that Dana experiences when she is transported to the 1800s is dependent largely on the social practices of a particular point in American history. The devaluing of Dana's body from a twentieth century black woman writer to "a poor dumb scared nigger" (Butler 48) is a result of a nation of people categorizing bodies solely on the basis of a categorical logic or system of distinctions of race and gender. One thematic effect of Kevin's role in the narrative and as the husband of Dana is to mark certain possibilities for race relations and gender relations in the 1970s.

On Dana's third trip back to antebellum Maryland, Kevin is transported with her. The year is 1819, and Rufus has managed to fall from a tree limb and has broken his leg. Dana and Kevin accompany Rufus back to his father's plantation under the guise of female slave and white slave owner. As her owner, Kevin is put in the position of protecting Dana by providing her body with the security that she no longer has the power to supply herself under the prevailing social terms. Dana realizes this and considers the negative results that might develop from such a responsibility.

> A place like this would endanger him in a way I didn't want to talk about. If he was stranded here for years, some part of this place would rub off on him. The place, the time would either kill him outright or mark him somehow. I didn't like either possibility (Butler 78).

Dana fears that the time and place would necessarily redefine the value of Kevin's body as it had done to her own. More importantly, Dana was afraid that Kevin would be afflicted by a white male ideology from the antebellum South, one that dictated that a white male body has much more value than that of a black female body. Dana is concerned that, among other possible effects, Kevin's entire understanding of the body will be negatively affected by the socio-historical practices of the nineteenth century. Thus, as a marker for race relations and gender possibilities of the 1970s, Kevin is in jeopardy ironically because of his race and because of his twentieth century socialization.

In positioning Kevin next to Dana in 1819, Butler encourages the participants in the narrative to juxtapose Kevin and Rufus, two white men in a black woman's life. Both are inextricably linked to the history of American slavery in a way that is similar to the way in or by which Dana is linked to Alice in the same historical frame. As travelers between two time periods and locations, Dana and the reader must consider the fact that Kevin is a white man with privileges and power in the past and present. And as a black woman, Dana must negotiate with this power if she is to survive in either time period.

The one time that Kevin is not present to protect Dana's body, she is caught teaching a slave child how to read. Tom Weylin, Rufus's father, finds Dana in the cook-house giving Nigel, Rufus's black playmate, a reading lesson. Dana is caught breaking one of the most common proscriptions of slavery in the antebellum South. Tom Weylin drags Dana out of the cook-house and attempts to beat her to death. Dana says, "I thought Weylin meant to kill me. I thought I would die on the ground there with a mouth full of dirt and blood and a white man cursing and lecturing as he beat me" (107). The shock and fear of the experience causes Dana to return to 1976. Kevin is left in the past to wander until Dana returns for him.

Dana remained in the year 1976 for eight days until she was summoned to the past by Rufus again. Dana finds an adult Rufus being brutally beaten by an Isaac, Alice's husband. Apparently, Rufus had attempted to rape Alice and was being punished by her husband when Dana appeared on the scene. After conversing with Rufus, Dana realizes that the "time and place" has shaped Rufus into a typical racist, misogynist male far beyond her influence. Rufus has developed into an adult male who is firmly entrenched in the customs and values of the antebellum South. His once free and independent playmate Alice has become the object of his desire. In the years of Dana's absence, Rufus has developed a lust for Alice that will lead to the rape that will result in the birth of Hagar Weylin and eventually Dana.

In Butler's fourth chapter entitled "The Fight," we learn that Alice also undergoes a social reformation—one set in motion by brutality. Rufus's violence toward Alice transforms her social position from that of a free born, married black woman into that of a widowed slave. Alice's husband, Isaac, was tortured and sold further south. And because Alice was captured with the runaway slave, Isaac, she also was sold into slavery. Like Dana, Alice is forced, in the course of the narrative, to lose what little security she possessed before her encounter with Rufus Weylin.

As Rufus's recently purchased property, Alice is subject to the advances of her new owner. Alice is a slave and by law has no authority over what is done to her body in a period that allows no support by law of the agency or humanity of black female bodies. Dana realizes that her survival is dependent on Alice's decision either to submit to being raped by Rufus or to run away and risk being killed. Dana goes to Alice with the intent of cajoling her into the arms of Rufus, but Dana hesitates when Alice asks her if she would sleep with a man whom she hated as much as Alice hated Rufus. After considering Alice's situation, Dana offers to distract Rufus while Alice attempts another escape to freedom. Alice responds to Dana's offer in the following passage:

> "I'm lying. I can't run again. I'm going to him. He knew I would sooner or later. But he don't know how I wish I had the nerve to just kill him!" (Butler 168)

Alice's decision to submit to Rufus's sexual advances highlights some important facts about the social coding of her body. The first is that Alice's character is not defined solely by the location of her body. Although Alice's physical body is subjected in the 1800s to the social authority granted to Rufus Weylin by right of legal and economic ownership, her mind remains free to hate and covertly plot against the man who has stolen her freedom. Rufus may own Alice's physical body, but he never truly possesses all of her. Alice maintains the control of her spirit. Furthermore, Alice's refusal to run away is an overt example of passive resistance. In choosing not to attempt another escape, which could very possibly be an act of suicide, Alice actively chooses to survive in a system that is designed to subjugate and then destroy black bodies. In this way Alice is able to maintain some control over her body despite its physical location and condition.

When Kevin returns to the Weylin plantation, he attempts to rescue Dana and travel North. Rufus stops the two before they can escape the plantation and threatens to kill both Kevin and Dana. If Rufus is to be content, he believes that he must possess both Dana and Alice. Alice has lived and played with Rufus since childhood and represents physically and socially constructed desires. The institution of slavery has dictated to Rufus that he has every right to possess any black female body that he can afford to buy. Alice is accessible, affordable, and most importantly stationary.

Dana, on the other hand, represents a potentially mobile intellectual superior to Rufus. One of Dana's primary functions in the course of the narrative is to save Rufus from life threatening situations. In many ways, Dana is Rufus's guardian angel. Dana plays the roles of mother, friend, and guardian so well throughout the course of Rufus's life that he inevitably convinces himself that he both deserves and desires Dana as well as Alice. The fact that Dana is neither accessible nor stationary only complicates Rufus's already distorted perception of reality.

As Kevin and Dana attempt to leave the plantation Rufus displays an outburst of emotion that clearly reflects his inability to control his fear and anger: "You're not leaving!" he shouted. He sort of crouched around the gun, clearly on the verge of firing. "Damn you, you're not leaving me!" (Butler 186). Rufus fears Dana's absence for another random period of time, and he is angered because Dana's body is beyond his control. Where Alice has literally "nowhere to run," Dana, on the other hand, has a refuge far beyond the Weylin plantation and Rufus's adolescent temper tantrums. All that Rufus knows of Dana's refuge has come to him in visions just before she materializes to rescue him from whatever danger he is facing in his time frame. Rufus is very conscious of the fact that he cannot control this phenomenon and is frightened by his lack of agency.

Rufus's inability to possess Dana's body completely and indefinitely is symbolic of the fact that Dana's body has not been fully constructed within the time frame or historical period in which Rufus exists. Dana's body cannot be completely "real" to Rufus because in the historical sense, she has not yet been born. She is an unborn specter from the future trying to ensure its birth into a twentieth century reality, a time and place that will identify her as a black woman writer and a human being.

Rufus's attempt to shoot Kevin and Dana enables both to return to their home in Los Angeles. Dana's eight days in 1976 equated to five years for Kevin in antebellum America. Kevin tells Dana that "Five years is longer than it sounds. So much longer" (Butler 193). He implies that the five years that he spent away from 1976 and Dana were, in many ways, analogous to being in prison. Kevin wonders "how people just out of prison manage to readjust" (197).

Kevin's time in antebellum America offers the participants in the narrative the opportunity to make observations about the treatment of a white male body versus that of a black female body. Although we learn that Kevin has suffered during his stay in the 1800s, it is clear that Kevin's gender and race must have played a crucial role in his survival. Aside from some unexplained scars on his forehead and witnessing "a woman die in child birth once" (Butler 191), Kevin experienced a freedom and mobility that Dana's black female body could not have afforded her in the early 1800s. During his "prison sentence" Kevin "had a job as a teacher" (193), was able to wonder "farther and farther up the east coast" (192), and "would have wound up in Canada next" (192). Thus, by allowing Kevin to travel back in time with Dana, Butler illustrates a few of the complicated boundaries founded on race, gender, and power that is specific to a time and place.

Dana's final trip back to Rufus's time and place occurs because Rufus manages to destroy Alice's body. In an attempt to punish Alice for running away again, Rufus misleads her to believe that he has sold her two children, Joe and Hagar. After hearing the tragic news Alice commits suicide by hanging herself. Dana is conjured up because Alice's death has pushed Rufus to the point of committing suicide himself. Alice's absence rekindles Rufus's desire to possess Dana both physically and permanently. Rufus wanted Dana to become his substitute Alice; he wanted Dana "to take the place of the dead" (Butler 259). With this desire, Rufus transforms Dana into a fetish that represents not only Alice, but his control over black bodies and over the decaying Weylin plantation and his security. Alice's death makes Rufus aware of a very disturbing fact; Dana is the only bit of security that he has left beyond his race and gender. Thus, Dana's threat to leave or hate Rufus in the final chapter of the narrative is paramount to a direct threat on his life.

For the first time in the narrative, Rufus is forced to truly consider the consequences of his actions. Sense his childhood, Rufus has been taught by Dana's presence and actions that his life was valuable and would be protected if placed in the face of danger. When his personal guardian angel threatens to stop rendering her services permanently, Rufus experiences the fear of loosing his life for the first time in his life. Thus, Dana's threat signifies both death and loneliness, the two things with which Rufus Weylin has never had to concern himself with until the death of his father and Alice.

In a final battle, Dana tells Rufus, "keeping you alive has been up to me for too long!" (Butler 259). Dana realizes that Rufus's desire to possess her body has transcended any discussion of reason. Either Rufus must die or Dana must forfeit her body and identity as a free black woman from 1976. The ability to prevent her body from being raped was one of the few boundaries not yet crossed that prevented Dana from completely becoming a slave in antebellum America. In the process of defending herself, Dana stabs Rufus to death with a knife. The fear and shock of her act of lethal self-defense sends Dana to July 4, 1976 (the day of her independence), without her left arm. "From the elbow to the end of the fingers, my left arm had become a part of the wall. It was the exact spot Rufus's fingers had grasped" (Butler 261).

Rufus's death by Dana's hands can be interpreted as the closure of an obscure symbiotic relationship or as the beginning of another unwritten narrative. The term "symbiotic" is useful here because both Rufus and Dana benefited from their relationship. Rufus obtains moments of security and a piece of Dana's body, but loses his life. Dana obtains the security in knowing that although the birth of Hagar Weylin was the result of Rufus' raping of Alice, her progeny will be given the opportunity to exist and eventually reproduce free children in a better time and place. By keeping Rufus alive over the years, Dana secured her existence in the year 1976. She has also shared an experience with her ancestors that would not have been possible without Rufus's existence. By using Rufus as a conduit, Dana is enabled to experience first-hand the horrific elements of American slavery. Even the loss of Dana's left arm can be interpreted as an unforgettable reminder of how the past necessarily forms the present and can also dismantle it. Dana's left arm in a more literal sense was the price for crossing boundaries of time, place and body. In her comparison of *Kindred* with Assia Djebar's *La femme sans sepulture* Anne Donadey asserts that

Although the text stages many aspects of violence, physical, emotional, and psychological, the most physically disabling violence experienced by Dana in *Kindred* is arguably her loss of an arm. There is a very rich symbolism to this loss, which powerfully inaugurates the novel and symbolizes the hold of the past on the present. The history of slavery and white supremacy is a wall that continues to have disabling consequences for African Americans because today's racism has its roots in the slavery system. Dana's experience evinces the need to face the past, then wrench ourselves from it, without being able to escape the mutilation of that past (71–72).

OTHER POSTMODERN TEXTS

Kindred also speaks to more contemporary narratives that investigate issues of black women's bodies. Butler's novel illustrates several points of relation with Toni Morrison's *Beloved* (1987) and Gayl Jones's *Corregidora* (1975). Despite the science fiction element of time travel, *Kindred* is primarily about the movement of a body through historical moments and memories much like *Beloved*, or *Corregidora*. In this sense *Kindred* brings together the past and present to a point that necessitates a refiguring of our understanding of history.[1] In regards to *Kindred* and *Beloved* Vint asserts that both novels "urge a rethinking of the relationship between African American and fantastic literature" (241). In order for the narrative of *Kindred* to function, both Dana and the reader must share some remembrance of the antebellum South and the time and space in which it occurred. Without such a memory, the narrative would not be possible, because the participants would not have points of reference. Dana's experience only opens on the basis of the fact that her knowledge or memory of the histories of her family and country are and must be incomplete. Yet, there are traces and there are memories. Without Dana's vague memory of "grandmother Hagar, Alice Green-something and Rufus Weylin" (28) she would have been rendered completely dysfunctional in a time and place that was utterly foreign.

Because Dana remembers fragments of her past she is able to recognize this foreign context and to make sense of what is happening to her in her present. In this way *Kindred* transforms what is generally referred to as history into something that necessarily includes memory. Where history was defined as things that happened in a past time and place, Dana's adventure implies that those past events must also be attached to the present by memories (Rushdy 134).

Where Dana is forced to visit the past in *Kindred*, Sethe from Toni Morrison's *Beloved* undergoes the opposite imperative and must face a visitor from her past in her present. Dana must experience first-hand many of the hardships and tribulations that led to her contemporary existence. That is to say that Dana's travels through time and space to the past form new memories that enable her to better understand her existence in 1976. Similarly, Sethe must remember (or relive) a tragic past in the present in order that she might recover from the physical and mental wounds she has carried with her from the past into her present. However, it must be recalled that Dana must remember what is so present—everywhere and nowhere—that it has almost been forgotten. Whereas Sethe must remember in order to forget, what is so present that it cannot be forgotten.

After escaping from the Sweet Home plantation in Kentucky to the free state of Ohio, the pregnant Sethe enjoyed a month of freedom in Cincinnati before slave catchers came after her and her three children. To spare her children the grief and torture of slavery Sethe cut the throat of her eldest daughter, Beloved, tried to kill her two boys with a shovel, and threatened to dash out the brains of her infant daughter, Denver. Sethe was condemned to hang for her acts, but was able to gain release and return to her home with her freedom and her children. After the death of Sethe's mother-in-law, the two sons were forced out of the house by the ghost of Sethe's dead daughter, Beloved.

Beloved materializes in Sethe's present almost as mysteriously as did Dana within her own past, with Rufus and within the social order of the Weylin plantation. Beloved is part child and part woman, but for the most part she represents the suppressed memories of horror and pain involved in her death. These memories must be faced by Sethe if she is to attain her sanity and general health.

Morrison's *Beloved* demonstrates a revisionist plot through the character Sethe, who not only demonstrates passion, complexity and moral ambiguity of character by taking the life of one of her children, but by presenting a kind of perspective and system of values that Harriet Jacobs for example, could not have imagined in her narrative. Taking the life of her children would have lost many, if not all of Jacobs' sympathetic readers. Such an inhumane act would have undoubtedly contradicted the most dominant and proclaimed moral values of her audience and defeated one of the main goals of the text, which was to vouch for the humanity and sensibility of the African American and especially the African American woman.

Similar remarks can be made with regards to Butler's *Kindred*. Dana not only defies the rules of the antebellum South, but engages in an "unethical" sexual relationship with her white husband, Kevin. Dana and Sethe practice liberties that the subject of the older feminine autobiographical narratives of slavery could not afford. If we consider Barbara Christian's point, that "re-memory is a critical determinant in how we value the past, what we remember, what we select to emphasize, what we forget" (Christian 326), then *Kindred* proposes such a re-engagement. In this light, it becomes a definitive declaration of two major insights: 1). that African Americans possess history and culture; and 2). that their history and their culture are interwoven with that of the slave owners, biologically, as well as psychologically, or we might say, in body and soul.

Gayl Jones's character, Ursa, from *Corregidora* uses her memory as an historical document that will exist in her presence for as long as she can sing her story. As a daughter from three generations of mothers and daughters Ursa finds herself at the end of a genealogical line. Because she cannot produce a daughter of her own Ursa is unable to pass down the oral record of her mothers' enslavement and rape by Corregidora, a Portuguese plantation owner. In 1948 Ursa's husband, Mutt, pushes her down a flight of stairs which results in the removal of her womb. Ursa's inability to produce a daughter of her own threatens her family's tradition of passing down the memory of a series of incestuous rapes that eventually produces the Corregidora family.

Both *Beloved* and *Corregidora* are novels invested in the notion of memory and its ability to link bodies to the past and present. Although each of the novels accomplish this difficult task differently than *Kindred*, the images of slavery, the presence of black women at the center of the narrative, and the common theme of survival places the three narratives in a similar location. Like *Kindred*, *Beloved* and *Corregidora* function in a revisionary capacity which speaks to a larger literary tradition and the bodies of women in the past and present. Thus, Butler, Morrison and Jones are all concerned with a "truer" identity of women on both a literary and individual level. As Barbara Christian states in her "Trajectories of Self-Definition," "African American women writers in the seventies and eighties have been able to make a commitment to an exploration of self, as central rather than marginal" (Christian, 234), and in so doing have helped reconstruct the history of female identity. In each novel the notion of historical identity is inextricably linked to memory and the revision the black female body.

Unlike traditional SF novels, *Kindred* presents a version of a time travel narrative in which memory and imagination are the most important means of transportation. There are no machines involved in Dana's movement throughout the narrative unless we consider our imaginations and Butler's narrative as organic mechanisms. Ashraf Rushdy says "Butler treats time as a flexible structure and takes more seriously than most the theory of mind-body continuum"(Rushdy 137). In other words, Dana's time travel is less important to the way she defines herself and her place in history than her actual experience of surviving the past in the present. I find Rushdy's observation to be insightful but too simplistic because the notion of the mind-body continuum in *Kindred* acts as an axis from which to think Dana's experiences.

The idea that the body is only bounded by the human imagination seems to be what makes Dana's travels possible. Dana and the reader are led to believe that Rufus caused the present and past to somehow fold, but such an explanation seems both simplistic and presumptuous with regards to the agency of a five year old child. A more reasonable deduction might take into consideration the imaginative capacity of a professional fiction writer and a child who obviously believes that anything is possible, such as swimming without knowing how to swim.

Kindred, like the rest of Butler's works, originates from a complicated location of ambiguity. It is imagination which allows Butler to manipulate boundaries of the real world without relying on SF or the impossible. As a (re)visionary writer, Butler allows Dana to attempt to rewrite the feminine slave narrative by means of her memory. "Dana's memory is a performance of history, a performance of such potency that it incorporates her into the past, leaving 'no distance at all' between her and the remembered events" (Rushdy 137). In other words, because of Dana's ability to create through the use of her imagination as a professional writer, the folding or overlapping of time and space becomes the ambiguous location. Through *Kindred*, Dana is transformed into one of the many contemporary black women visionaries who have written African American historical novels, as a sign of desire to re-vision African American history from an imaginative and informed point of view (Christian, "Somebody Forgot" 327).

If we accept the connection that Fredric Jameson finds between SF and historical fiction, which is that both SF and historical fiction create a violent formal and narrative dislocation in their methods of representing the future or the past in order to restore life and feeling to our capacity to organize and live time historically, the classification of Butler's work seems of minor importance (Rushdy 136). In Butler's narratives, bodies, especially those functioning under the guise of historical fact or fiction, it seems, will always cross boundaries.

KINDRED'S LACK OF BOUNDARIES

In the telling of Dana's adventure, a subtext consisting of body politics and a critique of the agency attached to the black female body are established. The same might be said for autobiographies such as Jacobs's *Incidents in the Life of a Slave Girl*, Lucy Delany's *From the Darkness Cometh Light*, and Mary Prince's *The History of Mary Prince, a West Indian Slave*. Both the feminine slave narrative and American historical fact play crucial roles in Butler's re-writing of a complicated black heroine's genealogy. Everything from the "groups of young whites who ostensibly maintained order among the slaves" (Butler 37) to the vivid description of the Weylin plantation and its operation and the difficulty involved in finding Rufus Weylin a rich white wife show signs of historical research on the part of Butler. By introducing the possibility of time travel into a narrative structure that was initially designed to speak to a relatively small sympathetic nineteenth century audience, on the basis of references to a temporal and spatial domain considered relatively immediate, Butler considerably expands the value and accessibility of the slave narrative form.

Reading *Kindred* as a revised slave narrative necessarily sheds new light on the goals and boundaries of more traditional narratives. The narrative frame in which Butler situates Dana is not governed by the same ethical codes or social and political goals as documents produced in the late 1800s. Where Harriet Jacobs or France E. W. Harper might have been constrained in the portrayal of their female characters, Butler is able to fully develop Dana into an overtly empowered, sexual, and complicated female heroine.

In the chapter entitled "The Fight," we learn that in 1976 Dana demands both power and respect from her agency job and her future husband, Kevin. Dana remembers her way of life before her infamous birthday. The independence that she received from the agency was not what she considered to be consistent but she believed it to be real and tangible with no controlling strings attached. She recounts moments of independence and freedom which are not accessible to the nineteenth century black female but are things that she attempts to obtain despite this fact. Dana does not even allow Kevin to infringe upon her freedom and independence. When Kevin asked Dana to do some typing for one of his manuscripts, Dana refused so vehemently that Kevin became angry, and an argument ensued. "He said if I couldn't do him a little favor when he asked, I could leave" (Butler 109). When Dana returned to Kevin the next day she still refused to do his typing. Such acts of defiance help the reader to identify Dana in her present as a heroine who is willing to fight for her freedom on several levels.

The fact that Dana married Kevin despite the negative feelings of her uncle and aunt demonstrates her commitment to maintaining her independent lifestyle and way of thinking about the worlds she inhabits, past and present. Dana's description of her uncle and aunt to Kevin is filled with irony and humor considering their plight in antebellum Maryland.

> They're old. Sometimes their ideas don't have very much to do with what's going on now. I think they're still waiting for me to come to my senses, move back home, and go to secretarial school (Butler 110).

The above description that Dana gives to Kevin of her uncle and aunt is historically progressive compared to the belief system practiced on the Weylin plantation. It seems that Dana's relatives may be old, but their ideas are timely and potentially useful to the Dana who is to travel back in time.

Unlike traditional slave narratives, *Kindred* allows the reader to experience slavery with the protagonist, instead of merely identifying with the memoirs of an ex-slave second-hand. Dana carries us with her through time, through life threatening moments, including an attempted rape, and most importantly through her thoughts about the vulnerability of slavery. Dana's ability to travel through time allows twentieth-first century readers to experience a nineteenth century phenomenon as if they were doing the experiencing themselves. The readers' ability to access Dana's experiences is largely due to the fact that Dana is a professional writer by choice and trade, as opposed to an ex-slave writing an intentionally political narrative to end slavery. As a writer and storyteller of her fabulous journeys, Dana is able to reflect on her experiences in a much more vivid and believable manner than a Linda Brent or an Iola Leroy, because of historical hindsight.

Because we are given the opportunity to visit the Weylin plantation and know the complexity of Tom and Rufus Weylin personally, our picture of the victims and tyrants of the antebellum South are by far more vivid than those found in the traditional slave narrative. The character of Alice Greenwood develops into more than a typical victim of slavery pushed to suicide. Butler writes Dana and Alice as agents willing to sacrifice their lives in order to maintain control of the agency and identities that make up their bodies. Thus, Alice's suicide becomes an act of resistance to the brutality that Rufus has inflicted on her mind and body throughout the narrative.

Although Jacobs's Linda and Harper's Iola are not "allowed" to respond to their victimization in such extreme fashion as Dana and Alice, we as readers of *Kindred* can come to a better understanding as to why this was the case. Dana's twentieth century perspective on the antebellum South presents a much better explanation than does Linda's or Iola's nineteenth century avoidance or complete absence of issues of slavery. As readers who are from a time and place very similar to Dana's, we identify with her in a way that allows us to say, "I probably would have done what Dana did under those circumstances." Dana's language and voice are clearer and less inhibited than the voices of Jacob's and Harper were allowed to be during the nineteenth century. The reader does not have to assume an incident of rape or molestation in Dana's story because Butler allows Dana to speak what was once the unspeakable. In several ways Butler's characters fill in the gaps of older narrative structures by positing "black ladies" where there were once "white ladies." Through Dana and Alice we are able to better speculate on the sexual relations of Linda and the father of her mulatto children; or how Iola Leroy must have felt when her freedom was snatched away from her by a vengeful uncle. Butler gives Dana license to reveal all of the unspeakable sins of slavery that her ancestors were unable to pass down. In this way the body is positioned as a scene on the unspeakable in the *Kindred* narrative.

NOTES

1. In "Only by Experience: Embodiment and the Limitations of Realism in Neo-Slave Narratives," Sherryl Vint explores how fantastic neo-slave narratives like *Kindred* and *Beloved* revise and resist tropes of nineteenth-century slaves narratives.

2

Wildseed: The Paradox
of Bodily Inscriptions

The novel *Wildseed* is primarily a creation story centered around a matriarch and patriarch who battle for either the enslavement or independence of unusually gifted individuals. It is the employment and creation of these individuals that fuel the plot of Butler's narrative and raise the question of what constitutes a body and its identities. Identities attached to the body are highly unstable notions that are subject to ambiguity and variation in different social situations. The body as it is presented in *Wildseed* and, perhaps, in most of the narratives of Butler is a surface of experiential inscription not limited to the material. That is to say that Butler's fiction suggests that the body can be interpreted as a blank canvas waiting for experiences to be painted on it, which give it form and meaning. Butler's *Wildseed* suggests that the body is constituted more by history and experience than the materials of flesh and bone.

"Wild seed," or the genetic materials needed to create a new race of people, is the decisive topic in Butler's narrative. As the term "wild" implies, "wild seed" is genetic material outside of the normal, whether that norm be a place, lineage or a species because it is wild or not understood by ungifted humanity. "Wild seed" is the potential ingredients of a superhuman race, which may lay dormant in the genetic structure of an average individual until it is mixed with other genetic material, like itself. The results are individuals with special capacities, such as telepathy or shape-shifting among others. More accurately the term "wild seed" refers to the bodies that contain a special genetic make-up. By gathering and wearing the bodies of individuals regardless of their "race, sex, physical appearance, or health" (Butler 178) the antagonist of *Wildseed*, Doro, raises difficult questions about the foundation and employment of identities attached to the body. How can an individual exist without a material body, let alone be identified by others without a body? And if an individual can exist without a material body by preying on the bodies of others, how are we to imagine such an individual?

Patricia Melzer addresses the problem of race and power in her discussion of Doro and the *Patternist* series.

> The close connection between race relations and power structures becomes apparent the *Patternist* series. Here, new markers of difference create stratifications that result in control mechanisms reminiscent of those during slavery. (82)

Doro takes advantage of the historical moment, the triangle slave trade, in order to achieve his goal. The primary goal of Doro in the *Wildseed* narrative is to gather wild seed and through eugenic engineering and selective breeding, to create an entire race of people to become his servants, prey, and family. Oddly, Doro seems to be outside the confines of racial markers. Melzer continues, "through his un-human, bodiless existence he transgresses external markers, such as race" despite his attempt to create a "super race" (82). It is through this systematic practice of employing the bodies of individuals that Doro is identified. Similarly, the protagonist of *Wildseed*, Anyanwu, can be identified by her desire and ability to reproduce bodies and nurture them. By reproduce, I mean the protagonist can give birth to other wild seed and nurture them as a mother would a child. She also has the ability to take the shape of almost any body she chooses and to maintain the health of that body. Unlike Doro, Anyanwu never forfeits her body; she merely manipulates the physical identity of the body. On one hand, Doro's character suggests that the physical body is simply subject to oppressive manipulation and a finite existence. He demonstrates this throughout the narrative as he plays the roles of slave catcher, executioner, lover and genetic engineer. On the other hand, the ambiguity of Doro's body suggests a productive power and an unbounded existence. Doro does after all exist beyond his physical body as shown by his people's ability to identify him regardless of the flesh and bone he is wearing at any given moment. Anyanwu describes Doro's inner body as "a great light, a fire that had enclosed her" (Butler 256). This moment in the narrative suggests that Doro has a body beyond flesh and bone. What Anyanwu describes as a great light can be interpreted as a celestial body or a visualization of Doro's body in its indefiniteness. Doro's body is written as a paradox of bodily inscription. Doro's body is constituted by contradictions of how we traditionally imagine the body. He inscribes his identity with the physical shells of others in order to establish his body. Elizabeth Grosz might refer to

Doro as an example of a metaphor of the *"texualised body"* (Grosz 62): that is Doro's identity becomes a text upon which cultural practices give meaning to his existence.[1] Thus, when Doro is inscribed, not only is his personal inscription upon that body alone important: equally important are the inscriptions placed on the bodies that surround him within his *Wildseed* culture, because "bodily inscriptions serve their most significant purpose in placing the body within a cultural matrix" (62).

Questions of the body have had an upsurge of popularity in the field of philosophy over the past few decades and include philosophical inquiries stretching from Nietzsche, Darwin, and Freud to Descartes and Hegel (Hodge 31). As the scope of discourse on the body is so rich I will limit my critical commentary to two of the most contemporary and insightful theorists of the body as it pertain to the fiction of Octavia Butler. Elizabeth Grosz has expanded questions of the body in the direction of feminist and psychoanalytical theory. She has considered the thinking of Lacan as it impacted feminist thinking in her text *Jacques Lacan: A Feminist Introduction* (1990),[2] and a study of the transformations of thinking of the body entitled *Volatile Bodies: Toward a Corporeal Feminism* (1994). With these texts Grosz has brought much attention to the tension between de Beauvoir's analyses and Sartre's thinking about the distinction between the body and the flesh in *Being and Nothingness* (1943),[3] and of Merleau-Ponty's development of this in his thinking of the relations of touch and of meaning in the posthumously published *The Visible and the Invisible* (1964)[4] (Hodge 32). In Judith Butler's essay entitled "Foucault and the Paradox of Bodily Inscription," she identifies the body as a site where regimes of discourse and power inscribe themselves in a location that seems to be pregiven. In other words, the body somehow constructs itself before it actually becomes an identifiable body. This assertion speaks directly to Doro's existence in the *Wildseed* narrative as he seems to exist before he is able to inhabit a body of flesh and bone. In many ways both Doro and Anyanwu are blank pages waiting for inscriptions of physical identities. If Doro is a completely blank page waiting to be inscribed with a people like himself, i.e. a potential history, Anyanwu is a page already inscribed with a partial history waiting to be revised by Doro and her own experiences.

Judith Butler poses several questions that Octavia Butler's character seems to address. For example, "Which body, if there are two, qualifies as 'the' body? Does the existent body in its anonymous universality have a gender, an unspoken one? What shape does the body have, and how is it known? Where did the body come from?" (J. Butler 601). Although Doro does not completely answer the particular questions of historical inscription and construction of the body Judith Butler raises, his character does shed some light on the possibilities of such questions. For example, if someone or something like Doro can be imagined without a physical body, then perhaps the body is more than Foucault's "inscribed surface of events"(603). Perhaps Doro's and Anyanwu's bodies are somehow simultaneously independent and dependent of the history and culture that surrounds them. "A body is both dependent upon others and subject to violation by another" (Chambers 49). By animating the problematic of the body through literary characters Octavia Butler makes a significant contribution to thinking about complexities of the body outside the fields of philosophy and literary theory.

It is through an investigation of these two main characters and the structure of the *Wildseed* narrative that I will examine the construction of the body and the kinds of identities that usually accompany the body. By engaging such issues through close textual analysis, I will also provide a consideration of Butler's use of slave narrative motifs such as the notion of a middle passage and plantation social organization to illustrate how the value of marginalized bodies tend to shift dependent upon context. And since Butler also produces a cast of characters in *Wildseed* who exist literally on the boundaries of several identities, somewhat like *Kindred*, but perhaps more elaborate, I will examine the question of the physical recuperation of memory in *Wildseed*, just as I have done for *Kindred* in chapter one.

Wildseed is a narrative written very much in the traditions of creation mythology and the slave narrative, and this chapter will address some of the implications of this inheritance. Thus, this chapter sets out to provide a close reading of Butler's novel structurally and thematically, keeping in mind how the body of the novel itself responds to the paradox of the complicated bodily inscriptions that constitute the characters of the narrative. In this chapter I assert that it is in the *Wildseed* narrative that the value and malleability of marginalized bodies is made most evident, via the readers' introduction to its body-wearing/shape-shifting antagonist and protagonist, Doro, and Anyanwu. Although it cannot be claimed that Butler intentionally amplifies her narratives with the problems of the body, such concerns are nevertheless consistently present in her fiction. And apart from of the intentions of Butler, this chapter will show that *Wildseed* houses fundamental assertions concerning the formation of racial, sexual, and gender identity.

THE GENESIS OF A PEOPLE

The narrative of *Wildseed* is organized under three headings reminiscent of Genesis in the Old Testament of the Hebrew/Christian *Bible*. These three headings are "Covenant (1690)," "Lots Children (1741)," and "Canaan (1840)." As a unit these three moments (re)construct the biblical story of the genesis of Jewish people. In extremely lucid prose, Butler interweaves the creation story with a (re)visionary narrative of slavery in a new world. It should be remarked that this narrative utilizes elements from both the masculine and the feminine traditions of the African American slave narrative. The result of this intermingling of thematic devices is a mythical story of the birthing of a new community of people, Doro's people.

Wildseed begins at the end of a seemingly unsuccessful search for family and bloodline by the antagonist, Doro. The family that Doro was seeking referred to one of his many seed villages scattered around the globe. It had been under construction for thousands of years, along with a bloodline that would produce a new breed of unusually gifted people. After finding his seed village destroyed and in ruins, Doro accidentally stumbles onto the awareness that someone with the special abilities that he is seeking was not far from him and might prove to be useful in the completion of his continuing mission. By beginning her narrative with Doro, Butler challenges the reader to imagine a character who has lived over a thousand years and possesses villages of humans or communities of people with the sole purpose of reproducing. Whether the reader is successful or not in identifying who or what Doro is, Butler makes it very clear from the outset of the narrative that Doro is a possessor and producer of bodies. Doro is possessor because he buys and sells the human bodies as if they were produce in a market or chattel slaves. Doro is also a producer of bodies in the sense that he is a genetic engineer bent on creating a family of bodies that will be most like himself.

Doro is far more complicated than a slaver who is simply interested in catching bodies and selling them to the highest bidder (Alaimo 127). Doro seems to have much more at stake than the material gain that can be acquired by the ownership of a slave. Through his bodies Doro is exposed to his people, and the vulnerability of the bodies he wears ties him to his people (Chambers 49). The people who populate Doro's seed villages represent genetic experiments in a project designed to create people like himself. Unlike the slavers who had destroyed his village with guns and greed, Doro has more at stake than the loss of profit. The village represented an investment that was both paternal and proprietary for Doro. Despite Doro's almost tyrannical control over the people in is his villages he felt responsible for them because they gave him their bodies and their loyalty. Doro's feelings went beyond a classic "white man's burden" in many respects he felt the burden a father feels for his children. Butler places Doro in the role of patriarch, one who has a complicated and ambiguous persona focused on accomplishing his goals with the least amount of resistance and interference from his charges.

The reader learns by the third paragraph of chapter one that Doro cannot be completely or simply human. As Doro wanders from the village, being pulled by an unexplained "awareness," "he was killed several times—by disease, by animals, and by hostile people" (Butler 3). Thus, Doro's existence is independent of the birth or death of body but is dependent upon the inhabitation of body for life. What this phenomenon does is raise the questions of who or what is Doro and how is his or its identity constructed.

Doro's identity is independent of flesh and bone. The body for Doro can act as a disposable mobile home to be used primarily for reproduction and transportation, not completely dissimilar to that of a "normal" person. However, for Doro, to dismiss death or being killed by animals or hostile people only necessitates mobility to another body. In this way Doro's essence or true identity is not limited to a single or individual body. His physical identity changes depending on the body he inhabits, but his "essence" remains constant. In many respects Doro's lack of a permanent physical body suggests a state of utopian identity. Doro is not bounded by the physical yet he has power within the material world. The concept of essence will be the guiding topic of this chapter; whether this concept can include something like "body" is one of its primary questions.

As we learn in the later chapters of *Wildseed* and Doro's final battle with Mary in *Mind of My Mind*, Doro is unable to assert his will unless he actually inhabits a body. It is the ritual of wearing bodies and employing them as reproductive material that makes Doro's character unique in the Patternist series.[5] To construct a race of people like him, Doro must obtain the proper raw materials. Although the physical identity (race, sex, and age) of the body is relatively unimportant, Doro does need a material body to function and to complete his genetic engineering. In this way Doro's dependency upon the body only requires that he treat the body as genetic material. He is or can be relatively unconcerned with a person as body, with emotions, self-initiative or personality. Melzer reminds us that,

> According to Foucault's theory of discursive power, gender roles and functions that supposedly are based on sexual differences in reproduction and in desire do not develop from "biological facts" but are produced through discourse. Bodies themselves (and desire that supposedly comes with them, based on their "natural" sex) do not determine relations between the genders, but their interpretation does. Paralleling Foucault's insistence on the "de-naturalization" of categories relating to sex, Butler undermines Western dualistic thinking, which assigns social value to sexual difference and is extremely inflexible. (83–84)

Doro's instinctive "impulse" for unusual bodies leads him to the protagonist of the narrative, Anyanwu. Doro finds an old and harmless looking woman working in her garden, but he is not deceived by what he observes. Doro immediately makes the statement (enters a discourse), "You are something more than an old woman" (Butler 6). In other words, Doro understands that the body that Anyanwu is wearing is much more complicated than it appears to be at the moment. Anyanwu is indeed more than an old woman, despite her bodily appearance. Anyanwu is a three hundred year old shape-shifter living near the Benin Empire in Nigeria in the year 1690.

Anyanwu is a black woman who possesses the ability to take the shape of any animal (human or beast) that she understands genetically or intuitively. Such understanding is obtained by visual assessment or by ingesting the flesh of an animal and simply reproducing its genetic structure and physical form. In explaining her ability to Doro, Anyanwu says,

> . . . I could see what the leopard was like. I was not a true leopard, though, until I killed one and ate a little of it. At first, I was a woman pretending to be a leopard—clay molded into leopard shape. Now when I change, I am a leopard (Butler 80).

A more accurate assessment of what Anyanwu becomes after tasting the flesh of an animal and imitating its form externally and internally is something very similar to what Doro is, an essence of an individual in the shell of a temporary body. Thus, it is this act of incorporation of another body and becoming that body that is at the foundation of the questions that will be examined in this chapter. Is the body dependent or independent of the notion of essence or self if there is no "bodily integrity" present? According to Sherryl Vint *Bodies of Tomorrow*,

> Gail Weiss's work on body images suggests a different perspective from which we could view the process of inhabiting many body images. Weiss argues that it is normal, and in fact healthy, for individuals to have multiple body images that they move between in response to the context that the body/subject occupies. These images help us to retain a constant sense of self throughout many changes to our cultural context. (76)

Anyanwu's ability to become a leopard (which is not to be confused with merely taking the shape of a leopard) implies that Anyanwu's self is not limited by the material forms that she incorporates. The elements that identify Anyanwu are not necessarily attached to a particular structure of flesh and bone or a specific material body but do involve something that is material. What I mean by this is that Anyanwu's self is real and ideal, perhaps spiritual, simultaneously. The exact shape or color of Anyanwu's and or Doro's self is insignificant, because until it takes a physical form there are no consequences to be dealt with in the real world.[6]

Stacy Alaimo's research on the body in *Wildseed* reveals some important insights on Doro and his method of defining himself and modes of knowing.

> In a passage that could serve as an epigraph for Octavia Butler's work, Trinh T. Minh-ha writes: "Ego is an identification with the mind. When ego develops, the head takes over and exerts tyrannical control over the rest of the body...But thought is as much a product of eye, the finger, or foot as it is of the brain" (39).[7] Butler's *Wildseed* dramatizes a battle between two modes of knowing and being: the tyrannical force of an egotistical, disembodied mind and the transformative powers of an utterly embodied woman. (Alaimo 126)

The point that Alaimo is emphasizing is that the identities of Doro and Anyanwu are different and similar simultaneously. Where Doro is a mind/ego first attempting to control the bodies that he possesses; Anyanwu is a brain/material matter attempting to control the ego. Ultimately, only human morality and conscience can be used to distinguish the bodies of Doro and Anyanwu. Alaimo goes on to note that

> Cartesian thought defines nonhuman nature as that which is devoid of mind or intention, so that humans can fashion themselves as the only creatures endowed with reason and, moreover, to justify reason's unchecked use, alteration, and even destruction of nonhuman nature. Doro extends the Cartesian territory of *terra nullius* onto human bodies, bodies that he can colonize, breed, and control with his disembodied mind. For Doro, both a Cartesian and a capitalist, bodies are nothing but vestments and investments. (127)

I agree with Alaimo's assertion that Doro's ability to empty or clean out the bodies that he colonizes is both Cartesian and capitalist in nature, but it is also very human, as it is dependent upon Doro's desire to survive. Despite his nonhuman form Doro is largely defined by his desires to possess and belong to bodies of his creation. In other words, Doro's humanity is dependent upon his quest for a family.

Because of a special ability to understand and manipulate her external and internal structure, Anyanwu possesses the power to heal herself as well as others. Butler supplies the narrative with several graphic examples of how Anyanwu actually accomplished the changes with her body. The following passage is taken from Anyanwu's voyage to North America and explains how she prevents herself from becoming a victim of seasickness.

> She focused on her inner ear and remembered perfection there, remembered organs and fluids and pressures in balance. Every change she made in her body had to be understood and visualized. If she was sick or injured, she could not simply wish to be well. She could be killed as easily as anyone else

if her body was damaged in some way she could not understand quickly enough to repair (Butler 54).

These abilities suggest to the reader that Anyanwu's less-material self is both real and is constantly working with her material body. For all intents and purposes Anyanwu is an immortal (someone who does not have to die) and the very thing that Doro has traveled so far off his course to obtain. When Doro first sees a demonstration of Anyanwu's shape-shifting ability he understands that the two together could very well become the matriarch and patriarch of a race of people who would defy the laws of physics and the boundaries of the body.

Shortly after Anyanwu's demonstration, Doro informs her that he has come to take her away to another land. Anyanwu initially rejects Doro's enticement to leave her people and to travel to a foreign land. It is at this moment that Doro makes the conditional promise that convinces Anyanwu to comply.

> "If you come with me, I think someday, I can show you children you will never have to bury. A mother should never have to watch her children grow old and die. If you live, they should live. Let me give you children who will live!" (22)

This covenant is the agreement that binds Doro and Anyanwu for the duration of the *Patternist* series. It is also a basis of conflict between the two characters, for as the patriarch of Anyanwu's children, Doro will always be the cause of their deaths directly or indirectly.

"The Covenant," Book I of *Wildseed*, introduces Anyanwu and Doro as matriarch and patriarch and then tells of their journey to North America. The middle passage motif is the most resonant structure in the architecture of the novel and is a commonly reoccurring motif in Butler's work. Butler reuses the middle passage motif in *Pattern Master* and the Xenogenesis series, and *Parable of the Sower* is almost completely dependent upon the events that take place on a trek up the west coast of North America. As in *Kindred* the notion of transporting the body over time and space is an important tool in developing Butler's main characters and story line. In the second chapter, at the beginning of their trek to the coast of West Africa, we find that Doro values the productive possibilities of the body more than the life of the body. In an altercation with a disgruntled tribesman Doro demonstrates for Anyanwu his method of destroying life and obtaining bodies.

Doro takes the body and life of a young village child in an attempt to warn off a young tribesman who does not wish to submit to Doro's authority. The event both shocks and frightens Anyanwu. After Anyanwu calms herself and is removed from the village, she realizes the potential danger Doro's powers could pose for anybody who contradicts his intentions and how much danger he would have posed for her people if she had refused to leave with him. It is at this moment in the narrative that Anyanwu begins to fear Doro and his ability to steal her body on a decided whim of "sacrifice, annoyance, or regret" (Butler 36).

On arriving at the coast, Doro and Anyanwu meet with a one-handed slaver, Bernard Daly. Daly is a servant of Doro and relays the massage that Doro's ships have been awaiting his arrival. What is significant about Daly's presence in the narrative is that it comes with the introduction of "race." Until Doro and Anyanwu arrived at Daly's slave camp there was no discussion of "racial distinction" in the narrative. The reader was left to assume that because the setting was on the African continent all of the bodies mentioned shared the same phenotypical characteristics. This suggests that race is an important marker for the body but that it is relatively unimportant when it is not accented by difference.

Because of Daly's white skin he is referred to by Anyanwu as a "white animal" (Butler 42). Likewise, Daly refers to Anyanwu and her people as "heathen savages" all guilty of cannibalism, if given the opportunity (43). Because of the difference in the racial identity of the two characters, they devalue each other's body on such a basic and primitive level that Doro's practices seem almost humane. Doro seems indifferent to racial categorizations of the body and demonstrates his impartiality through business transactions and his occupancy of different kinds of bodies across many phenotypes throughout the narrative.

On Doro's ship, headed to the New World, Anyanwu encounters one of his sons, Lale. Lale attempts to invade Anyanwu's mind, but she takes the form of a leopard and kills him. Doro tries to stop Anyanwu from feeding on Lale's corpse and is almost forced to take Anyanwu life in the process.

> He stood inches from her, head back, as though offering her his throat. Which was exactly what he was doing, of course. "Come, he challenged. Kill again. It has been a long time since I was a woman" (74).

Here we learn that Doro is unconcerned with racial identity and that gender is a boundary that does not influence his body snatching practices. Just as Anyanwu had taken the guise of an old woman and a "well-muscled man" (15) at the beginning of the narrative, Doro demonstrates equal willingness to cross gender boundaries without hesitation. Thus, Doro is an equal opportunist when it comes to achieving his goals of survival. The same may be said for Anyanwu, who is obviously willing to do whatever is necessary to survive. Neither seems to place any value in the notion that the racial and gender identities attached to a body necessarily dictate the level of authority and power wielded by a particular body. At this early moment in the narrative it is made clear that for both Doro and Anyanwu power is defined by one's ability to manipulate bodies.

The point that I want to emphasize about power is not necessarily how it is employed by either character but the fact that each character is powerful because he or she can look beyond the forms of the bodies that they employ. Both Doro and Anyanwu possess objectivity about the body that allows them to see beyond the boundaries of lesser individuals because of their shape-shifting abilities. In other words, because Doro and Anyanwu are not limited by the forms of their individual bodies (material and spiritual) they automatically have an advantage over characters without such abilities. Doro and Anyanwu, along with the reader, see and know better than others in the *Wildseed* narrative what constitutes the notion of a body and a self.

By the end of book one, both Doro and Anyanwu learn a great deal about the capabilities and weaknesses of each other. More importantly, Doro learns that unlike his children, Anyanwu possesses powers and a will that he can not completely dominate. Doro becomes aware that Anyanwu has more power than he would like one of is charges to enjoy. The threat of death was not viable in the same way as it might have been with his other wild seed. If Doro was forced to kill Anyanwu he could only wear her body for a short period of time and would not reap the full benefit of her body's reproductive capabilities. Doro's hesitancy toward Anyanwu occurs when he realizes that his "awareness" does not function when she takes the internal and external form of anything other than a human. After eating the meat of a dolphin Anyanwu transforms herself into a female dolphin and leaves the ship temporarily to learn more about the species. After being hoisted back onto the ship by the telekinetic abilities of Isaac, Doro's most competent adult son, Doro realizes that he could not sense or detect Anyanwu's presence in animal forms.

In "Becoming Other: Animals, Kinship, and Butler's *Clay's Ark*" Sherryl Vint notes that,

> Agamben, Derrida, and Haraway each call for a thinking of the human's subject's relationship to its animal other as part of a transformation of ethics and politics. Their scholarship also makes clear that the category of the animal is important to our philosophical heritage precisely for the ways in which it informs various discriminatory hierarchies established among humans to designate the Other and thereby used to exclude certain humans from the realm of ethics. (281–82)

Anyanwu's ability to take the form of animals lends to her ability to negotiate the hierarchies of the "humans" she encounters throughout the *Wildseed* narrative. As a political device this ability seems redundant considering Anyanwu's "natural" form is that of a black woman. However, in the context of a SF narrative the state of an animal distances her from Doro's ability to evoke *terra nullius* or to colonize her mind and body.

Without his mental radar the location of Anyanwu's body is unattainable and thus subject to be more mobile than Doro sees fit. As an obtainer of bodies, just as a common slave owner, a crucial aspect of Doro's power is his ability to enforce his authority. This can only be done if the body can be located with ease and accuracy. While Doro has the keen ability to locate and identify specially gifted bodies despite their racial and gender identities, he is unfamiliar with the identity markers of the animal kingdom. As a result he is not in the position to enforce his rule over Anyanwu. In this way we are able to see how the narrative advocates a re-thinking of the construction of race and gender and their relationship to power. Perhaps it is not the shape or color of the body that evokes power or agency but the self within or underneath the flesh and bone of a body that necessarily calls for agency or authority. Doro immediately understands the implication of his inability to identify Anyanwu's animal markers and feels threatened. Although Anyanwu is not aware of Doro's fear at this moment in the narrative Doro is fearful, because he understands that his threat of consuming her body and those of her children may not be enough to absolutely control her actions in the long run. Doro's belief that "if he could not breed stupidity out of them [his children], he would frighten it out" (87), would not work for his new wife Anyanwu.

At the end of chapter six of book one, we learn that Doro intends to break his covenant with Anyanwu in order to secure his hold on Anyanwu and her unborn offspring.

> Her children would hold her if her husband would not. She could become an animal or alter herself enough to travel freely among whites and Indians, but several children would surely slow her down. And she would not abandon them. She was too much of a mother for that. (92)

In this passage Doro identifies Anyanwu's point of weakness to be her inclination to nurture. Doro understands that such a weakness can be used to drastically limit the mobility of the female body and if necessary threaten a body that may otherwise be impervious to external forces. Thus, despite all of Anyanwu's special abilities and super human strength, it is her maternal instincts that make her controllable, perhaps susceptible to subordination.

In this way Doro seems to take on an element of masculinity. Despite Doro's practice of changing bodies, references of "he" or "him" and Doro's masculinity are never disrupted in the narrative because his character is consistent with the notions and actions of the masculine. Notwithstanding this latter observation, Doro's opinions about Anyanwu's weakness also imply that maleness and masculinity should not be too easily equated in the case of Doro's identity. Because Doro changes bodies so arbitrarily throughout the narrative the notion of maleness is subject to shifts toward the ambiguous with regards to masculinity.

When Doro tells Anyanwu of his intent to have her marry Isaac she initially rejects the idea but is eventually cajoled by a seemingly sympathetic Isaac. By the time Doro's ship arrives at the end of its middle passage to Wheatley, his seed village in the new world, Anyanwu was well on her way to "making the children who would prolong her slavery" (Butler 131). What I mean by this is that by producing children with special abilities Anyanwu makes herself even more valuable to Doro as a slave and as a producer of rare goods. At this moment in Butler's narrative the possibilities of the female body with regards to reproduction and power exposes a paradox. The characteristics that mark Anyanwu's body as valuable, powerful, and potentially dangerous to Doro are also at the root of her vulnerability and general susceptibility to servitude to him. As readers we are left to contemplate the very complicated, if not contradictory, elements of motherhood in the second half of *Wildseed*, the narrative of which begins 51 years after Anyanwu's arrival in Wheatley. Here we find Anyanwu playing the role of the mother and nursemaid. She has apparently adapted to the ways of Doro's people and has merged herself into the business of helping her new families reproduce and survive the trials and tribulations of belonging to Doro. I use the term belong here because Doro is their benefactor and patriarch. Doro's rights of ownership come from the fact that he controls the bodies that inhabit his villages with regards to life, death, reproduction, and law.

Anyanwu's healing skills have designated her as the resident witch doctor.[8] Upon his arrival in Wheatley, Doro asks Isaac for the whereabouts of Anyanwu. His response is, "helping the Sloane Baby" (Butler 137). Although Anyanwu has chosen to adapt to her new environment some of the newer arrivals to Wheatley like the Sloanes had not yet overcome their racialisms and other superstitions. "They're afraid of her blackness and her power. They think she is a witch, and the mold-medicine she made [penicillin for the pneumonia] some poison"(137). Eventually, they would learn to accept and even love Anyanwu despite her racial identity and her power. For the past fifty-one years Anyanwu and Isaac have acted as the overseers and caretakers of the Wheatley village while Doro traveled abroad working on the development of his new race of people. Wheatley is filled with dysfunctional families of gifted people who act as Doro's reproductive material and prey. Apparently many of the parents in Wheatley and other seed villages of Doro make very poor guardians for their children. Like the Sloanes, many of the couples placed together by Doro for breeding purposes experience a chemical imbalance that disallows them to interact normally with their children, especially during transition periods. Because of excessive interbreeding among siblings and other incestuous practices the wild seed families of Doro are fragmented and dysfunctional. In this way Doro's seed villages are similar to some African American slave communities during America's antebellum era. It is one of many along the east coast of America, in Pennsylvania, Maryland, Georgia, and Spanish Florida. However, it is presented as a sort of home-base for Doro because it is the home of his favorite son, Isaac, and Anyanwu. Wheatley is also the home of Anyanwu's youngest daughter, Nweke.

Doro's primary reason for returning to Wheatley, on this occasion, was to visit Nweke during her transition. In this section of *Wildseed* we learn that the children of Doro must go through a transitional stage similar to puberty but one that is much more unpleasant in order to fully develop their special gifts. The transition is dangerous for both the child and the individuals around the child and often results in the death of one or the other. Doro sensed that Nweke was something new and different from his other wild seed. "It was as though from New York City he had sensed another Anyanwu—new, different, attracting him, pulling him. He had never followed a feeling more willingly" (145). For these reasons Nweke's transition is the center of Book II "Lot's Children." In this moment of the narrative we learn that Doro has "refrained from preying on Anyanwu's least successful children, refrained from breeding her daughters to her sons—or bedding those daughters himself" (143). Anyanwu has learned to negotiate with Doro's power. And although Doro believes that he can take Anyanwu's life at any moment, he has developed a tolerance for her resistance and has let her live longer than any other wild seed woman after child birth. Despite their concessions a great hatred developed among the two characters over the years. It is this hatred that will result in Anyanwu's escape from Doro's Wheatley.

Nweke's transition was a horrific failure. Before her body was smashed into the ceiling by Isaac, Nweke managed to destroy several of Anyanwu's internal organs. She also manages to wound Isaac mortally in the same fashion before her own demise. Doro was not injured, but he was unable to prevent Nweke's death. "Nweke had been all Doro had hoped and more" (189). She had become a healer with powers that Doro had never seen before. Unfortunately, Nweke had lost control of her abilities before she could complete her transition.

Through this event we are informed that Doro is more than a paternal slave trader, in fact he is first and foremost a genetic manipulator, an individual completely invested in the production of particularly gifted bodies. The loss of Nweke was little more than the failure of a promising experiment to Doro. Although he does experience some physical and emotional stress from the incident, Nweke and Isaac were merely examples of "good stock" (195).

On the day of the funeral Anyanwu took the form of a bird and flew away from Wheatley and beyond Doro's special awareness. She eventually decides to live among a group of dolphins. "She was a dolphin. If Doro had not found her an adequate mate, he would find her an adequate adversary. He would not enslave her again. And she would never be his prey" (Butler 198). With this covenant to herself Anyanwu escapes to a temporary freedom that is contingent upon the shape and identity of her body.

The third book and final section of *Wildseed* is entitled "Canaan 1840." After almost one hundred years away from Doro, we find that Anyanwu has settled in Louisiana. Doro's seed villages have spread across the globe and the abilities of his wild seed has grown considerably since Anyanwu's time at Wheatley. As before, Doro stumbled into an awareness of Anyanwu on a trip to collect more wild seed for his villages. After arriving on her plantation, Doro intended to take her life but was distracted by his observations. "Anyanwu had come almost as near success as he had—and with far less raw material" (206). After interrogating Anyanwu's son, Stephen, about his ability to read minds, heal himself and the abilities of the other people on Anyanwu's plantation, Doro decided to make Anyanwu a silent partner instead of killing her.

Through his usual threats on the lives of Anyanwu's children Doro managed to take over her settlement. He used Anyanwu's plantation as he had used Wheatley. He brought the worst of his genetic experiments to breed with Anyanwu's children and to disrupt the order and serenity that had once reigned over the settlement. It is in this final moment of the narrative that a mutual understanding between the antagonist and protagonist is established. Doro allows Anyanwu to see who and what he is beneath his temporary flesh. Doro's true body is described as being blinding sunlight filled with anger and solitude (257). The encounter between the two enabled Anyanwu to understand why Doro had always been so intent on creating a race of people like himself. Doro was constructing a family for himself; a family that would fill the gaping absence that he had experienced since his own transition. Such a family needed to be immortal. Doro's ultimate family needed to be able to exist somewhere between the real and spiritual world. Anyanwu was finally allowed to understand this aspect of Doro's character. Thus, for the first time in the narrative Anyanwu was allowed to visualize her role as the matriarch and companion who would help Doro achieve his goal and keep his covenant that he had made to her almost two hundred years before. On some levels this concession is disappointing as Anyanwu is forced to attain a sense of personal worth only by taking part in what appears to be masculine values. Instead of aspiring happily to the worthy estate of motherhood, she is cajoled to be contented within a patriarchal family (Barbara Walker 693).

WRITING THE BODY

Butler's writing of the body in *Wildseed* is largely accomplished through her employment of biblical references, African American folklore, American history, African history, history of colonialism and speculative elements of SF. Biblical references literally give structure to the outline of the entire narrative, as the three sections of the novel are entitled "Covenant," "Lot's Children," and "Canaan." African and African American folklore presents itself in Doro's resemblance to *Elegba* of Nigeria, A.K.A. *Anansi* the Spider of Ghana, A.K.A. *Brer Rabbit* of the United States of America. And although all of Anyanwu's abilities may not be common in the either African or African American oral traditions, root workers and witches have been known to show up on occasion.

It is on the basis of these elements that Butler manages to produce such identifiable characters with such complicated bodies. Doro and Anyanwu are made identifiable to the readers of the *Wildseed* narrative by way of character flaws and struggle. What I mean by this is that despite the fact that Butler writes the two characters as extraordinary, they are not perfect and they struggle to survive and accomplish their goals throughout the narrative. By writing characters who are both extraordinary and yet common, Butler makes it possible for the reader to identify with characters who are constantly changing in ways that do not always make sense. The act of placing Doro and Anyanwu in familiar biblical scenarios, (which also may not make sense) allows the characters to become less unfamiliar and more believable.

The second section of *Wildseed*, "Lot's Children," makes reference to the biblical city of Sodom and Gomorra. According to the King James' version, Gen. 19:1–38, Lot, his wife, and his two daughters were ordered to leave the doomed city of Sodom and Gomorra by angels from heaven. On their departure, the wife of Lot looks back at the destruction of the city (after being told not to do so by God; Gen. 19:17) and is transformed into a pillar of salt. Lot and his two daughters escape the city to dwell in an abandoned cave. With Lot being the only male present and the end of a family bloodline, his daughters plot to produce offspring by way of the father's loins. The two daughters proceed to get the father drunk hoping that he will become disoriented enough to engage in coitus with them. One night after another, the daughters manage successfully to obtain their father's seed and the potential longevity of their bloodlines.

In this act of survival, questions of morality and immorality are usually raised and then discounted because of a necessity to procreate. As in the time of Adam and Eve, the taboos of incest are negated when they conflict with attempts to construct a new race of people. Lot's story is both an allegory of the moral obligations of fatherhood and a story that preserves a memory of intermarriage among ancestors of the Israelites. The Lot narrative ends with a theological motif that demonstrates God's providential guidance of the patriarchs, His judgment of sin, His accommodation to man's weakness, and His saving grace. The fathers and daughters of Doro reenact the story of Lot as a socially acceptable chain of events necessary for their survival. Doro's written resemblance to the biblical character of Lot perhaps makes him more believable as a character in the eyes of readers who might have questioned his ultimate goal and his position in the narrative.

By demonstrating the violation of certain taboos such as the incest taboo and the interdiction against and interracial coupling in a familiar Christian context, Butler's narrative suggests a reevaluation of the sense of the proper way of reproducing the body. More precisely, Butler's writing of certain bodies necessitates a discussion of the moral ethics that surround any body in a social setting. This is most clearly demonstrated by the way Anyanwu is repulsed by Doro's refusal to adhere to her cultural taboos.

To identify with the protagonist, Anyanwu, is to identify with conservative and traditionally Christian notions of morality, despite the fact that her character supposedly originates far from any place that can be connected directly with Christianity. Anyanwu's character is written such that the social ethics of her native people are in many ways similar to that of the western world of probable readers of the *Wildseed* narrative. "Lot's Children" is a crucial moment in Butler's text because it is the section of the narrative that both elaborate the power and production of the antagonist and the struggle of the protagonist to adapt to difference. Anyanwu is forced on several occasions to overlook what she understands as taboo in order to survive. "Lot's Children" begins, "Doro had come to Wheatley to see to the welfare of his daughters" (Butler 135). The significance of this introduction lies in the fact that, by this time in the narrative, Anyanwu has long since been "given away" by Doro to Isaac, one of his more powerful sons. Thus, Anyanwu has had to mate with her son-in-law and is forced to tolerate the incestuous relationships that are common in Doro's Wheatley. Doro's desires, no matter how perverse to outsiders, were accepted by his people. And more importantly, Doro's people understood his practices as the norm and the only social standard of any importance.

The necessity to interbreed in order to strengthen certain genetic characteristics has been socialized into all of the communities that Doro constructs. His practice of eugenics has no moral boundaries and therefore, attaches no taboo to father-daughter procreation. In fact, such bonding has been practiced by Doro and his children for centuries. "In Wheatley, young girls usually saved themselves for husbands, or for Doro" (151). At this moment in the narrative, it is clear that Doro is not the traditional good father concerned with preserving his daughter's virginity for a young male suitor, nor do his daughters perceive him as such. Where the biblical story of Lot vaguely speaks to issues of the moral obligation of fatherhood, Doro's story pertains to the production of the most advantageous genetic combination.

Anyanwu comes to understand this procedure beyond her moral experiences in Nigeria. But while she understands it and learns to adapt to it, she does not accept the practices as normal for her own three hundred years of existence. The representation of Anyanwu's accommodation and ambivalence, suggests that we reconsider the construction of the moral and the immoral. Anyanwu's lack of acceptance or reluctance to give herself totally to Doro's cause and methodology, however, results in her flight from both Wheatley and Doro.

This scenario can be understood analogous to the situation of Lot's wife with the exception of several points of deviation. Of the differences, the first and most obvious is that Wheatley is in no immediate danger of being destroyed by the hand of God. Secondly, no angels reside in the town of Wheatley who represent those without sin; in fact the town of Wheatley is filled with "abysmal parents" (137). Good and bad exist in all of Doro's children. Furthermore, Anyanwu is not turned into a pillar of salt. Instead, to escape her angry god, she uses her own agency to transform herself into a bird then a dolphin.

As for the comparison of Lot and Doro, on many counts it is Doro who acts as a god. And as a god, Doro has very little if any saving grace; he judges no sin but disobedience of his will; and he manipulates weaknesses of his people instead of making accommodations for them. In addition to the biblical reference of Lot, Doro can also be compared with figures found in the creation stories of the Nation of Islam. In the *Autobiography of Malcolm X*, Mr. Elijah Muhammad told his followers of a mad scientist who became embittered with Allah and created an evil race of white people, "a devil race" (Haley 165), to obtain revenge. "Yacub's History," serves as an example of demonology that attempts to explain the origin of both the black and white race. As a member of the "original black race," Mr. Yacub was one of twenty-four wise scientists. Known as "the big head scientist," Mr. Yacub, much like Doro, learned how to breed races scientifically and discovered that black men contained two germs, black and brown. After being exiled from the Holy City Of Mecca, Yacub began to upset the laws of nature through the employment of eugenics on a small island called Patmos—described in the Bible as the island where

John received the message contained in Revelations in the New Testament (Haley 165). With the assistance of 59,999 all-black followers, Mr. Yacub created a colony with laws that would eventually bleach-out the black race and construct a weaker white race that would be much more susceptible to sin. Like Doro, Mr. Yacub does not live to see nor enjoy the completion of his project, but the rest of humanity is left to suffer the oppression of a devil race. In the case of the Patternist series, Butler constructs a race of superior humans (minor gods) who manipulate and punish humanity as if they were jealous and vengeful gods of the Old Testament.

Butler continues to employ biblical references in her final section, Canaan. Canaan represents the land to which Anyanwu temporarily escapes in order to elude Doro. She starts a small agricultural community in New Orleans (a parental site of creolization or blending of race and culture) where she houses her "special" children and other wild seed. As in the biblical Canaanite social structure, there are essentially three social groups: freemen, clients, and slaves. The people who hold a status analogous to the slave in Anyanwu's "community of the cursed" are those who have no control over their abilities or who have no special abilities at all. The freemen include Anyanwu and her healthy offspring and those surrounding her community. The client element in the analogy does not develop until Doro arrives in the community: He went to complete his unfinished business of killing her and gathering up any new human descendants (Butler 203). The moment Doro enters her community it becomes a community of merchants. The merchandise is wild seed and the ability to nurture and grow the seed into useful tools for Doro's cause and appeasement. At this moment in her text, Butler moves away from the traditional slave plantation motif found in Wheatley by complicating the roles of the slave with agency and hope.

Although Anyanwu is clearly in a position to be manipulated by Doro, she uses her mobility and leverage to resist Doro actively. This is significant because with these seemingly small allowances, Anyanwu is placed in a position of an active writer of the history of an entirely new race of people. She is becoming more like Doro on one hand and less like him on another. Anyanwu's plantation can be interpreted as her allegorical diploma for genetic engineering or as a symbol of her ability to mother children that Doro can only oppress.

It is not until the end of the second book in the Patternist series, *Mind of My Mind* that we find that the covenant does come to pass. Doro and Anyanwu eventually procreate a new race of people, but the arrival of the first true Patternist results in the destruction of both the mother and father. Doro is made victim to his own creation and because of his death his wife Anyanwu (now Emma) follows. The children of Adam (Doro) and Eve (Emma) take the Garden of Eden for themselves through the use of lethal force.

Wildseed can be understood as a retelling of the biblical story of Genesis on several levels. As Adam and Eve, Anyanwu the sun rises from the Doro, the East. The two are destined from the beginning to create a new world. As a serial body possessor, Doro (The Serpent) takes on the guise of a seducer that leads Eve/Anyanwu away from the path of the straight and narrow, into sin. Butler alludes to this metaphor often in the Covenant section of the novel: "Give me food, Anyanwu," he said. "Then I will have the strength to entice you away from this place" (Butler 17). Genesis tells of the serpent enticing Eve away from the word of God. In Butler's version "this place" is Anyanwu's homeland, Africa, the location of her family, her Eden.

Butler's writing of the body as object and subject is dependent on our understanding of how the body is to be formed biologically and socially. Although genetic manipulation is clearly near the center of the *Wildseed* narrative, the social values that we use to bind the body are also crucial to both the story line and any allegory that might be present. Through *Wildseed* it is suggested that the body acts as a holder of several identities at once. The race, sex, age, and gender of a body do not necessarily have to permanently restrict the holder of a body. The body is not the individual nor do the identities held by or written upon a body necessarily constitute the personality of an individual. The self is not dependent upon a physical body.

Doro, and eventually Anyanwu are not simply the realization of the Western logos: spirit freed from body, because they affect the real world in all of the forms that they hold. Furthermore, neither Anyanwu nor Doro seem to perceive their bodies as enclosures or prisons to be freed from. In fact it is Doro's ability to move from body to body and Anyanwu's ability to change her body that identifies the two as the most mobile characters in the *Wildseed* narrative. If we accept the body as more than flesh and bone, possibly "the condition of a process of construction only externally related to the body that is its object" (J. Butler 601), Doro's character takes on an even more complicated role in understanding how we construct a body in our imaginations and how we attach identities to a particular body. Notwithstanding the latter, in Octavia Butler's deceptively lucid creation story about the father and mother of a new race of people the body is left in question and steeped in ambiguity.

NOTES

1. In his discussion about the individuals' perception of their own racial identity McKnight provides a partial explanation to how Doro might perceive his

body(s). "The body is developed as a conception central to the definition of membership with others in the polity (Grosz 1994, p. 119). By fixing the representations of the body, this allows for the introduction of aural elements, including the voice, and social behaviour to differentiate between the acceptable and unacceptable practices that then describe membership by type. These discursive practices elaborate a racial subject without the need to reference traditional attributions of human phenotypal difference" (65).

2. Elizabeth Grosz, *Jacques Lacan: A Feminist Introduction* (London: Routledge, 1990). *Volatile Bodies: Toward a Corporeal Feminism* (Indiana: Indiana UP, 1994).

3. Jean-Paul Sartre, *Being and Nothingness* (1943), English version (Washington Square Press, 1993).

4. Merleau-Ponty, *The Visible and the Invisible* (Paris Gallimard, 1964), Trans. Alphonso Lingis (Evanston: Northwestern UP, 1968).

5. *Black Critics and Kings*, by Andrew Apter examines how Yoruba forms of ritual and knowledge shape politics, history, and resistance against the state. Focusing on "deep" knowledge in Yoruba cosmology as an interpretive space for configuring difference, Andrew Apter analyzes ritual empowerment as an essentially critical practice, one that revises authoritative discourses of space, time, gender, and sovereignty to promote political—and even violent—change. Butler's writing of Doro, and Anyanwu lends a Yoruba sensibility to the *Wildseed* narrative.

6. Both Doro and Anyanwu seem to contradict the theories expressed by Lacan and his "Mirror Stage." Where Lacan's theory typifies an essential libidinal relationship with the body image, Butler's characters do not require a static reflection in society's mirror to define and validate their egos. More detailed information on Lacan's "Mirror Stage" can be found in *An Introduction of Lacanian Psychoanalysis* by Dylan Evans, Routledge Press, 1996.

7. Trinh T. Minh. *Women, Native, Other*. Bloomington: Indiana University Press, 1989.

8. Anyanwu's situation in the Wheatley village is reminiscent to the experience a Maryse Conde's witch Tituba found in her 1992 novel *I, Tituba: Black Witch of Salem*.

3

Patternmaster:
Hierarchies of Identity

This chapter is an examination of relationships existing between the body and the hierarchies that surround it in Octavia Butler's Patternmaster series, which begins with *Patternmaster* (1976) and concludes with *Survivor* (1978). In this reading of the Patternist series I am primarily concerned with the notion of race as an essential marker for the body. I argue that race is an involuntary structure of hierarchy that is both conceived and maintained in order to identify bodies in a given social structure, which in the case of the Patternmaster series is largely dependent upon the flexibility of the science fiction narrative that Butler employs. Her narratives are not dependent upon the notion of a black or brown body in conflict with a white body. On the contrary, the differences among the bodies used in Butler's work attempt to move a few steps beyond "normal" geological and biological difference which might be connoted by things such as phenotype and pigmentation. Furthermore, the term race is a consistently ambiguous term in Butler's writing because it is treated as a historical process that changes according to the social and historical context in which it is used. As Butler's speculative narratives are varying according to historical time frame and social organization, race becomes something more—a description of the social and cultural development of what Butler calls the Patternist race, i.e. a technology of identity.

Butler's Patternist series is essentially a collection of stories that speak to the work of creating a genetically distinct community of people with a collective identity. In Butler's writing the term race is not limited to biological difference. In fact, I am proposing that the notion of race, in

Butler's fiction, is often employed as a moving marker for collective identity as well as individual biological difference. By this I mean, the Patternist race that Butler writes into her speculative reality changes and develops into something slightly different as her narratives jump further into a speculative future. The notion of a technology of identity works here because technology changes and becomes more complicated as time progresses. Butler creates bodies which are different with respect to a generic racial identity, as her characters are frequently marked as Black, White, Latin, Asian, and Other. With every narrative in the Patternist series a new technology of identity is developed because a new "Other" is added to the plot. Yet through a narrative history, the Patternmaster series, biological difference, cultural practices, and social behavior specific to descendants of Doro and Anyanwu form what might be referred to as an ethnicity.

With regard to the term ethnicity, Hortence Spillers presents some very useful insight in her essay "Mama's Baby, Papa's Maybe," that I would like to borrow as I proceed with my examination of Butler's fiction. In her essay, Spillers questions the condition of the African American family with regard to its capacity to function as a matriarchal structure despite the pressure which this state places on the males and females of the community. Ultimately, Spiller concludes that the complexity surrounding such a condition does not have to be debilitating for male or female. And in fact, a matriarchy may very well supply the African American family with some things not necessarily available from a traditional white male patriarchy, namely a black female subjectivity that is completely capable of yielding a more conscious and developed male subjectivity aware of the "female within" (Spillers 480).

As Spillers discusses the term, "ethnicity" has been used to identify the total objectification of human and cultural motives. As such, it is a static notion, applied in a way that allows it to be used as a code that translates into vulnerable objects. What interests me about Spillers interrogation of the term is that she allows it to be placed in an historical context that speaks to ethnicity's availability to metaphor and its utter dependency on the historical placement/movement of bodies in an historical context. What I mean by this is that ethnicity can describe the changing practices and behaviors of a collective body, which might include gender and sexuality as well as other characteristics beyond the "normal." Undoubtedly, Butler's Patternist race is something I want to posit as beyond the normal even within the vast bounds of SF. However, it also must be understood that all such notions in Butler's fiction within or beyond the genre are likely to be metaphors applicable to the real.

In response to Spiller's article but also applicable to Butler's writing, Elisabeth Krimmer suggests that the defining of gender roles is closely connected to political and social changes of the time (Krimmer 257). In other words the roles of mother and father are social constructs that may shift from time to time, depending on the condition of a particular environment. This is especially important when considering the matriarchal birth of the first pattern and its shift to a patriarchal pattern in the *Patternmaster* narrative. Butler's narrative questions how the body is used to prescribe social and moral tasks based on gender distinctions.

> The new association between body and gender was made possible by redefining of the gendered body itself. In his study of gender constructs from the Greeks to Freud, Thomas Laqueur postulates the existence of two different models of gender identity, the earlier one-sex model, and the later two-sex model. In the one-sex model. The difference between male and female is interpreted as one of degree, not of kind (Krimmer 259).

Thomas Laqueur's one-sex model can be observed in most of the gender relations written in Butler's fictions. Women and men share many of the same impulses and desires in Butler's Patternist series. The genders are made distinct by the varying degrees of intensity in which the characters act upon certain impulses and desires. Laqueur's two-sex model seems to be based on the very principles that Butler's narratives attempt to combat with the characters of Mary and Amber, irrational gender hierarchy and old-fashioned misogyny.

> Women's bodies became the primary anchors of women's underprivileged position. With biology bolstering the new gender order, women were relegated to the house and home while the newly created public sphere became the domain of men (Krimmer 260).

Krimmer's investigation of the importance of and power attached to the notion of paternity in nineteenth century Europe, suggests that the role and identity of the father is often unclear. This may partially explain the patriarchal construction of the True Cult Womanhood and its confining four cardinal virtues—purity, piety, submissiveness, and domesticity.[1] What Laqueur's two-sex model fails to explain is how the public domain can exclude the importance of the family and its role in shaping society. Ultimately, Krimmer's discussion suggests that by distancing the father from the mother and family a question of paternity is made significant. Although uncertain paternity is not a major theme in the Paternmaster series, the role played by the father in establishing social order is of great importance to this discussion, particularly with regard to the *Patternmaster* novel.

All of the narrative moments that I will explore in this chapter are dependent upon identifying differences among particular bodies. Whether the Patternist people are categorized as a race or an ethnicity, their distinctions are ultimately functions of difference that continuously change with continuities and discontinuities as Butler's series progresses. In examining Butler's narratives, however, consciousness of bodily difference and the body are two inextricable elements that necessitate a struggle for power and the formation of hierarchies. One of the primary functions of this chapter will be to unearth the results of race/ethnicity as a marker used to construct and maintain hierarchies of difference. In accomplishing this clarification the value of the body is made more lucid in Butler's fiction. That is to say, this chapter will attempt to engage these terms of bodily difference as processes that are not static in definition or employment in Butler's writing.

Through the Patternist series Butler has constructed body after body over a period of time (and or a series of SF narratives) and given them a unique group identity and a genealogy. In doing this, race has become a process of narrative history extending from scenes and backgrounds in the Patternmaster series. In addition to being a mobile phenomenon and a marker for the body, the idea of race, in Butler's fiction, is also a function of gender and the production of bodies. In Butler's writing the Patternist race is definitely a sort of historical development over a period of narratives and is therefore analogous to Spillers ethnicity.

Hierarchies are clearly delineated in the Patternmaster series, but they are most explicitly present in the *Patternmaster* narrative. In Butler's first novel tiers of power and authority are based on both the identities of the body and the agency of the body. By this I mean that the characters in Butler's narrative are, for the most part, neatly positioned within a pattern or web structure that symbolizes the value of that character depending on gender, genetic possibility and the ability to preserve or destroy other bodies. In order to gain a clearer understanding of how Butler's narratives employ the terms of race and the body in *Patternmaster* I briefly examine the texts leading to it and following it in the series.

The series begins with *Wildseed*, where Doro and Anyanwu are first introduced as the patriarch and matriarch of a genetically engineered group of people known as Doro's wild seed. It becomes evident by the middle of the narrative that Doro's wild seed is a euphemism for Doro's guinea pigs in his ruthless attempt to create a community of people like himself upon which he will feed and continue to breed. The narrative that follows *Wildseed* is *Mind of My Mind*, and it is in this moment of the series that Doro accomplishes his goal. The protagonist, Mary, is the result of centuries of interbreeding and the brutal objectification of anyone possessing the genetic material needed by Doro. Mary inadvertently creates the first pattern and is forced to destroy Doro at the end of the narrative.

As Mary's pattern grows and the Patternists become a highly organized and distinct community of people, an exploratory spaceship called Clay's Ark has managed to return to Earth with an infected pilot in the *Clay's Ark* narrative. The pilot is infected with a virus-like extraterrestrial organism that does some genetic engineering of its own. The Clay's Ark organism combined with human DNA produces a new species called Clayarks. Their primary function is to reproduce and spread their virus to as many carriers as possible.

Meanwhile, the descendants of Mary and her pattern have become a highly organized and powerful community of people in the *Patternmaster* narrative. In this novel the Patternists brothers, Coransee and Teray, battle for the position of Patternmaster while killing large numbers of their arch enemies, the Clayarks. When the Clayarks are on the verge of infecting all of humanity, including the Patternists, spaceships filled with Christian missionaries are sent to find a new home for humanity. In the *Survivor* narrative the protagonist, Alanna, only finds more of the same kind of power struggle that she and her missionary parents thought they were leaving behind on Earth.

By examining the *Mind of My Mind* (1977) narrative the reasons behind Doro's desire to create a new race of people is made clearer. Understanding the role of a specific character, Mary, a daughter of Doro, in his race-building plan begins to explain the need and origins of racial identification which seems to be identical with the notion of practicing an ethnicity. And seeing Mary give birth to the first pattern allows the reader to image what it must be like to hold the absolute identity of a race of people in the palm of ones hand. When Mary constructs the pattern she unlike most of humanity has much more than an intuitive knowledge of what belonging to the Patternist race, or any race for that matter, is like. Mary is allowed to understand the bodies of her people on both a material and abstract level which easily transcend any intuitive understanding of ones identity.

By understanding the genesis of the Clayarks the order of the Patternist hierarchy is placed in a better perspective alongside those of the ordinary human. The readers of the *Clay's Ark* narrative are allowed to see how the mixing of different bodies can create a completely new species and race of bodies. This narrative also explains some of the hostility between the Patternists and Clayarks that is not fully explained in the other narratives surrounding it. The struggle of the protagonist, Eli, to maintain what few human characteristics the Clay's Ark organism leaves him, raises several reoccurring questions of whether or not humanity is dependent upon a physical body.

My examination of the *Patternmaster* narrative is the most detailed because it is in this structure that the hierarchy of a race/ethnicity is most clearly configured. With the body as its central concern (flesh and other),

Patternmaster presents several questions about how race works in a social structure and how gender works in the function of race and how together the two connote a unique ethnicity. Although Amber, the character I will argue to be the main protagonist of *Patternmaster*, is a member of the Patternist race, her gender acts as a subdivision that may influence her status in the larger hierarchy that can only be referred to as a Patternist ethnicity.

I conclude this chapter with a brief examination of *Survivor*. It is in this text that Butler's narrative seems most didactic in its message. Through Alanna, the judgment of humanity's understanding and use of racial hierarchies is made lucid. In this final moment of the Patternmaster series the message seems to be that by creating a structured and stagnant system of valuing the body, humanity is doomed for extinction. By locating these examinations in a larger narrative of race/ethnicity, the readers of Butler's fiction are presented with opportunities to learn how and why there is a need to categorize our bodies. The allusive logic of racial difference and structures of hierarchy among various bodies are called to task. More importantly, we as readers of fiction are placed in a position to consider the advantages and disadvantages of continuing such practices in our real society. The readers of Butler's fiction are given the gifts of foresight through her adroit use of metaphor and the opportunity to change direction, if we choose. Thus, the primary assertion in this chapter is that the ability to acknowledge and then adapt to the changing nature of the body and its identities is at the core of human survival in Butler's speculative worlds.

COMPLETION OF A RACE/ETHNICITY

The organization that exists in the *Patternmaster* narrative is made possible only after the narrative work done in *Wildseed, Mind of My Mind* (1977), and *Clay's Ark* (1984). As I have discussed in chapter two, *Wildseed* is the genesis of the Patternmaster series. The two main characters Doro and Anyanwu come together, as did Adam and Eve, to begin the construction of a genetically superior human population, i.e. a new body of beings. Throughout the *Wildseed* narrative Doro and Anyanwu battle over issues of morality, sexuality and power only to learn inevitably that they desire the same things. Both Doro and Anyanwu want to be loved by each other unconditionally and to create a people like themselves.

The narrative that follows *Wildseed* is *Mind of My Mind*, and as discussed in chapter six, it manifests the dreams of both Doro and Anyanwu. *Mind of My Mind* produces the child that Doro desired and creates a pattern that surpasses his expectations as well as Anyanwu's maternal needs for familial bonds among her special children. If *Patternmaster* explains the operation of the Pattern among older and more developed genera-tions of Patternists, then *Mind of My Mind* presents the rise of the Pattern as a reality in the development of the daughter of Doro, Mary. Mary is a young telepathic experiment who Doro has created in the attempt to bring his active telepaths together.

> I'm going to try to mate her with another telepath without killing either of them myself. And I'm hoping that she and the boy I have in mind are stable enough to stay together without killing each other (*Mind of My Mind* 9).

For Doro, Mary initially represented an opportunity to bring the "warring tribes" (9) he had developed over the centuries together into a unified and powerful family. Mary was supposed to be a controllable tool in Doro's plan to move closer to his race-building dream. I use the term control-lable because Doro intentionally desired a young girl to play the role he had written for Mary. In the Prologue of *Mind of My Mind* Doro tells Emma (Anyanwu) that "I wanted a girl, and I wanted her to be one of the youngest of her generation of actives (telepaths who have control of their abilities). Both those factors will help keep her in line. She'll be less likely to rebel against my plans for her" (12). In his declaration to Emma, Doro both describes the importance that Mary will play in the following narra-tive and foreshadows some of the conflicts around gender and power that Laqueur's two-sex model facilitates.

The fact that Doro perceives Mary as an experiment implies that he does not know exactly what the outcome of her presence among his dis-jointed family will be, but he does believe that she will be the catalyst for some kind of unification. It is through this line of reasoning that Doro be-lieves that if he controls Mary, he will control whatever family Mary pulls together. He has followed this logic for nearly four thousand years and it has proven successful, even with his most powerful adversary, Anyanwu (Emma). As the *Mind of My Mind* narrative progresses the reader learns that Doro's premise that gender and age are easily manipulated is proven false. It is, however, through such realization that what comes to be known as the Pattern is created. What I mean by this is that, ironically the assumptions made by Doro about the body and how it can be manipu-lated by his powers will not be enough for him to lead the people who he has ultimately engineered for over four thousand years. Doro failed to recognize the fact that with the construction of race, there is the practice of race, which is a performance that inevitable leads to an ethnicity. Doro's hegemony over his wild seed marked them as targets for his consumption and terrorism, but due to the nature of their bodies, did not leave them completely defenseless. In fact, without a material body of his own, Doro is only half of what Mary has evolved into.

This idea directly contradicts Hortense Spillers assessment of how the term ethnicity is used in the Moynihan Report. Ethnicity in the Moynihan Report, according to Spillers, is a sort of concrete-laced identity that is stagnant and debilitating with regards to time and perspective. In Butler's Patternist series I perceive ethnicity to be a process that is fluid and progressively changing from narrative to narrative. As the Patternist people evolve the performances of their group identity also evolves. Mary's move away from Doro's way of doing things in *Mind of My Mind* is one of the starkest examples of the progressive fluidity and liberation that I am suggesting. If Mary's performance is placed next to that of Anyanwu, and Amber the tendency to break, bind, and or change the rules of being affiliated with Doro (the Patriarch) or being a Patternist is revealed as a common motif throughout the series.

Where Doro's form once represented an advantage because of his mobility of identity, it now becomes a handicap that marks him as an incomplete being in the shadow of Mary and her new group. It is because of his "half ness" that Doro will not be able to thrive as he had in the past, as Mary and her people can travel in both the material and non-material realms as freely as Doro, via telepathy. It will be Mary who becomes the founding mother of the first Pattern and the first Patternmistress/ Matriarch. That is to say, it is Mary who takes on the role of ethnic leader of a new people. The pattern is definitely Mary's baby, but Doro's papa status, with regard to the pattern, is clearly in question. The pattern that she creates is symbolic of the ethnic practices that will continue to evolve as the series moves on.

This outcome is a result of Butler's speculative fiction. Things might have worked very differently in the real world for Doro and his wild seed because traditionally ethnicity along with racial distinction more than often places its subjects in a position of objectivity and vulnerability.

> "Ethnicity" perceived as mythical time enables a writer to perform a variety of conceptual moves all at once. Under its hegemony, the human body becomes a defenseless target for rape and veneration, and the body, in its material and abstract phase, a resource for metaphor (Spillers 456).

There are a number of racial metaphors that could be extracted from Doro and his wild seed. The most obvious would be the identities of the African American and Native American, but the experiences of immigrants from Southern European and Asian countries could also be interpreted as references for Butler's metaphor. What seems to be most important is that until Mary came along in the narrative history of Doro's wild seed, they were indeed defenseless targets of Doro's rape and consumption. Thus, one of Butler's conceptual moves has been to take a fact of history and transform it into something different by way of introducing a fantastic female character through the genre of science fiction. The results have yielded a group of people distinguishable from "normal" people only by their performance of special mental and physical abilities and their practice of a way of life unique to people like themselves. Thus, despite the fact that the term race is used in the narratives that I will be examining, it does not seem to be commensurate in describing what the Patternists are becoming. The term ethnicity seems to do more work in the way of assessing what Butler is doing in the Patternmaster series.

THE GENESIS OF THE CLAYARK

When Doro's final eugenic experiment had proven successful beyond even his expectations, the pattern produced a rival species, which I will refer to as a race with an ethnicity of its own. The Clayarks are a race of beings who continued to push the boundaries of difference and the imaginations of Butler's readers. The genesis of the Clayarks begins in Butler's 1984 novel *Clay's Ark* and continues to unfold throughout the Patternmaster series until its final episode, *Survivor* (1978). *Clay's Ark* is an essential component in understanding the relationship of the Patternist and the Clayark race. The *Clay's Ark* narrative presents vital information about the origin of the Clayarks, and begins to explain their conflict with the Patternists. The Clayarks play a significant role in the understanding of how race and ethnicity are constructed in Butler's writing and how images of the body figure in notions of humanity. Ultimately, the term race is moved beyond the business of connoting difference within categories of humanity and introduces the allegory of the extraterrestrial. The Clayark race, as well as the Patternist ethnicity is a result of eugenic experiments. The Clayarks are the result of symbiotic microorganisms from Proxima Centauri, the second planet in the Centauri system, successfully invading the human body of Asa Elias Doyle (*Clay's Ark* 42). Unlike the Patternists, the Clayarks are easily distinguishable from the "normal" human, and for this reason cannot simply be just another ethnic group. The Clayark is another species that includes bits of humanity, but is at length a human/ extraterrestrial hybrid. However because the Clayark is partially human and does develop distinct cultural and social practices, an ethnicity of sorts, does evolve as the Patternmaster series progresses.

The product of this mixing is initially a small Arizona ranch of individuals in the year 2021, who are "the sporangia of the dominant life form of Proxi Two—the receptacles that produce the spores of that life form"(*Clay's Ark* 192). What this seemingly horrific state of being translates into is being the parents of a new race of people, who resemble sphinx (beings with sleek cat-like bodies and human faces). The role of Eli, the main character in the *Clay's Ark* narrative, is not dissimilar to the complicated paternal/maternal role that Doro plays in *Wildseed*. Both characters carry and spread the seed or microorganisms necessary to create a new body of beings. Furthermore, Doro and Eli are both assisted reluctantly by female characters who they claim as their permanent wives, Anyanwu and Meda respectively. More importantly both Doro and Eli are written as relatively neutral catalysts for great change. Both have complicated characteristics attributed to them that disallow them and their actions to be categorized as simply "good" or "bad." This same description also applies to Mary and her proprietary feeling about her pattern and the individuals it enclosed. The point that I am making here is that in Butler's writing the impetus for new bodies and the need to distinguish difference among bodies seems to be rooted in the arbitrary elements of circumstance. Thus, despite any planning or eugenic experiments, race seems to be a result of hap and circumstance which is inadvertently and inevitably caused by change. The *Clay's Ark* narrative demonstrates how race is often a random phenomenon that can be used to subjugate groups of bodies in the hands of the powerful. It is not until race and the differences that it alludes to are transformed into practices that are accepted by all under its category, does it become an ethnicity, a potentially empowering identity. And as Mary has shown in *Mind of My Mind*, an ethnicity can be used to unify groups of people in a manner that is far more stable than a bond based on some vague notion of racial identity.

The *Clay's Ark* novel is divided into two separate narratives, the "Past" and the "Present," that inform one another as the plot progresses. The "Present" narrative tells of the abduction of Dr. Blake Maslin and his two sixteen year old daughters, Keira and Rane. The "Past" narrative tells the history of Asa Elias Doyle after his return to Earth from Proxi Two by way of a starship named Clay's Ark. In this narrative the reader learns that the entire crew of Clay's Ark had been infected/invaded by virus-sized symbiots and that all but Eli were killed in a crash upon returning to Earth. In the "Present" Blake Maslin's family of three had set out to visit relatives and were stopped on the side of the highway by a sand storm. As they waited for the storm to pass they were high-jacked by a group of three, led by Eli. During the abduction it is revealed to the reader that Keira is dying from leukemia. Eli and his assistant Ingraham are disappointed to learn that Keira is not completely healthy because the point of their mission was to obtain "a descent car with two or three healthy, fairly young people in it" (*Clay's Ark* 13). Despite Eli's hesitancy, he proceeds with the kidnapping by putting Rane in a separate vehicle driven by his female assistant Meda, and takes his three abductees back to a desert ranch where the rest of his people await him.

As the two narratives progress, the reader learns that the symbiots that have infected Eli's body encourage him to spread the organisms to other humans. As the extraterrestrial organisms are symbiots, they endow their host bodies with superhuman strength, speed and healing abilities, which all assist in the process of spreading the organisms as efficiently as possible.

By the time Eli abducts Blake's family he has become the patriarch of a small desert ranch of individuals whom he has infected directly or indirectly with the symbiots. Upon arrival at Eli's ranch Blake and his daughters learn that the virus-like organisms can be spread through contact with blood, sweat, or saliva. "Emaciation, trembling, bad coloring, sweating—plus surprising strength, speed, and coordination" (*Clay's Ark* 27) were all symptomatic of the Clay's Ark disease. As Meda told Blake more about their illness, he began to compare it to Earth diseases that he had heard about.

> Some of what Meda had said about the disease reminded him of another illness—one he had read about years before. He could not remember the name of it. It was something people had once gotten from animals. And the animals had gone out of their way to spread it. The name came to him suddenly: rabies (27).

Blake's initial diagnosis of the Clay's Ark organisms was ironic because of the implication that the illness or disease was not initially of the human variety. Blake's confusion and fear stems from the fact that the virus with which he and his daughters will inevitably be infected is so different from what he understands as a physician, that it may not be human or terrestrial. Thus, the fear of difference in the *Clay's Ark* narrative moves so completely beyond Earthly differences like color and phenotype that they are kept in the shadows of the narrative. The traditional racial identification of the characters in the narrative is rarely mentioned.

For example, during the abduction of Blake and his two daughters, Eli is described as being "a tall, thin black man with skin that had gone gray with more than desert dust" (*Clay's Ark*). This description is significant only because it does not occur until the second chapter of the narrative. His assistant Ingraham is referred to as "Green Shirt" for more than half of the second chapter until the reader learns by deduction that he must be a white man. Green shirt was described as being shorter and smaller-boned than Eli. "He was blond, tanned beneath his coating of dust, though his tan seemed oddly gray. A sick man" (9). The reader is given no clue that Blake is white until Eli questions whether or not Blake is the father of Rane and Keira. "What is this, anyway?" Eli demanded, glancing back at Keira, then staring at Rane. "What kind of cradles have you been robbing, Doc?"(*Clay's Ark* 9). Eli's question is focused upon his observation that both Rane and Keira are black while the man claiming to be their father is clearly white. We learn that Blake's wife, Jorah, had been black and that Eli's question had been a reoccurring issue when the three traveled together.

In the first chapter and third paragraph of the narrative the reader is told that after hiding himself for five days and two nights, Eli had only three goals. Eli and the organisms that had infected his body desired only food, water, and human companionship. The element of human companionship was not limited by superficial racial distinctions. Thus, it seems that race in the *Clay's Ark* narrative is primarily used to connote difference of species as opposed to the more traditional physical differences among terrestrial bodies. The construction of a new race in the *Clay's Ark* narrative refers to the children of those infected with the symbiot organisms. Jacob Boyd Doyle, the son of Eli and Meda, was the first Clayark to be born.

> He was a beautiful, precious child, but he was a quadruped. His senses were even keener than those of his parents and his strength would have made him a real problem for parents of only normal strength. And he was a carrier. Eli and Meda did not learn this for certain until later, but they suspected it from the first. Most important, though, the boy was not human (175).

Jacob represented a threat to the race of humanity and other life on Earth because the virus-like organisms that created him killed four out of seven of the humans that it infected and left almost no chance for the survival of any canine, rodent, or reptile. Because Jacob was a carrier, he and all of his kind would live to spread the virus to uninfected humans. And in addition to the need to spread the virus Jacob would also grow to reproduce more offspring like himself. Thus, ultimately the survival of the Clayark necessarily meant the extinction of humanity.

As the *Clay's Ark* narrative unfolded Blake and both of his daughters were infected with the symbiont. Unfortunately, only Keira was able to survive through the horrific events of the narrative. Apparently Keira's leukemia was cured by the symbiont organisms and worked to make her healthier than before her infection. Both Blake and Rane were killed in an attempt to escape from a hostile car family after they had infected most of the group. Ironically, it was Blake not Eli who allowed the microorganisms to infect a private hauler who ran over Blake with the intention of robbing him. The epidemic that Eli had gone to such great lengths to restrain had been given to an individual who would "go all over the country, all over the continent . . . and would deal with people who go all over the world" (208).

As the Patternists were still physically human despite their telepathic or psionic abilities, the Clayarks represented a logical threat to the structure of the pattern as well as the abilities of the Patternists. As the children of Jacob Doyle were not physically human the telepathy of the Patternists could not be used to control the minds of the Clayarks. The Clayark's insatiable need to spread its virus to all non-infected humans threatened both the Patternists' labor force (mute humans) and their own existence. The Clayark species inevitably evolves into an ethnic group of its own. With Eli as its father/mother/host and Doro and Anyanwu all wrapped into one, the Clayarks mimic the genesis of the Patternist people.

Beyond the similarity in genesis and the fact that the Clay Ark starship was a product of Patternist technology, the *Clay's Ark* narrative does not offer a great deal to the plot of the Patternist series. The *Clay's Ark* narrative does, however, act as a foreshadowing of things to come in Butler's Xenogenesis series which began with the 1987 publication of *Dawn*. Where the evolution of the Clayarks is only touched on in *Clay's Ark* and *Patternmaster* because of their extraterrestrial identity, Butler thoroughly engages the evolution of an analogous group of people know as the Oankali in her Xenogenisis series. In the Xenogenesis series Butler speaks of a group of extraterrestrials who travel through space with the sole purpose of gene trading with other dissimilar species as method of survival. The pervading premise of this series is that hybridity and the acceptance of difference is the best way to survive in hostile environments. This series also suggests volumes about human sexuality and the nonsensical importance placed on superficial aspects of the material body.

STRUCTURE OF THE *PATTERNMASTER* NARRATIVE

The *Patternmaster* narrative lends a great deal of insight as to how boundaries formed by hierarchies can be dismantled. It is through the main characters of the narrative, Teray, Coransee, and Amber, that questions of the body are formulated. By examining Butler's writing and employment of the three main characters in the *Patternmaster*, I am able to present a clear picture of the structure and function of the pattern from top to bottom. In doing this the values and protocol of the Patternist race and its ethnic practices will reveal how the body is figured into the narrative. It is through Amber's body that the rules of this structure are disrupted and shown to be much more complicated than a mere male dominated hegemony resembling an Antebellum Southern plantation. It is through Amber's control over her own body and the bodies of other characters in the narrative that her value and identity becomes unbounded. But more importantly to my discussion of ethnicity, Amber's partial rejection of the

ethnic practices in place during her particular point in time of the Patternmaster series lends further evidence that my suggestion of ethnicity
in Butler's narratives is indeed a pliable and applicable notion.

Although she may not appear to be at the center of the narrative at its
beginning, it is Amber's character that presents the most important questions of identity and power in the narrative. As a healer, a bi-sexual, and a
mother, Amber proves herself to be the most complicated character in the
Patternmaster narrative. Furthermore, it is through Amber that the questions of the body and hierarchy are most thoroughly engaged. *Patternmaster* is a tale of two brothers seeking to hold the throne of their father,
while a wiser and more powerful sister foregoes her claim to the throne
in favor of motherhood and freedom. It is through this non-traditional
narrative that the body is deconstructed and its identities are complicated
beyond the boundaries of a male dominated hierarchy. Through Amber's
character the reader of this narrative is shown how racism, heterosexism,
and patriarchy can be resisted and overcome.

Patternmaster begins with a prologue that introduces Rayal and his lead
wife Jansee. Rayal is the reigning Patternmaster and Jansee is his sister-
wife, the two most powerful descendants of Doro and Anyanwu to date.
The primary functions of the prologue are to introduce the plot through a
prophetic discussion between the husband and wife and to render a brief
history of the customs surrounding the Pattern As Rayal and his lead
wife relax in their bedroom Jansee begins to worry about her two sons
who have been sent to school some 480 kilometers away from where she
and Rayal reside. Despite the fact that she was linked to them through
the Pattern and would be one of the first to know if they were not safe,
she wanted to send someone to check on her two sons. If a mute were to
run this errand Jansee would be able to read his/her mind as easily and
clearly as if she was seeing her sons herself. There would be no mental
barriers constructed to prevent the invasion of privacy nor would there
be any other form of resistance, because mutes were powerless humans
with no special mental abilities. Rayal suggests that if she must send
someone, it should be an outsider; someone who would be better able to
defend himself from the Clayarks. Rayal realizes that his suggestion is un-
satisfactory to Jansee because anyone more powerful than a mute would
complicate and probably hinder the memory reading processes that Jansee intended to inflict upon whoever carried the images of her children.

The ability to read minds and to prevent one's own mind from being
read is an important characteristic for anyone in this world. Such abilities
speak to the non-physical power of the bodies in the world and help to
avoid any binary divides in the negotiation of power. Later in the narrative of the world of the pattern the reader observes that the power of the
body does not have to be limited to the physical world. Mind reading acts

as proof that the identities of the body can be founded on non-physical differences. With a smile Rayal makes another suggestion that further agitates Jansee's discontentment. "You should have more children. Perhaps then you would be less concerned for these two" (*Patternmaster* 2). Jansee quickly retorts with the implication that Rayal would have her mate with one of his outsiders to produce more children. "Have them by a journeyman, or at least an apprentice" (2), is Rayal's indifferent response.

It is through this brief lover's quarrel that the hierarchy of the pattern in partially revealed. Ordinary humans are powerless mutes who are only involved with the pattern as slaves, concubines, and reminders of what humanity once was. "Outsiders" are Patternists who have powers, but are not as powerful in the pattern as apprentices and journeymen. Because of the power hierarchy Rayal has no intention of allowing Jansee to produce another child. He tells Jansee that, "You are so strong that even your child by a weaker man might be able to compete with our two sons" (*Patternmaster* 3). With this remark Rayal reminds Jansee that it is the nature of Patternists to fight for control of the pattern, even if it entails killing one's siblings. He reminds Jansee that he had had to kill two brothers and a sister in order to become the Patternmaster and he might have killed his "strongest sister if she had not been wise enough to ally herself with me and become my lead wife" (3). Just as Rayal and his siblings battled for the power of the pattern, the sons of Rayal and Jansee are destined to do the same. Rayal's comment also brings to mind the fact that during Antebellum America it was imperative that the patriarch controlled female bodies in the household and or on the plantation in order to maintain its hierarchal structure, as the condition of the mother often defined the condition of the child.

Without the oppression of all women, the planter class could not be assured of absolute authority. In a biracial slave society where "racial purity" was a defining characteristic of the master class, total control of the reproductive females was of paramount concern for elite males. Patriarchy was the bedrock upon which the slave society was founded, and slavery exaggerated the pattern of subjugation that patriarchy had established (qtd. in Carby 24).

Spiller's title, "Mama's Baby, Papa's Maybe" alludes to an historical context that Butler's narrative is clearly evoking. Rayal doesn't want his heirs to be tainted with anything other than his own royal/pure bloodline. After convincing Jansee that she would not be strong enough to watch more of her children kill themselves, Rayal announces his lack of sensitivity about the issue. When Jansee asks Rayal about his children by his other wives he responds, "I don't have your sensitivity. Those of my children who don't compete to succeed me will live to contribute to the people's strength" (*Patternmaster* 4). It is this prophecy that complicates an otherwise standard narrative of two brothers battling for their father's kingdom.

The children or child who inherits the strength of Rayal and chooses not to succeed him promises to play a much more interesting role in the pattern's future than does the main protagonist and antagonist. Such a character would introduce an element of hope for a seemingly violent race of people and those who are oppressed by the powerful. It is with the hint of this unnamed character in the Prologue that situates the *Patternmaster* narrative outside of traditional Cane and Abel tales of two brothers, one representing good and the other representing evil, battling for power. In making this biblical reference I also want to consider the narrative archetypes mentioned in Thelma J. Shinn's essay "The Wise Witches: Black Women Mentors in the Fiction of Octavia E. Butler." In this essay Shinn identifies archetypal patterns common to three centuries of women's fiction, which preserve female knowledge within the enclosure of patriarchal society. Shinn locates thematic patterns which have been used to translate masculine literary experiences into feminine narratives. In her analysis Shinn posits that women's fiction could be read as a mutually illuminating or interrelated field of texts reflecting a preliterate repository of feminine archetypes, including three particularly important archetypal systems—the Demeter/Kore and Ishtar/Tammuz rebirth myths, Arthurian grail narratives, and the Craft of the Wise, or witchcraft (Shinn 204). I would like to argue that derivatives of each of these patterns constitute the complexity of the *Patternmaster* narrative.

The Prologue ends abruptly with an attack on Rayal's House by an army of Clayarks. Because the Clayarks are not completely human, the Patternists are not able to read or control the minds of the Clayarks as they would a mute. Thus, "Rayal's sentries noticed them, but, lulled by the peace and unaware of the cannon; they paid no attention to Clayarks so far away" (*Patternmaster* 6). The sphinx-like Clayarks were given enough time to load and fire a cannon shot through the private apartment of Rayal and his lead wife. The shot beheaded Jansee and severely wounded Rayal. Because the attack found Rayal's sentries so completely off guard the Clayarks were able to fire a second shot at the disoriented Patternist House. Finally, the Clayarks abandoned the cannon and stormed the House to kill who they could and to infect Rayal with the Clayark virus.

The Prologue leaves Rayal in a very difficult position, but at the beginning of chapter one the reader is able to deduce that Rayal did indeed survive his perilous plight for what appears to be at least twenty years. The pattern is still in order and Rayal's youngest son, Teray, is in the process of graduating from the Redhill School for Patternist youth. The narrative that follows the prologue is largely centered on the capture and escape of Teray, the younger of the two sons of Rayal and Coransee. Teray's location in the narrative as its hero is placed in question by Amber, a female healer and maternal figure. Because both Teray and Amber are crucial to the outcome of the narrative, the task of identifying one as the protagonist and the other as a supporting character is difficult to accomplish. What is most important about both characters, however, is that their bodies and understanding of the body feeds the plot of the *Patternmaster* narrative. It is through Teray's understanding of the tiers within the pattern and Amber's ability to heal and destroy bodies that the reader is able to make sense of the Patternists as a people identifying themselves beyond the physical.

SUBVERSIVE MATRIARCH

In the final pages of the *Patternmaster* narrative the reader is left with the question of why Amber does not rise to take over the pattern. When Teray is revived after his battle with Coransee, Amber tells him, "If you had been anyone else, Teray, you and Coransee would have burned together" (*Patternmaster* 194). Amber's declaration to Teray can be interpreted as a response to the reader's question. Despite her wisdom and obvious advantage over the still inexperienced Teray, Amber's love for him and concern for the well being of their child out weigh her desire for the power of the Patternmaster. It is because of love and motherhood that Amber's character seems to disrupt the hierarchy of the pattern. Despite the fact that Amber has proven herself to be the most able person to succeed Rayal, because of her wisdom and strength, she decides to pass the position of power to a lesser candidate, the father of her child. In doing this Amber continues to distinguish herself as a clever negotiator of power in a patriarchal and heterosexist society.

With Teray indebted to Amber and concerned about their unborn child, Amber insures its safety. In other words, by placing Teray in a position to become the Patternmaster, Amber has bought her and her child life insurance from anyone who might want to harm them. As Patternmaster, Teray will be in a position to protect the people who he cares for. Whether this was the reasoning behinds Amber's openness to impregnation is not completely clear in the narrative. What is important is that Amber made all of the decisions pertaining to her body alone. Amber tells Teray that she is pregnant long after the fact in the following passage:

> I decided that I wanted a child by you. And since I didn't know how long we'd be together, I didn't want to wait (161).

It is through this statement that Amber's character declares that she and she alone controls her body and its functions. By impregnating herself without the consent of Teray, Amber has taken the traditionally debilitating title of motherhood and transformed it into a symbol of liberation and power of the female body.

Motherhood is a reoccurring theme in the narratives of Butler. It is through this narrative of motherhood that the notion of womanly authority is developed and demonstrated through Amber's subversive negotiations with the powerful. Amber's womanly authority can be interpreted as a form of feminism if one chooses to limit her identity to gender. If, however, Amber's sexual difference is included along with her healing abilities, the authority or power that Amber exhibits can only be named as exceptional. Amber's actions have complicated her gender role within the Patternist ethnicity. In no way does she play the Southern Belle in the "big house" on Coransee's plantation, because Butler does not allow such a role to solidify in her fiction. In Butler's fiction there is always a female complicating gender through her performance, and the *Patternmaster* narrative does not present an exception to this rule. Amber is "less interested in joining the ranks of gendered femaleness than gaining the insurgent ground as female social subject" (Spillers 480). The point that I want to accent here is that the Patternist ethnicity/race/culture that has evolved through the Patternmaster series necessarily produces and encourages characters like Anyanwu, Mary, and Amber to defy dangerously narrow definitions of body and identity.

Amber's guidance continues to benefit Teray when Coransee and his Patternists catch the two just outside of Forsyth's borders. In order to avoid their final conflict for a few more days Teray agrees to travel into Forsyth with Coransee as his outsider to be evaluated by Rayal. Coransee agreed to free Teray if Rayal finds that he is not a contender for the pattern. Unfortunately for Amber, Coransee intends to take her back to Redhill regardless of the outcome. As Teray is both indebted to and in love with Amber, Coransee's ultimatum is both distressful and unacceptable. Teray's situation is further complicated when Amber informs him that she is pregnant with his child and that Coransee probably intends to take Teray's life despite Rayal's assessment. Fortunately for Teray, Amber has observed that he is a latent healer unlike Coransee. Amber's observation presented an advantage of which Teray was completely unaware and that meant the difference between life and death for Teray and Amber.

In the final conflict between Teray and Coransee it was Amber's observation about Teray's healing ability that allowed him to emerge as the victor. In his battle with Coransee, Teray used what he had learned from Amber about focusing on the body of Clayarks to kill them. In doing this with Coransee, Teray was able to send Coransee's body into violent convulsions and a horrific death.

He did not know when Coransee's body went into violent convulsions. He did not know when Coransee's muscles contracted so violently that they snapped one of the Housemaster's legs. He did not know when Coransee bit off a large piece of his own tongue. He knew nothing until just before he lost consciousness completely [*of the physical world outside of the pattern*]. Only then did he realize that he had won. Coransee was dead (*Patternmaster* 191).

Despite the perilous battle that Teray wins he loses consciousness and is revived and healed by Amber. In this way Amber continues to play the role of a matriarch rather than a mere female companion to Teray. It is at this point in the narrative that Amber's role is most lucid. Amber tells Teray, "While you were unconscious, they [Coransee's 10 Patternists] asked me which of us would lead them—you or me" (194). Teray's questioning silence clearly identifies him as a foil by which to illuminate Amber's strength and position in the narrative. Teray's dependency on the knowledge and strength of Amber throughout their middle passage to Forsyth disrupts the possibility of a single hero independently earning the throne of his dying father. After Teray regains his consciousness he links with Coransee's ten Patternists and sweeps the area for Clayarks.

Before, with Amber, he had killed dozens of Clayarks. Now he killed hundreds, perhaps thousands. He killed until he could find no more Clayarks over all his wide range. He even checked the system of underground tunnels. When he was finished, he was certain there were no more Clayarks anywhere near enough to affect him or his party. (198)

It seems that this act of massive destruction is the first independent act that Teray performs, short of leaving the Redhill School with Joachim at the beginning of the narrative. When Teray completes his violent sweep Rayal opens a mental channel with him and informs him that his journey to Forsyth was Rayal's way of testing Teray's worthiness. Through this father-son conversation the reader learns that Rayal has been using Teray as a sort of pawn to protect the pattern from Coransee. It is also revealed that Teray, despite his victory over Coransee, will not become the Patternmaster until Rayal forfeits his life.

I will never gather the strength of the Pattern in my mind again, sent Rayal. It would kill me. When the need arises next, young one, the Pattern will be yours. That will kill me, too, but at least I'll die alone—not take thousands of people with me (201).

Teray's acceptance of his father's promise or covenant makes it difficult to identify him as the hero of the narrative, as he does not truly achieve his unspoken desire to become the Patternmaster. Furthermore, the narrative ends with Teray once again following the instructions of Rayal. "Hurry and get here. You have no idea how tired I am" (202). As a naive child might follow the instructions of an adult who has deceived him/her more than once, Teray hurries to Forsyth as a naive boy instead of the seasoned hero that his journey should have constructed.

Butler continues to push questions of social identity throughout her narratives even after her creation of the Patternists and Clayarks. Race, whether it distinguishes differences of phenotype within a species or the differences among species, is the most commonly used method of identifying bodies. Where there is no race or no identifiable difference, there is no body. Thus, all bodies are dependent upon difference and an individual's ability to recognize difference. My primary concern in considering the Patternmaster series has been to examine race as a technological tool. In other words, I want to know what race does to and for the body and how it is constructed. Through examinations of Butler's narratives, specifically the development of her main characters such as Doro, Anyanwu, Mary, Eli, and Amber it has become clear that race is constructed by chance and it is constructed to identify bodies and power. Beyond what Butler's Patternmaster series has proven to be a superficial method of identifying a body—giving it a race, the notion of ethnicity seems to do much more work in the way of speaking the significance of substantial differences like cultural practices and the operation of unique social systems.

Since the first pages of *Wildseed* the question of humanity has been posed in Butler's narratives as a question of race. Because Doro had no physical body that he could call his own permanently; he and his people wondered if he could be classified as human. It was Doro's lack of humanity that forced Anyanwu to flee from him for her independence. That same element of inhumanity also forced Mary to consume Doro's life force at the conclusion of *Mind of My Mind*. After Eli was infected by the micro-organisms from Proxima Centauri, in the *Clay's Ark* narrative, he constantly spoke of salvaging pieces of his humanity. And although Amber and Teray spend little time contemplating the humanity of their Clayark enemies, both Clayarks and Patternists sit on the border of the inhumane with regards to their bodies and deeds. It seems that even when the body is not identifiable as belonging to the human species the notion of humanity is not completely evacuated. The race of humanity can be made to be as ambiguous as Doro's state of being.

NOTE

1. "The attribute of True Womanhood, by which a woman judged herslf and was judged by her husband, her neighbors and society, could be divided into four cardinal virtues. With them she was promised happiness and power" (Carby 23).

4

✛

Discussing Duality and the Chthonic: Octavia Butler, Wole Soyinka, and W.E.B Du Bois

Octavia Butler's speculative fiction suggests that ambiguity is both empowering and necessary for the survival of humanity. The notions of racial purity and cultural commonality are written as archaic detriments to humanities' history and future. In Butler's *Xenogenesis* series, [*Dawn* (1987), *Adulthood Rites* (1988), and *Imago* (1989)], the importance of ambiguity with regards to sex, race, gender, class, and human identity is immeasurable in any quest for survival. In each of the novels mentioned, one's ability to act as a bridge between two (or more) distinct identities suggests a new way of thinking about the figure of a multiple referenced identity. In this sense, the trope of "mulatto" is complicated in denotation and connotation in that it takes on broader distinctions other than racial origin and social status. The representation of racial hybridity in American film and literature has famously congealed around the cliché of the tragic mulatto.[1] While this trope has allowed writers and social critics of various stripes to highlight the contradictions in our present system of racial classification, its flaw is that instead of locating the tragic destinies of its biracial subjects in a U.S. social body that penalizes racial indeterminacy, it writes tragedy onto the body of the mixed-race person. Also, by forging such close ties between the hybrid and the tragic, it forecloses other possibilities of a potentially utopian nature that might also be explored under the sign of the hybrid. By recontextualizing hybridity within an alien and uncertain future and displacing the "interracial" with the "interspecies," "The hybrid is a usefully slippery category, purposefully contested and deployed to claim change" (Hutnyk 80). Butler bypasses the pitfalls associated with the literary representation of racial hybridity in order to suggest that the perspective of the "Other" is essential in understanding the body of the "Other."

Through the genre of Science Fiction (SF) and the imagination of its readers, Butler's *Xenogenesis* series suggests that understanding the perspective of the "Other" is essential in overcoming superficial and superfluous boundaries used to establish destructive hierarchies and hegemonies. Malleability is written as the desirable, if not perfect, state of the survivor. Consequently, Butler's literature disrupts the idea that ambiguity is a device of chaos and destruction. In an interview with Butler entitled "Radio Imagination: Butler on the Poetics of Narrative Embodiment," Marilyn Mehaffy and AnaLouise Keating arrive at several insights that speak to Butler's writing of ambiguous bodies.

> Octavia Butler's work is thematically preoccupied with the potentiality of genetically altered bodies—hybrid multi-species and multi-ethnic subjectivities—for revising contemporary nationalist, racist, sexist, and homophobic attitudes (Mehaffy and Keating 45).

Mehaffy and Keating's use of the terms "multi-species" and "multi-ethnic" speak directly to the issues of the body that I would like to interrogate in this discussion. I agree with Haraway's and Boulter's assessment that the reproduction of bodies and the language used to define and propagate those bodies are of paramount importance in understanding the critical work of Butler's fiction. In fact, I would like to suggest that bodies that do not participate in the processes of reproducing other bodies that are ambiguous, directly or indirectly, have little or no value in Butler's fiction. I will be considering another close reading of Butler's *Xenogenesis* series by Donna Haraway that supports my assertion later in this discussion.

Butler's stories deploy characters that are between races, cultures, and species, in addition to being between sex and gender identities. Melzer supports this assertion with the observation that, "Butler counters the construction of dualisms by assuming multiple, contradictory notions of self that undermine the binary and by creating an alternative way to view difference—as an essential part of the self, not something to create boundaries against"(Melzer 67). None of the topics that Butler discusses in her narratives possesses simple binary explanations; every subject or conflict is complicated with several possibilities. The actions of her characters always influence the lives of communities and histories, never sole individuals. In fact, Butler's individual characters rarely move independently or in a single direction. Thus, both the narrative and reader seem to be located in at least two spaces simultaneously. "Her writings respond to Audre Lorde's call for 'new patterns of relating across difference' (Lorde,

"Age, Race, Class, and Sex" 123)"[2] (68). Many critics have overlooked this particular aspect as it relates to the critical value of Butler's fiction. Charles Johnson accuses Butler's fiction of "plunging so deeply into fantasy that revelation of everyday life . . . disappears" (115–16). Such an accusation seems to overlook the realism and historical research present in the novel *Kindred* or short stories "Near of Kin," "Speech Sounds," or "Crossover."[3] And although Eric White's article "The Erotics of Becoming: Xenogenesis and *The Thing*" renders a positive critique of the *Xenogenesis* series, his depiction of the series as being race-blind SF suggests a narrow reading of the potential of the three novels. Failing to acknowledge the realism and the discussions of race in Butler's fiction limits the scope and value of extremely rich literature, in addition to negating the things that makes Butler's fiction unique in a genre that has historically been marred with ideas of escapism and fantasy.

In a practical sense, Butler's writing can be located between traditional African American literature and traditional SF. Both genres have historically included elements of social commentary and allegories that involve spaces/scenarios that are uncommon in mainstream (white) American literature. However, as Mehaffy and Keating note, "Butler's work has never simply 'fit in' with conventional expectations for either canonical or science fiction literature" (46). These spaces/scenarios are uncommon primarily because they are focused on people and metaphors who have been traditionally marginalized and who have not yet been thoroughly theorized from a black aesthetic.[4] Butler's fiction is successful largely because it produces narratives that are easily comparable to African American experiences but also because it considers the perspective of a universal marginalized body. To theorize such subject matter there must be an engagement of aesthetics that allow duality and multiplicity with regards to race, gender, and sex; an aesthetic that presents a space of ambiguity that is both acceptable and logical. Modern "Western" literature and thought have no problem with considering the notion of ambiguity. Modernism seems to be very much invested in the consideration of ambiguity and difference, as demonstrated by militant French philosophers such as Gilles Deleuze and Pierre-Felix Guattari. However, Butler's postmodernist fiction begs a perspective that completely embraces ambiguity and difference as normative.[5]

W.E.B. Du Bois's and Wole Soyinka's theories of identity engage questions of complicated identities in a fashion that is very pertinent to Butler's fiction. Both Du Bois and Soyinka have authored fiction ["The Comet" (1920), *The Strong Breed* (1963)] that can be compared to or defined as SF, but it is their aesthetics of identity that most readily speak to Butler's texts. Where Butler tends to employ characters who are between several identities at once, Du Bois and Soyinka speak of the double-consciousness of the

Negro and a "transitional yet inchoate matrix of death and becoming, the chthonic realm" (Soyinka 28). Butler, Du Bois, and Soyinka present three examples of the type of theoretical hardware necessary to interrogate the identities of the marginalized as well as the self.

Du Bois's pseudo-apocalyptic short story tells of a passing comet that casts a shadow of death over Manhattan. Only two survive: a black man (Jim Davis) whose world has been one of poverty and hard work and a white woman (Julia) who knows only leisure and privilege. The two are led to believe that the future of humanity is dependent upon their repopulating the planet, despite their socially constructed differences. Du Bois engages the discourse of race and class difference with "Death, the leveler!," "And the revealer . . ." ("The Comet" 15). Sadly, by the end of the short story, the narration reveals that the comet only destroyed Manhattan, while the rest of the world is still intact along with racism as demonstrated by the comment of a bystander. "Well, what do you think of that? Of all New York, just a white girl and a nigger!" (17). Although Du Bois does not complete "The Comet" in the guise of an apocalyptic creation story his belief in the permanence of racism is very clearly established.

Soyinka's play *The Strong Breed* presents a narrative topic far more invested in the tradition of SF and folklore than that of Du Bois's "The Comet." The play reenacts an annual ritual where a member of the village community is chosen to be sacrificed for the sins of the community. Soyinka's protagonist, Eman, decides to take on this deadly responsibility when he learns that Ifada, a youthful and unwilling village idiot, has been marked for sacrifice. The play is based on the Yoruba festival of the New Year and the ritual of sacrificing a "carrier" of the previous year's evil. The ritual is designed to rid the village of evil through a mutually agreed upon sacrifice. Shirley Jackson's 1948 short story "The Lottery," acts as a western version of a similar ritual designed to maintain the semblance of a utopian society. Lilith's new Earth is far from a utopian society yet the similarity of position of the Yoruba "carrier" and the role that she plays in the Xenogenesis series is remarkable. In each narrative a member of a community is charged with sacrificing themselves for the greater good.

Using Du Bois's notion of double-consciousness and Soyinka's idea of chthonic realm as theoretical tools, I would like to suggest that Butler's narratives present similar approaches to understanding the problematic of marginalized identities. In the process of this investigation I hope to show Butler's approach to be not only accessible, but practical. By practical I mean, theory that can be applied and acted upon, as praxis. While Butler's literature is clearly cautionary, it also infers plausible solutions to contemporary problems outlined in her fiction. The first moment of this discussion will entail drawing parallels with Wole Soyinka's notion of ambiguity with that of Butler's writing of the main characters in the novel *Dawn*. I would like to suggest that Butler, like Soyinka, writes with a Yoruba sensibility that necessarily transcends the boundaries of traditional Western thought and characterization. According to texts such as Henry Louis Gate's *Signifying Monkey* (1988) and Robert Farris Thompson's *Flash of the Spirit* (1984), such influences are commonly found in African American culture. Du Bois's theory of "double consciousness" explains the conflict that Butler's protagonists endure in all three novels of the Xenogenesis series. Butler's characters employ their double consciousness as an advantage that allows them to move within and beyond human and racial identity. By drawing parallels between these three writers, I hope to demonstrate that the body in Butler's fiction is written as a location designed to refigure the borders of identity and survival.

THE CHTHONIC AND DAWN

Wole Soyinka's "The Fourth Stage" is both an example of critical hermeneutics and an examination of Yoruba aesthetics. This examination addresses what appears (from a western viewpoint) as the paradox of uniqueness and Oneness or a conflation of the material and the spiritual in the Yoruba cosmology. In discussing such issues of aesthetics, Soyinka juxtaposes the notion of Yoruba tragedy to that of the Greek tragedy. He uses the Dionysos-Apollo brotherhood from Nietzsche's *The Birth of Tragedy* to reveal continuities and discontinuities between the Yoruba and western aesthetics.

Interestingly, book one of the Xenogenesis Series might indeed be interpreted as a tragedy. *Dawn* tells the tragic story of an apocalyptic Earth that has been stumbled upon by god-like organisms who have decided to resurrect the planet and some of its human population. In the text Butler juxtaposes the tragedy of the past with a struggle for survival in a potential future. The continuities and discontinuities that are revealed speak to the nature of humanity's tragically *flawed* aesthetic. I place stress on the term "flawed" because the narrative suggests that this term is synonymous with "contradiction" and or "ambiguity." The Oankali, Jdahya, explains humanity's flaw to Lilith in the following passage:

"You are hierarchical. That's the older and more entrenched characteristic. We saw it in your closest animal relatives and in your most distant ones. It's a terrestrial characteristic. When human intelligence served it instead of guiding it, when human intelligence did not even acknowledge it as a problem, but took pride in it or did not notice it at all . . . That was like ignoring cancer" (*Dawn* 37).

In the above passage, the tragic "flaw" of humanity is revealed as its inability to acknowledge and wield its genetic contradictions. The inability to embrace that which is multidimensional and ambiguous as normative is the narrative's explanation for humanity's failure in its potential future. Tragically, the humanity of the past was not able to accept ambiguity even when it resided at the core of human existence on a genetic level. It is the non-Western thinking/non-human/alien Oankali characters who teach the sole survivors of humanity to embrace something very similar to Yoruba aesthetics. Consequently, Butler transforms the tragic mulatto tradition by relocating tragedy from the body of the mixed-race subject to the social. Thus, Butler relocates issues of miscegenation to a normative space. Jdahya explains this to Lilith in the following passage:

> "Your people will change. Your young will be more like us and ours like you. Your hierarchical tendencies will be modified and if we learn to regenerate limbs and reshape our bodies, we'll share those abilities with you. That's part of the trade" (*Dawn* 40).

In *Dawn* the mixing of races and species is no longer an isolated occurrence. It has become a fact of life and survival for the humans who would repopulate the rejuvenated earth. The setting of *Dawn* and the entire Xenogenesis series is a space that is conducive for a re-figuration and revaluing of hybrid bodies. This space is made possible not solely because of the genre of SF, but by the very plausible possibility of a nuclear holocaust rendering any human survivors sterile. In fact, we learn that the Oankali have removed the ability of reproduction from the human body in hopes to controlling and encourage the human/Oankali "trade."

Soyinka's deconstructionist methodology begins with an analysis of Apollo's resemblance to the serene art of Obatala. He argues that "Obatala finds expression, not in Nietzsche's Apollonian 'mirror of enchantment' but as a statement of world resolution" (Soyinka 27). Western art's ability to imitate is accompanied by its ability to, delight, but functionality is essential in Yoruba art. It is not merely the idea that is being imitated by means of physical material or interpreted by sound and movement but a spiritual essence which exists within and affects both the spiritual and the material world. The Oankali are artists with genetic material; they do not simply mimic the material they trade, it is manipulated precisely (Butler, *Dawn* 39).

Ogun, the urge and essence of creativity, is placed next to Nietzsche's Dionysos and shown as a more composed and powerful image. Ogun is not merely a fictive nature spirit that only has authority in one realm. Rather, Ogun is an entity that propagates an art that is both race specific and politically charged. Soyinka notes that the Greek tragedy was developed on the principle of illusion. This places the Greek tragedy and the notion of art in a space with only one dimension, the intangible or unreal. The Yoruba tragedy, however, is multidimensional or of the "chthonic realm." This chthonic realm is the "transitional yet inchoate matrix of death and becoming" into which Ogun once plunged and emerged (Soyinka 28). "Obatala is the serene womb of chthonic reflections (or memory), a passive strength awaiting and celebrating each act of vicarious restoration of his primordial being" (29). The actor who experiences the chthonic realm by becoming the voice of Ogun or Obatala is said to have known the sublime aesthetic joy. This is a sublime joy that is not found within Nietzsche's heart of original oneness but can be located in the "distanced celebration of the cosmic struggle within the chthonic realm" (29).

What Soyinka refers to as Ogun can be likened to characters identified as *ooloi* Oankali in the *Dawn* narrative as well as the character, Doro, found in the Patternist series. Jdahya explains the nature of the Oankali and their non-gendered genetic engineers, the *ooloi*, to Lilith in the following passage:

> "We acquire new life—seek it, investigate it, manipulate it, sort it, use it. We carry the drive to do this in a minuscule cell within a cell—a tiny organelle within every cell of our bodies . . . One of the meanings of Oankali is gene trader. Another is that organelle—the essence of our selves, the origin of our selves. Because of that organelle, the ooloi can perceive DNA and manipulate it precisely" (Butler, *Dawn* 39).

The ooloi are the Oankali who are most chthonic in nature. The ooloi are the third sex of the Oankali. They are neither male nor female, yet they are essential in any and all reproductive processes. The ooloi are the eugenic scientists/gods who will help refigure human identity in the Xenogenesis series.

The actor who is chosen to become the voice for the Oankali is Butler's protagonist, Lilith.[6] Like the character from Hebrew mythology with the same name, it is Lilith's role to reject the rules of patriarchy/mankind by choosing to survive outside the boundaries of purity and homogeneity. Like Adam's first wife, Lilith will be put in the position of a trader to mankind despite her quest to save the existence of human identity. From Lilith's perspective, there is no experience of sublime joy in delivering the message to fellow humans that the old world has been traded away for a new beginning. Lilith is written as the messenger of very bad news. Humanity has failed to the point of near extinction and must redefine itself if it is to survive. Lilith's roles as matriarch and messenger force her into the position of a social pariah filled with guilt and self-loathing. Thus, a gift from the gods comes with a heavy price that must be paid by the strongest and most malleable.

The gods are the Yoruba's final measure of eternity, as humans are of earthly transience (Soyinka 29). Despite this fact, Soyinka is careful to note that eternity in Yoruba aesthetics does not have the same quality of remoteness or exclusiveness as it does in Christianity and Buddhism. Unlike the European, "the Yoruba is not concerned with the purely conceptual aspects of time" (29). The past, present, and future or the ancestors, the living, and the unborn are all woven together in a oneness that permeates Yoruba aesthetics. Each mode of time helps to explain the next in contexts of art, religion, life, and the metaphysical order of the Yoruba world. Butler's trilogy plays out in much the same fashion as the Oankali have a genetic memory that is passed down from generation to generation. The ooloi are able to read the history written on the genetic structure of organisms. Likewise, Lilith's brain chemistry is altered by the ooloi Nikanj to remember all that she has learned and experienced: "She remembered all that she had been taught, all that she had picked up on her own . . . she was alarmed, pleased and frightened . . ." (Butler, *Dawn* 79). Lilith's new ability to remember allowed her to better read the past so that she could cope with her present and shape her future.

Soyinka's "The Fourth Stage" defines the Yoruba aesthetic and Tragic Drama as concepts based on a committed, collective, and functional premise that is not constantly present in Western Art. Yoruba *art* is also revealed as a term that does not necessarily imply separation from Yoruba music, religion, or cosmology. In the shadow of Nietzsche's Apollo and Dionysos, Ogun and Obatala appear to be extremely complex, interrelated, and most importantly, valid ingredients of something non-western.

I would like to suggest that what Soyinka so clearly identifies as the foundation of West African aesthetics can also be compared to Butler's method of operation. The Oankali aesthetic found in *Dawn* is analogous on several levels to that of the Yoruba aesthetic that Soyinka discusses. Furthermore, it is Western practices/aesthetics that are written as the root cause of humanity's demise in *Dawn*. And like Ogun and Obatala, it is the Oankali and ooloi who will be at the foundation of any attempt at recreating a new and different life for humanity.

THE AMERICAN NEGRO'S
CONSCIOUSNESS AND THE OANKALI

In his 1903 publication *The Souls of Black Folk*, Du Bois used the term "double consciousness" to refer to an internal conflict between what appeared to be two (spiritual entities) identities housed in a single African American body.

> The history of the American Negro is the history of this strife,—this longing to attain self-conscious manhood, to merge his double self into a better and

truer self. In this merging he wishes neither of the older selves to be lost. He would not Africanize America, for America has too much to teach the world and Africa. He would not bleach his Negro soul in a flood of white Americanism, for he knows that Negro blood has a message for the world. He simply wishes to make it possible for a man to be both a Negro and an American, without being cursed and spit upon by fellows, without having the doors of Opportunity closed roughly in his face (Du Bois 11).

In Du Bois's employment of the terms "strivings" and "strife" there is a clear implication that an identity grounded in multiplicity is both alien and unacceptable to a normative (white) masculine American identity. At this point in Du Bois's meditation, it becomes clear that the *Souls of Black Folk* is a query of identity and its complexities; it is not a declaration of monolithic African American identity, for such a thing cannot exist where the terms "normative" and "identity" have no rational relationship. Duality enough isn't reason enough to read Butler through the already overused lens of double-consciousness. *Adulthood Rites,* the second book of the Xenogenesis series takes up the issue of racial duality via the character Akin, Lilith's son and the first male human/Oankali construct. Akin is a being who can initially "pass" as human, but is in actuality is a result of several merged identities. Ultimately, Akin does not "Oankalinize" humanity, for his humanity has too much to teach the alien Oankali. He does not negate his Oankali insight in a flood of so called humanity, for he knows that without the Oankali trade, humanity is doomed to revisit its destiny with self-destruction. Akin is stuck in a dangerous yet potentially empowering state of duality. Nikanj speaks of the advantages and disadvantages of Akin's human likeness in the following passage:

> "That won't do him much good with some Humans. They'll resent him for not being completely Human and for looking more human than their kids. They'll hate him for looking much younger than he sounds. They'll hate him because they haven't been allowed to have sons. Your people have made Human-looking male babies a very valuable commodity" (Butler, *Adulthood* 9).

In Nikaj's declaration *it* (s/he) is speaking of the humans of Lo, a village of humans who have accepted a symbiotic relationship with the Oankali. Nikanj's statement suggests that even the humans most likely to tolerate Akin's multiple identities have reasons to show hostility toward the talking infant. Humans who reject the idea of living with the Oankali and reproducing with them, "resisters," represent an even greater threat to Akin.

Resisters were humans who had decided to live without Oankali—and thus without children. Akin had heard that they sometimes stole construct children, the most human-looking construct children they could find. But that was stupid because they had no idea what the child might be like after metamorphosis. Oankali never let them keep children anyway (19).

The village of the resisters is called Phoenix and is ultimately the location that Akin will develop his dual identity as a tool of negotiation and collaboration among the humans and the Oankali. Akin employs the ambiguity written upon his body to transcend both human and Oankali difference.

In its critique of the African American condition during America's post-civil War Era, *Souls of Black Folk* redefined the terms of three hundred years of interaction between black and white people and influenced the cultural and political psychology of peoples of African descent throughout the western hemisphere. It represented a long tradition of African American texts that used autobiography and personal essays to explore themes of freedom and self-determination, to establish a cultural position and identity for a marginalized people. In short, the term "double consciousness" allowed Du Bois to talk about an African mode of thought and what is now called a cultural conflict between African (blackness) and American (whiteness), both of which are imaginary social constructs that possess very little, if any, stability in a rational reality. Du Bois used the idea of double consciousness because it allowed him to speak of another aesthetic; an aesthetic that endowed the African American with an intuitive faculty enabling him/her to see and communicate notions about American society that could not be seen by white America. The shortcomings of such a gift lay in the fact that the African American was too often only able to see the self through the eyes of the white masculine other.

Double consciousness in Butler's fiction is not limited by the eyes of the other. By constructing characters that are mixed beyond the human race, Butler reconfigures the problems of miscegenation. According to Fredric Jameson, the success of such refiguring is partly due to the conventions of science fiction: "[As] for race [in Butler's writing], its thematic is relatively neutralized by the presupposition of the alien life in the first place—which can, to be sure, stand as the allegory of race—although it can also return, within an alien world, as the representation of interspecies coexistence and rivalry . . ." (140). Akin from *Adulthood Rites* and Jodahs from *Imago* see themselves from several perspectives at once and negotiate their positions in a manner that offers a great deal of insight to the tragic mulatto or Du Bois's Negro American.

Adulthood Rites is the second book in the Xenogenesis trilogy, and like the first and last, it is primarily a tale of human survival. More specifically the trilogy speculates about the survival of humans, culturally and biologically. In *Dawn* we find that humanity has managed to destroy most of the Earth by way of nuclear bombs and industrial pollution. The Oankali (or gene traders) have helped Earth to regenerate itself in exchange for genetic information and mutual benefits necessary for the survival of the new Earth and the life forms which will coexist in its environment. The Oankali are vaguely reminiscent of displaced Africans, not seeking a return to home and origin but seeking and embracing difference as a method of survival. Donna Haraway draws similar parallels with African Americans.

> Unlike Lessing, Piercy, Russ, LeGuin, Atwood, Wolf, or Tiptree, Butler's uses of the conventions of science fiction to fashion speculative pasts and futures for the species seem deeply informed by Afro-American perspectives with strong tones of womanism or feminism (Haraway 378).

In addition to Haraway's assertion that Butler's fiction is invested in the experiences of the African Americans and their struggles, Haraway also declares catastrophe, survival, and metamorphosis to be constant themes in Butler fiction. Thus, like the mulatto, tragic or not, "origins are precisely that which Butler's people do not have access . . . [Thus], Butler's fiction is about miscegenation, not reproduction of the One" (378–79). Butler's fiction demonstrates quite vividly how the term miscegenation transcends most conventional notions of race. Her employment of miscegenation disrupts the possibility of a pure racial identity being written upon a body primarily because the bodies of the Oankali, for example, have no known singular location of origin. More importantly, the Oankali and the human/Oankali constructs have no desire to limit the narratives of identity that constitute there bodies.'YHUIR''

The central character in this section of the trilogy is Akin Iyapo. Akin is the child of Lilith (Latin-African American, female human), Joseph (Chinese, male human), Dichaan Ishliin (male Oankali), Ahajas Ty (female Oankali), and Nikanj Ooan (oolio Oankali). At best, Akin can be described as one of the first human-born male constructs. Another way of locating Akin's identity would be to say that he is a child in sexual and gender limbo until puberty. Akin has the intellect of an adolescent human child in the womb of Lilith. He looks like the "perfect" male human infant (with the exception of his tongue), yet for a large portion of the novel Akin demonstrates the reasoning and logic skills of an adult five times his age. Akin also occupies several identities at once and is in possession of a multiple consciousness.

As the first male child born of a human woman since the war destroyed Earth, some three hundred years ago, Akin's growth into adulthood acts as the central plot of the novel. It is revealed late in the novel that the Oankali intentionally allowed Akin to be born so that he might become a conduit between humanity and the Oankali. As the plot unfolds, Akin is kidnapped by raiders who hope to trade him to a resister village (where there are no children because humanity has been sterilized) for goods and women. After learning about the struggle of the raiders and resisters, Akin arrives in the village of Phoenix, which is lead by Gabriel and Tate (two of the main characters from *Dawn*). Eventually Akin's hybrid state allows him to understand and bridge the complexity of human nature and the scientific logic of the Oankali. Because he can identify with the human need to be independent of the Oankali, Akin becomes the voice for the human resisters and dedicates himself to the restoration and propagation of a wholly human society on Mars.

Akin is able to become a translator between the two races because his body is located at the center of what is human and what is Oankali. Butler posits Akin's character at the center of the Xenogenesis trilogy and on the cusp of a struggle focused around the miscegenation of two very different races of beings. Anatomically, Akin passes for the "perfect" human child, but intellectually and culturally he is far from being perfect or pure in his genetic origins. Even on the most superficial level, Akin is placed in the middle of adulthood and childhood. For most of the novel Akin holds the form of an infant who grows only to the size of an adolescent human by the end of the novel. In placing Akin at so many centers, Butler creates a negotiator of difference and a character who is multilingual on several fronts, namely body language, cultural moorings, and states of consciousness. Consequently, Butler has ultimately written an allegory that is significantly more complicated than Du Bois's troubled Negro American.

Akin's mobility and adaptability exist because of the form his body holds and the advanced state of his consciousness and ability to reason beyond notions that are purely human or purely Oankali. Thus, Butler endows Akin with the tools necessary to survive and negotiate the survival of others in spaces that can not be occupied by those who wield the powers of hegemony. Similarly, Du Bois's talented tenth is embodied in Butler's constructs/ mulattos because they are the individuals who have the tools to bridge the gaps of difference and ease the fear of change. With Akin the narrative suggests that the mulatto has a natural ability to negotiate difference because he represents proof that difference and change does not necessarily result in death or chaos. Akin is a symbol that suggests that there is little or no value "rooted in the fantasies of natural roots and recoverable origins" (Haraway 379).

The character Jodahs from *Imago* represents a completion of interbreeding or miscegenation between humanity and the Oankali. Jodahs is a human-ooloi, the Oankali third sex and the ultimate changeling Jodahs has the ability to change the form of its body at will. Jodahs can take on the appearance of male or female, but has no human identified gender or race to return to because it is both. Through Jodahs's character Butler shows some of the processes involved in the translation of difference into likeness. Jodahs tells a human in transit through Lo that "we feel our Humanity. It helps us to understand both you and the Oankali. Oankali alone could never have let you have your Mars colony" (Butler, *Imago* 14). At this moment Jodahs names itself and mulattos like itself to be the saviors of humanity, which in *Imago*, represent the marginalized.

THE INTOLERABLE PARADOX

Butler's narratives make manifest assertions about miscegenation and being in the middle of several identities at once. 1.) The state of the mulatto is potentially powerful. 2.) The mulatto is not someone who should be feared, for the mulatto potentially possesses a space of identity security. 3.) The varying appearance of the mulatto is at least subconsciously appealing because it represents a desired paradox of likeness and difference, a miscegenation resulting in something stronger and potentially more powerful than the "normal body," i.e. black, white, male, female, animal or homosapien.

Jodahs's character, despite its boundless anatomical forms, suggests a full range of experiences open to individuals who may, as women, be aggressive and, as men, be tender. Jodahs is the embodiment of a spectrum upon which human beings choose their places without regards to propriety or custom. Its fundamentally indefinable nature of androgyny is best evoked by borrowing the descriptions of Soyinka's *Obatala*. While Jodahs appears to be neither man nor woman, in the eyes of Tomas and Jesusa it is both. This is demonstrated when Jesusa tells Jodahs, "You look like Tomas, you know? You look the way he should look. You could be our brother—or perhaps our sister." Jodahs appropriately responds with the declaration that it is "neither" (*Imago* 109).

In a discussion involving the origins of *Esu-Elegbara* and the Signifying Monkey, Gates explains the nature of the Yoruba deity *Legba* and its relationship to sexuality. His description is notably parallel to the shifting and ambiguous sexual identity of the Jodahs' character in Butler's *Imago*. As Gates notes, "*Legba's* sexuality is a sign of liminality, but also of the penetration of thresholds, the exchange between discursive universes" (27). Jadahs's likeness to *Esu-Elegbara* is not coincidental and demonstrates the presence of a Yoruba sensibility in Butler's writing.

Jodahs, like its older sibling Akin from *Adulthood Rites*, is able to successfully build bridges of communication that were not present or possible before. Jodahs's androgynous body allows it to be pleasing to both sides of a battling binary, human and Oankali. Its state of being represents the best of several worlds. What I mean by this is that "It" embodies the survival instinct of humanity in addition to the intellect and ability to manipulate genetics of the Oankali. Images of androgyny and racial miscegenation in Butler's narratives are productive interactions in which different selves overreach their culturally prescribed identities to relate to one another in such a way that the boundary between self and other becomes blurred. According to Gates, Legba like Jodahs "is a principle of fluidity, of uncertainty, of indeterminacy even of one's inscribed fate" (28). Historically in America, little girls must wear pink and little boys must wear blue or they and their parents will be punished physically and verbally. In twenty-first century America, androgyny in any form is subconsciously equated with nonconformity and lawlessness or chaos. Perhaps this line of thinking exists because the lack of boundaries and identity markers pose the threat of a sort of power that can not be put in check.[7] Without constant identity markers, there can be no sure point of attack if such a notion of identity moves toward dominance. The idea of an unchecked power of malleability wielded by everyone is a thought outside of Western thinking. In fact, it necessarily disrupts the traditional notions of hegemony and hierarchy, because identity ambiguity constructs a playing field that brings new meaning to the notion of an "even playing field." The idea of power being derived from any notion of equality in a system founded on inequality constitutes an intolerable paradox. Alas, what would our world be like if everyone were free to be whoever and move in a space defined as wherever?

The answers to these questions are provided by writers like Du Bois, Soyinka, and Butler. Further analysis of their writing and thinking will yield the tools necessary to reflect beyond Western aesthetics. Like the identities discussed in their meditations, the theory of identity does not house itself in a single book, ideology, or fantasy. In this brief comparative analysis of three very different writers, it becomes apparent that the problematic of marginalized identities can and must be approached from diverse perspectives. The line between fact and fiction, figurative and abstract is as imaginary as the boundaries of racial identity. In fact, it would seem that the answers to most of the questions posed by Du Bois, Soyinka, and Butler are located squarely in a realm of ambiguity.

NOTES

1. Lydia Maria Child's 1842 short story "The Quadroons" is one of the first examples of literature to feature the female tragic mullato. Fannie Hurst's 1933 best selling novel *Imitation of Life* was adapted into two films of the same title by Universal Pictures: a black and white film in 1934 starring Fredi Washington and Claudette Colbert, directed by John Stahl; and a remake in 1959 starring Lana

Turner and Susan Kohner, direct by Douglas Sirk. A more contemporary example of cinema's treatment of the mullato can also be found in Spike Lee's 1988 musical drama *School Daze*, starring Laurence Fishburne and Tisha Cambell-Martin.

2. Audre Lorde, "Age, Race, Class, and Sex: Women Redefining Difference," *Sister Outsider*. California: Crossing Press, 1984.

3. All of Butler's short stories can be found in *Bloodchild and Other Stories*, New York: Four Walls Eight Windows, 1995, 2005.

4. Butler's writing has evolved out of the Black Womanist literary movement of the 1970s. In part, Butler's location of women of color at the center of her fiction is a response to the black-male-centric rhetoric of the Black Arts/ Black Power movement of the 1960s. Despite the black aesthetic origins of Butler's writing very few critics in the academy have begun to consider the inextricable ties of science fiction and the aesthetics of people of color.

5. I would like to make the point that modernist fiction doesn't embrace ambiguity and difference as normative but as a response to ideas of normative failing (Stevenson 2).

6. The Lilith character is likely a derivative from Hebrew mythology. According to the *Alphabet of Ben Sira*, Lilith was the first wife of Adam. When Lilith refused to constantly lie beneath Adam, she abandoned Eden and became a demon. Lilith was cursed to see her children die and was marked as the first woman to defy the laws of man. Butler's choice in naming her protagonist seems appropriate as *Dawn's Lilith* is also a feminist and a mother.

7. According to Gates, "above all else, Esu, as the originator of a uniquely African mode of reading, is the Yoruba figure of indeterminacy itself, ayese ayewi, or ailemo, literally "that which we cannot know" (Gates 11).

5

Religious Science Fiction: Butler's Changing God

"[Science Fiction is] a realistic speculation about possible future events, based solidly on adequate knowledge of the real world, past and present, and on a thorough understanding of the nature and significance of the scientific method"(Robert Heinlein 21).

"Science-fiction is the search for a definition of man and his status in the universe which will stand in our advanced but confused state of knowledge (Science)" (Brian Aldiss 8).

"Science-fiction is relevant; it is important; it has something to do with the world; it gives meaning to life; and it enlightens the readers. And it has all these characteristics as no other form of literature has" (Isaac Asimov xi).

In defining the boundaries and utility of a genre the above passages suggest that three of the most dominant voices in the genre of science fiction (SF) agree that it can be a device used to understand the real world. Despite the elements of fantasy, time travel and utopian societies, the genre of SF is very much a literature that directly reflects the society that produces it. "Derrida argues that all Literature addresses the nuclear condition: the risk of absolute efficacy" (Luckhurst 103). Consequently, it is also a literature that has the ability to critique and police the boundaries of the real world in a fashion that is comparable to that of religion. Heinlein's observation about realistic speculation based on the past and the present is reminiscent of biblical revelations. Aldiss's assertion that SF is necessarily an existential quest coincide with what is generally understood as the function of religion;[1] and Asimov's declaration of SF's relevance to the real world reads like a Sunday school sermon. Indeed, SF is far from a juvenile literature designed for escaping reality. According to Freud religion was an attempt to control the mental world by means of a world of the oldest and most compelling wishes of mankind (Walker 850). Religion is a tool intended to critique the real world in the unbounded laboratories of our imaginations. Discussions of utopian or heavenly societies do not negate discussions of an imperfect world with imperfect representations of humanity. Given these observations the discussion examining relationships between religion and SF seems more than fitting as both seek to provide assistance in navigating our imperfect real world.

Adam Roberts's *The History of Science Fiction* asserts that science fiction would be better named "technology fiction" as the term "'science' is generally understood to be a discipline which seeks to understand and explain the cosmos in materialist (rather than spiritual or supernatural) terms" (4). Roberts continues his assertion by observing that SF is *"a mode of doing science* (or 'philosophy' more generally conceived) as well as a mode of doing fiction" (6). Ultimately, through terminology supplied by the German philosophy Martin Heidegger, Roberts arrives at the notion that SF is a process that thinks: "not only in the sense of rehearsing a great many concepts, possibilities, intellectual dramas and the like, but in the deeper sense of textually enframing the world by positing the world's alternatives" (12). Thus, by associating SF with what is traditionally understood as the pondering and explanation of the real world Roberts argues "that the reemergence of SF is correlated to the Protestant Reformation" (Preface ix). Consequently *The History of Science Fiction* is largely founded on the notion that the borders of SF and religion have been blurred for a very long time. Roberts dates SF as far back as the Ancient Greek novel and cites seventeenth century examples of ancient science fiction such as "Johannes Kepler's *Sominum* (1634), Francis Godwin's *The Man in the Moone* (1638) and Cyrano de Bergerac's *Voyage a la lune* (1655)" (Introduction ix). More importantly, Roberts make note of that fact that religion and science (technology fiction) has been at odds since René Descartes.

During the late sixteenth and early seventeenth centuries the balance of scientific enquiry shifted to Protestant countries, where the sort of speculation that could be perceived as contrary to biblical revelation could be undertaken with more (although not total) freedom. René Descartes, for instance, settled in Holland in 1629, in part because his native French Catholic culture was proving to be hostile to his scientific inquiries. In Descartes' mind was the recent condemnation of Galileo's astronomical work by the Catholic Church, a shocking development for many scientific thinkers at the time. Indeed, there were more troubling developments that this, especially for the more imaginative minded (which is to say, science-fictional) thinkers. (Introduction ix)

The speculative fiction of Octavia Butler often targets issues of religion and spirituality as a way to raise questions about how the body is valued in the real world as well as the spiritual world. As a writer known for her cautionary tales that question social ethics, religion seems an appropriate location from which to begin dismantling fundamental social values. In interviews, Butler has suggests that her slant toward religion has partially been a result of her grandfather being a Baptist minister and her mother raising her as a Baptist in order to install her moral conscience at an early age (Zimmer 1) (Zindell 3). Religion is ultimately a mechanism that polices the borders of social value and disvalue. In her narratives Butler employs the integration of postmodern slave narrative forms with feminist creation stories to question the political and spiritual value of marginalized bodies. By outlining practical behavior that advocates the end of oppression rooted in hierarchies of identity via clear paths of spirituality, the fiction of Butler expands the parameters of the genres she writes across. Butler's use of SF in conjunction with religious references allows her to rewrite history and the future with plausible fantasy and faith based mythology. By mixing SF with religious themes, Butler's fiction encourages readers to question social values that mark marginalized bodies. This is made evident through Butler's harsh critique of patriarchy, capitalism and any form of oppression that appears to be based on the rejection of change or a universal notion of God.

In this chapter I assert that the employment of religion and religious themes in the fiction of Butler makes her fiction both assessable and plausible as a source of social commentary and advice to an increasingly marginalized and especially African American audience. I contend that Butler's consistent employment of black bodies and spiritual references in her fiction appeals to a marginalized populous that identifies with archetypes on the borders of the secular and the religious. The humanitarian and universal elements of Butler's religious and cultural references allow her audience to identify with archetypes that are appealing and familiar. As the "Black Church has historically demonstrated its institutional genius in its ability to shape itself according to the needs of its congregation" (Toth 213), it is not surprising that the malleable and eclectic spiritual institutions imagined in Butler's fiction would appeal to readers culturally linked to institutions that embrace the marginalized. Through close readings of *Parable of the Sower* and "The Book of Martha," I consider the value of religious and spiritual references as persuasive devices used to bridge a mystical gap between religion, SF, and the real world.[2] Because of the probable source and employment of religion, SF and folklore in our society is a mixture that yields speculative fiction that is paramount to an mythology that is commonly accepted as truth by the populous as a means of survival.

Among Butler's many approaches to religious themes, two of her most contemporary narratives, *Parable of the Sower* (1993), and "The Book of Martha," found in the second edition of *Bloodchild and Other Stories* (2005), speak directly to the policing of social values via the employment of religion. In *Parable of the Sower*, Lauren Olamina leads a community of individuals up the Pacific coast while writing and teaching a religion based on the acceptance of change and difference as God. And in "The Book of Martha," God allows Martha Bes to develop a functional utopia for humanity by augmenting the experience of individual dreams. Butler consistently develops female characters who seek the end of all oppression by understanding the movement of change and its relationship to difference and the spiritual. In *Patternmaster* (1976), Amber avoids the feudal patriarchy of the Pattern; leads Teray through an Arthurian quest, and declines a place of security and power as one of Teray's wives. In "Near of Kin," (1979) readers are persuaded to reevaluate the social taboo of incest by identifying with a nameless protagonist and her uncle/ father. In *Dawn* (1987), Lilith is forced to become the spiritual leader and matriarch of a congregation that represents the only hope of survival for humanity. Religion and religious values are interrogated in all of Butler's fiction directly or indirectly because they necessarily influence the way a society defines, loves, hates, and reproduces bodies.

The female protagonists employed by Butler supports the generally accepted notion that women have historically been closer to concepts of God and religion both literally and metaphorically. "By now it is so taken for granted that women are more religious than men that every competent quantitative study of religiousness routinely includes sex as a control variable" (Stark 495). The bodies of both Lauren and Martha are crucial to the existence of the gods in their respective narratives. For Lauren, God has no shape and every shape, as God is change. For Martha, her body allows God to take the form(s) as it is the image of Martha and humanity which God uses as a model and referent point. Martha's god is only limited through the existence of her bodily experience. In speaking with her god, it is both her mind and body that allows an encounter to occur. Without the human body, God has no form or shape to be perceived—just a voice giving directions. Martha has agency and the ability to shape God. "You see what your life has prepared you to see . . . "What you see is up to you, Martha. Everything is up to you" ("Book of Martha" 191). The body of God shifts, but it is Martha's body that is the more interesting as she is a woman with a familiar biblical narrative attached to her name. Butler's choice in naming her protagonist was not coincidence. Martha, the sister of Mary and Lazarus is the perfect candidate to assist Butler's god in reconstructing the world. The Martha of Luke 10:38–42[3] is not easily distracted and is both a devoted and diligent worker defined by the household and the confines of the gender roles of the Victorian woman. Butler writes most of the Victorian out of her Martha by replacing the four cardinal virtues of purity, piety, domesticity, and submissiveness with independence, inquisitiveness, bravery, and a sense of self sacrifice that can only be described as biblical.

Women substantially outnumber men in conventional and non-conventional religious groups. Folklore as well as canonical literary tradition has long classified religion as "women's work" (Stark 496). Because of the female reproductive system and monthly menstrual cycles often associated with the moon and the power of "Mother nature," women have been imaged as having a closer link to God than their male counterparts (Walker 680). The examples of this phenomenon are numerous and widespread; Nathanial Hawthorne's Hester in the *Scarlet Letter* can frolic about in woods that men can only fear; Mary Magdalene is said to have been closer to Jesus Christ than many of his male disciples; and the Hebrew protagonist Lilith[4] (the first wife of Adam) has the power to speak the unspeakable name of God and defy the most sacred laws of man. Butler's writing of women necessarily engages the murky discourse of the "body" that has been a popular topic in the academy for more than a decade now. Locating the discussion of the female body in the church and religion further complicates the concept of the body as well as begins an excavation of how God is imagined with regards to gender.

> With the collapse of traditional patriarchy and the evolution of modern patrism, the changing status of women in society has been reflected in, among other things, the religious conceptualization of God and the social division of labour within the church between the (primarily male) priestly leadership and the (primarily female) lay membership. The old patriarchal God of traditional fundamentalism gave way initially to a more "democratic" vision of God as friend and confidant. In so far as Christianity is committed to the idea of a personal God, it has been difficult to imagine how this concept of personality could be degendered to give expression to a social equality between men and women (Turner 35).

Butler's fiction successfully "(de)genders" God, and in doing so, creates a "democratic" image of God that may not be a symbol of social equality but is definitely gender-friendly. Both Lauren and Martha confront gods that can be molded and shaped by the people (primarily women) who worship them. By investing her fiction in such religious themes, Butler's fiction begs the investigation of the already blurred borders of religious belief and SF.

Ingo Morth makes the claim in "Elements of Religious Meaning in Science Fiction," that religion and SF are not only comparable by means of the formal aspects of utopia and transcendence, but also by the transgressions of boundaries of knowledge, experience, and behavior. Morth suggests that SF establishes a fantasy world which literally transgresses the boundaries of everyday existence in the true sense of the word, constructing a world of different structures of meaning, based on the future or an alternative environment, into which the reader enters (Morth 88, 89). I would like to go a step further than Morth by suggesting the relationship of religion and science fiction, as deployed in the works of Butler, challenges the boundaries of everyday existence but does not completely transgress how religion and fantasy affect the value of bodies in the real world. Morth makes an insightful observation that when faced with the loss of closed concepts of the world in modern times, many writers fall back on earlier interpretations of the world which are no longer controversial and easily accessible within the general stock of knowledge (Morth 91). This insight is especially poignant in the case of Butler's fiction because it consistently seeks to persuade an audience of color to reevaluate the society's method of marking bodies via gender, race, class, etc.

The African American has historically used religion and places of worship as a devise of guidance and survival. In defense of her views on religion Butler says,

> Religion kept some of my relatives alive, because it was all they had. If they hadn't had some hope of heaven, some companionship in Jesus, they probably would have committed suicide, their lives were so hellish. But they could go to church and have that exuberance together, and that was good, the community of it. When they were in pain they had God to fall back on. I think that's what religion does for the majority of the people (Zindell 3).

As a producer of cautionary speculative fiction speaking to an audience that has not been traditionally targeted by the genre of SF, Butler's employment of religion seems to be a stroke of genius. Until the arrival African American writers like Samuel Delany and Butler onto the scene of SF, religion was easily considered to be more valid by most audiences than fantasy novels about white and metallic futures. What I would like to suggest with the term "valid" is that an audience is more likely to embrace the stories of the bible as more "legitimate" tools to navigate the real world than stories found in "illegitimate" SF novels despite the fact that the sources of mythology in both text and genre have a very similar foundation, our collective imagination.

According to Donna Spalding Andreolle, *Parable of the Sower* is a feminist narrative of self-awakening and self-fulfillment that blurs the boundaries of SF and religion by "combining it [SF] with specific religious overtones, to describe the ascent to divine status of a young, half African American, half Mexican American woman" (Andreolle 119). The presence of an Old Testament God in "The Book of Martha," further signifies a familial bond, in that Martha is commanded by a shape shifting god to avoid another apocalyptic flood by engaging in eugenic experiments which will lead to a genesis of a better humanity. Folklore, SF, and spirituality are shown to possess elements of one another and possibly to be located at the origins of each other. Butler's speculative fiction seamlessly weaves together 1.) What we think we know; 2.) What we don't know; and 3.) What we don't want to know about ourselves. Where Martha is given the power of God, according to Andreolle,

> Lauren is a new Christ, the sower of the new seeds of Christianity, after the Armageddon which destroys the wicked civilization that has abandoned the founding beliefs of the nation. Yet *Parable of the Sower* is more than just an allegory of Christ's life transposed into imaginary, dystopian near-future . . . (Andreolle 120).

Andreolle's acknowledgment of the possibility of Butler's fiction being more than allegory suggest that the fantasy world which Morth claims the reader enters, via SF, might not be so far away from the world in which the reader already exists. Butler's fiction has consistently suggested that she not only kept a watchful eye on world news and popular culture, but that she also analyzed it for dissemination into her startlingly speculative narratives. A society's daily response to religious beliefs along with folklore, superstition and supposed scientific fact suggest that the Western imagination is unclear on the relationship between Plato's realms of the real and ideal or the material and the spiritual. Andreolle's analysis of *Parable of the Sower* asserts that "Butler is not calling the Christian worldview into question but rather, is reflecting on the validity of Judeo-Christian values as the necessary ideological foundation of social order in the American imagination" (Andreolle 116).

In the fiction of Butler the spiritual beliefs of a character directly influence that character's ability to survive life threatening situations throughout the narrative as religion defines the boundaries of the body. In *Parable of the Sower* this is true for the main character Lauren Olamina, as her spiritual belief system not only acts as the key to her salvation, but the salvation of all those who choose to follow her on her migration up the West coast. It is Lauren's pilgrimage up the coast that acts as a bodily ritual which assists her in outlining the praxis of her beliefs and the symbolic order of the Earthseed religion. The bodies of Lauren and her followers play an essential role in the formation of their religion. To call Laurens group motley would be appropriate on several levels as they represent distinct difference in their varying race, class, gender, and sexual characteristics.

> Most feminist analyses of the construction of bodies attend primarily to social factors, such as gender, race, and class, but do not question how the body functions also as a map for the symbolic order (Torjensen 946).

I would like to agree with Torjensen's observation and suggest that the bodies found in Lauren's group represents the acceptance of ambiguity that is at the foundation of the Earthseed religion. The foundation of Lauren's religious beliefs deviate from those of her African American father's and his church, but still have their beginnings in a Black Church. Historically Black churches have been an extremely valuable resource for Black communities in America since the antebellum period. The Black Church was in many respects an example of Black Nationalism in that they were built, financed, and controlled by African Americans. The Black church is and always has been a valuable resource for individuals and groups whose entrance into traditional social institutions of the larger [White] society has been denied (Frazier 1971).

In Butler's narratives the church is a social construct designed to help maintain social order. This social order is often enforced by the employment of fear. In her discussion of how fear is used in Butler's fiction Claire Curtis observes that

> Butler uses the fear of Noah and Martha to raise questions for the reader about the meaning of subordination and the qualities of secure living. If fear is not universal, then peace is not possible. Fear, for Hobbes, is built on the universal emancipator: equal vulnerability in the face of death.
>
> So, we are all naturally equal; we all fear; we are all driven to act by the same basic set of motivations. Butler is a theorist of fear. ("Theorizing Fear" 416)

Lauren acknowledges the influence of her father's church in her community despite her fear of the unknown and her evolving individual beliefs. Lauren admits that her father's church and its beliefs have not been her own for at least three years, but because of her fear of being defined as an outsider to her father's church Lauren allows herself to baptized and initiated into a church she has no faith in (*Parable* 6). Lauren's father and his church act as the glue that holds their deteriorating Robledo community together, at least temporarily. Reverend Olamina is the heart of the neighborhood in that it is through his faith and focus that the organization and sanity of the community is maintained. The loss of Reverend Olamina is foreshadowed by his wife's question, "What are we supposed to do if you die?" (*Parable* 69) Lauren's shift away from her father's church is a critique of the system of faith practiced by his church.

Reverend Olamina's faith is dependent on an Old Testament God that is inflexible and utterly mysterious. For Lauren the God of the Old Testament is juvenile and mythical. She compares the Christian God to the Greek God Zeus—"a super-powered man, playing with his toys the way my youngest brothers play with toy soldiers" (14). Lauren questions both the function and practicality of her father's God.

Lauren and those who are to be the survivors of her community will need a church with a god that is not only flexible but malleable as well. Unlike the Zeus of the Reverend Olamino, Lauren's notion of God as change is both predictable and tangible. Change can be seen and accounted for in everyday life and death; change can be prepared for; change has no emotion or care to sway away from the objective. When Reverend Olamina does disappear from the Rebledo community and the change that Lauren has prepared for finally arrives, the new mobile church, Earthseed, replaces the old and the hope of survival is restored. What this replacement says to the audience of Butler's fiction is important on several levels. Lauren's new religion appears to be infinitely malleable and exclusionary only to those who do not value life and survival. Earthseed is a set of social values that seems to borrow its best aspects from several religions across the globe including many from her own father's church in Robledo. Several parallels can be drawn between Process Theology and the framework of Lauren's fictional religion. One of the main concepts of process theology is that the universe is characterized by process and change carried out by the agents of free will. Self-determination characterizes everything in the universe, not just human beings. God cannot totally control any series of events or any individual, but God influences the universal free will by offering possibilities. To say it another way, God has a will in everything, but not everything that occurs is God's will (Cobb 9). While there are indeed similarities between the two religious doctrines, there are far too many distintions to be identified in this breif meditation. Process Theology may be one of many sources visited by Butler in her creation of Lauren Olimina's very inclusive religion, Earthseed.

While clearly inclusive, Earthseed seems to embrace even those who might be rejected by more traditional religions and churches. Lauren's church is especially appealing to a marginalized audience because it seeks difference and is subject to change with the demands of its congregation. In addition, the demands that the Lauren's church places on its congregation seem far from taxing.

Once or twice
each week
A gathering of Earthseed

is a good and necessary thing.
It vents emotion, then
quiets the mind.
It focuses attention,
strengthens purpose, and
unifies people (*Parable* 192).

In other words, besides attendance and understanding the nature of a god that is change, i.e. shaping god; preparing for God; learning from God; all synonymous with understanding one's self, there isn't a great deal of material sacrifice involved in being a member of the Earthseed religion. There are no monetary taxes; no commandments etched in stone to follow and enforce; no rejection of individuals based on different sexualities, races, genders, ages, or classes. Earthseed sounds like a utopian religion accept for the very important fact that it exists because it acknowledges the impossibility of perfection and permanence. According to Claire Curtis' article "Rehabilitating Utopia: Feminist Science Fiction and Finding the Ideal," *Parable of the Sower* is an example of contemporary utopian fiction because it "recognizes the danger of perfection and in this sense differs from early more rationalist attempts to posit the best imaginable world," or in this case religion. "This is the key to the contemporary utopia: the fact that it incorporates into its own 'perfection' an acknowledgement that such perfection is simply unrealizable, but also ultimately dystopian" (Curtis 148). Lauren's church tries to systematize her observations and assumptions and act on them. With her bible, Earthseed: Book of the Living, Lauren creates a manual of praxis instead of mere faith and theory.

Butler's practice of critiquing the praxis of religion is manifest in "The Book of Martha," as Martha is asked to participate in the work of God. The marginalized audience identifies and perhaps believes in the plausibility of the "The Book of Martha" because Martha is utterly a representative of the ordinary person of color. She like most of Butler's characters sits on several fences with regard to identity. She obviously has faith in God, yet has not lived the life of a saint. She is an educated writer, yet not a member of the upper class elite because of her profession. Martha is not a traditional heroine yet she undertakes the Herculean task of saving the world. Martha is chosen by God and Butler for all that you [Martha] are and all that you are not ("Book of Martha" 194). Because Martha is written as a female Job or Noah, a vessel of God, readers who associate themselves with the church are more prone to personally identify with the fictional character of Martha. In other words, the religious references found in Martha's narrative make her experience less SF or fantasy oriented and more socially allegorical.

The fiction of Butler has always involved discussions of gods and the worshippers of gods. And these discussions have always addressed the struggles of the powerful and the powerless. It began with the shape shifting and body wearing of Anyanwu and Doro of the Patternist Series and continued with the Oankali of the Xenogenesis Series all the way to the Change of the Parable Series. Each representation of God interacted with those who accepted them as gods until the worshipers began to see the flaws of God via the reflections of themselves. Eventually the powerless began to understand that it was they who created and shaped the Doro, the Anyanwu, the Oankali and Change. In each of Butler's series the powerless began to see that power is always relative and always within who or whatever has the initiative to seek it. Consequently, the worshippers of God usually have the potential to share the power of God.

Martha's conversation with God does not seem to deviate from Butler's long standing narrative pattern. Martha's god needs her assistance to make humanity better. "You will help humankind to survive its greedy, murderous, wasteful adolescence. Help it to find less destructive, more peaceful, sustainable ways to live" ("Book of Martha" 192). Like the gods before, Martha's god needs the help of its creations. Like Doro, or the Oankali, the god in Martha's story is inexplicably dependant on the assistance of a worshipper who can hardly conceive of its image let alone its power. It is not coincidental that the same scenario plays out on numerous occasions in the Old Testament section of the Christian Bible. In many respects God resembles an adolescent child with great potential for creation and destruction but who is ultimately the creation of parents who can never really understand what or how they have been allowed to come into existence.

> "I have a great deal of work for you," he said at last. "As I tell you about it, I want you to keep three people in mind: Jonah, Job, and Noah. Remember them. Be guided by their stories" ("Book of Martha" 191).

Martha's god mentions the three well known biblical characters who readily and hesitantly sacrificed their bodies in the service of what they believed to be the God Almighty. Somehow a god that needs from its creations is a god that is easier to believe in and to worship. Humanity seems to need to be needed even by the god(s) of humanity, which suggests a paternal/maternal love between gods and mortals. Consequently, Butler's fiction seems to employ this understanding with extreme proficiency.

Like the Oankali, Martha's god gives her an advantage over the average mortal.

"You'll arrange it so that people treat one another better and treat their environment more sensibly. You'll give them a better chance to survive than they've given themselves. I'll lend you the power, and you'll do this" ("Book of Martha" 193).

Martha's god lends her the power to do what she thought was impossible for all but god. The Christian God gives Moses the power to part the Red Sea, Doro gives Mary the power to create the pattern, the Oankali give Lilith the physical strength and virility of a goddess and Change chooses Lauren as the recipient of foresight and wisdom beyond her walled Robledo community. Both King James and Butler translate and write such caring and compassionate gods considering the fact that they are also written as omnipotent, omniscient, as well as indifferent. The contradictory characteristics of the gods produced in religion, and fiction, and mythology appear to be due to the fact that gods reflect those who worship gods. Ludwig Feuerbach's *The Essence of Christianity* (1841) was the first book to argue that God or the gods represented man's ideal and unrealized potential. In the fiction of Butler, gods are reflections of characteristics or potential, not fully realized by the followers of the many faces of socially constructed notion of a god. Despite the fact that Martha's encounter supports these assertions about the construction of God as a reflection of humanity, "she had come to like this seductive, child-like, very dangerous being" ("Book of Martha" 213).

Morth reminds us that the relationship between fantasy literature and religious myth was first brought to light by Freud's analysis of "The Extraordinary," 1919, and the psychological development of individual unconsciousness. Carl Jung then expands on Freud's personal unconscious to develop an analysis of the collective unconsciousness and its archetypes. Jung considered the fantastic to be a further expression of a comprehensive mythology of mankind (Morth 88). In other words, religion has the same origins as SF; the collective unconscious of human society. Both social constructs, religion and SF, attempt to explain, predict, and to speculate the happenings of the real world by stimulating the imaginations of real people.

According the psychoanalyst Carl Jung, the part of the imagination or psyche that processes religion and folklore is the collective unconscious. Jung's collective unconsciousness is a sort of storage bend of human experience that all people are supposedly born with. This common reservoir of knowledge is the thing that Jung says influences all human experience and behavior. Religion, folklore, fantasy and literature all act as evidence that common pieces of knowledge are shared among humankind. The contents of collective unconsciousness are called archetypes or the unlearned tendency to experience things in a certain way. Butler writes characters that identify with her reading audience as familiar archetypes or spiritual instincts. Jesus, Moses, Job, Paul, and Noah for example, are all identifiable characters who demonstrate archetypes that a Black Christian audience can understand and associate with their real lives.

In his autobiography *Memories, Dreams, Reflections* (*MDR*), Carl Jung demonstrates through a telling of his own personal mythology how his understanding of the psyche and the psychology of religion come into being. According to Duane Bidwell's article Carl Jung's "Memories, Dreams, Reflections: A Critique Informed by Postmodernism," Jung uses images from 42 of his own dreams along with those of 13 clinical cases to develop his theories of the collective unconsciousness, the existence of archetypes (patterns of meaning that shape a person's life), and the ego or the supreme archetype (Bidwell 15). This is all to suggest that the construction of the self, God, and religion seem to be inextricable according to Jung.

Other scholars have also contemplated the relationship of myth, reality and religion and the real world and found that mythology is a response to the mysteries of reality. W.E.B. Du Bois for example is quoted by Don Hufford in an article entitled "The Religious Thought of W.E.B Du Bois," as saying,

> Religion is a theory of the ultimate constitution of the world, more particularly in its moral aspects . . . The church on the other hand, is the organization which writes down and from time to time rewrites the exact religious belief which is prevalent and which carries out celebrations and methods of worship (Hufford 74).

Du Bois' quote, taken from *The Crisis* (October 1933) speaks directly to what Butler's character, Lauren from *Parable of the Sower*, does throughout her trek up the West Coast toward Canada. Earthseed: the Book of the Living becomes an instructional manual on how to practice what seems to be an inclusive theology based on the acceptance of difference and the inevitability of change. In a very literal sense Lauren becomes a traveling evangelist spreading her brand of salvation like the Christian archetypes, Paul or Jesus. As a sort of "jack-leg" preacher Lauren easily identifies with African American Christian readers associating a fictional account with the historical fact of migrating black bodies up the East Coast as well as the mid-west United States. Lauren's pilgrimage mimics a familiar historical narrative reminiscent of the migration of marginalized people due to religious persecution.

> For any fictional narration to attain the level of cultural myth, it must possess three features: assemble common beliefs of culture which are grounded in

historical experience; give central focus to a historically representative figure of the community; be capable of evolving with the culture (Slotkin *The Fatal Environment*, 435). The utopian/dystopian narrative of survival and reconstruction, as epitomized in A Gift Upon the Shore and *Parable of the Sower*, illustrates the American cultural myth of progress and the powerful eschatological vision of the Puritan American self (Andreolle 115).

The historical experiences of African Americans are peppered throughout all of Butler's fiction. Butler's writing easily taps into the eschatological vision of the African American self because it necessarily considers the physical and spiritual condition of dark bodies in the past, present, and future. The African American soul is not in the jeopardy it was in before the arrival of African American SF writers. Butler's fiction does not require the death of marginalized bodies in her fiction as did more traditionally white dominated moments in the genre. Both *Parable* and "Martha," are narratives that assemble common beliefs that are grounded in a historically marginalized struggle for survival. Lauren and Martha represent common women in their respective communities who are identifiable with a contemporary reading audience. All of Butler's fiction is capable of evolving with contemporary American culture because it is necessarily a product of American experience.

As utopian/dystopian narratives of survival and reconstruction both the *Parable* novel and the short story "The Book of Martha," speak to a broad audience by virtue of universal points of appeal. However, the African American reader is uniquely targeted by the Butler's fiction via images, scenarios, and cultural experiences that are common to an African American experience that is shared more lucidly by marginalized people. The employment of religious and or spiritual archetypes functions as a devise of validation and transformation of cautionary tales to realistic speculation that might be heeded given the right circumstance. Consequently, Butler's employment of religious themes supports the reevaluation of an entire genre by marginalized audiences previously uninterested in SF.

NOTES

1. Walker suggests that religion is ultimately a quest to restore the bond between man and nature. The root religion is Latin for re-linking or reunion (Walker 850).

2. Religious references have been useful as a persuasive devise for African American writers since the slave poets and the slave narratives of the eighteenth and nineteenth centuries. The neo-classical slave poetry of Phillis Wheatley and the evangelical slave poetry of Jupiter Hammon commonly employed biblical

language and references to persuade their audience to consider the abolition of slavery. Frederick Douglass's classic masculine slave narrative also employs religion as a persuasive rhetorical device. (McKay and Gates)

3. As Jesus and his disciples were on their way, he came to a village where a woman named Martha opened her home to him. She had a sister called Mary, who sat at the Lord's feet listening to what he said. But Martha was distracted by all the preparations that had to be made. She came to him and asked, "Lord, don't you care that my sister has left me to do the work by myself? Tell her to help me!" "Martha, Martha," the Lord answered, "you are worried and upset about many things, but only one thing is needed. Mary has chosen what is better, and it will not be taken away from her" (Luke 10:41–42).

4. Lilith is the protagonist in Butler's novel *Dawn* and is a crucial character in all of the novels included in the Xenogenesis Series. Lilith's relationship to Hebrew mythology is explained in notes of chapter 4.

/

6

Migration of the
Hybrid Body

Despite the efforts of Negro farmers to adjust themselves to the rural economy, the farm ceased to be attractive to many. The return of ex-Confederates to power, intermittent agricultural depressions, unfair and, sometimes, cruel treatment by landlords and merchants, and rumors of rich opportunities in the cities and in other parts of the country stimulated an exodus of Negroes from the rural South that began as early as 1879 (Franklin 282).

Migration is usually a result of economic adjustment. Whether it is because of a world war, the end of a civil war or the desire to explore a western frontier, migration happens because a group of people want, and sometimes need to make an economic adjustment in order to survive within particular boundaries. Franklin speaks specifically of the African American in his historical text *From Slavery to Freedom* (1980), but his assertions hold true across racial, class, and national boundaries. Moving a body voluntarily in hopes of relocating it in a better economic situation or environment is a concept as old as the first nomadic cultures. It is also a concept that speaks to how we mark our bodies in socioeconomic systems as capital. Surely, the body as capital is a notion that has been inextricably tied into the past and the land of every marginalized people recorded in history. Any discussion of American slavery will undoubtedly reveal relationships between migration and cultivation of land and bodies as capital, but it is inside the pages of Octavia Butler's *Parable of the Sower* and *Mind of My Mind* that the complexity of such a relationship is engaged in a way that necessitates a reconfiguration of the notions of "body," "boundary," and "capital" as they relate to hybridity.

A topographical survey of the uses and misuses of hybridity and its synonyms has been established by John Hutnyk. Hutnyk makes the observation that the notion of hybridity has become crucial in political and cultural discourses of globalization and migration. "Hybridity is logically entwined within the coordinates of migrant identity and difference, same or not same, host and guest" (Hutnyk 80). What is most interesting about Hutnyk's observations in conjunction with the fiction of Butler is that the latter is very much invested in the process of diaspora. There is a seemingly mundane link between migration and the identity of a people that begs further analysis via the complexities involved in the discourse of hybridity. Hutnyk acknowledges the work of several scholars of Diaspora studies such as Paul Gilroy, Stuart Hall, Iain Chambers, Homi Bhabha, and James Clifford. Their findings reveal that "hybridity has come to mean all sorts of things to do with mixing and combination in the moment of cultural exchange" (80). In the genre of SF the motif of hybrid is extremely commonplace in reference to the body. In *Colonialism and the Emergence of Science Fiction* John Rieder asserts that the notion of a hybrid or artificial human has often been used as a motif to distinguish the civilized from the savage. Reider gives examples such as "Victor Frankenstein and his monstrous creation, Dr. Jekyll and Mr. Hyde, and Dr. Moreau and his Beast People" (Rieder 111).[1] In Butler's fiction "hybrid" is a term that consistently refers to identities that are biologically and culturally blurred. The blurring or mixing of character identities in Butler's fiction is facilitated by migration over land or through space. To be identified as a hybrid in Butler's fiction is, often times, synonymous with becoming a survivor and a signifier of the future.

As Stacy Alaimo and Donna Haraway argue, understanding the body and its relationship to its surrounding environment is inextricable from an understanding of its transformative possibilities. "Because the discursive links between 'nature,' the 'body,' and racist hierarchies have, historically, been so firmly forged, it is crucial not only to understand how these discourses have functioned but also to determine the possibilities for transforming this volatile space" (Alaimo 123). I believe Butler's fiction engages this volatile space by drawing attention to links between land, biology, and the historical oppression of marginalized bodies. Only by imagining the body as a function of the elements that confine it can a true understanding of its transformative possibilities be revealed.

In this chapter I demonstrate how *Parable of the Sower* and *Mind of My Mind (MOMM)* both focus on the migration of marginalized bodies across time and space as capital and as products of eugenic change. As the bodies migrate from space to space in each novel, their treatment and value also shifts depending on their ability to adapt. It is a body's hybridity that allows it to become valuable as a liberated subject as opposed to a subjugated object or mere capital in Butler's fiction. Land and nature are inextricable in the process of imaging the body and its boundaries. It is the crossing of boundaries of land and nature that allows for the production of history and the reproduction of bodies. By closely examining narrative moments in *Parable* and *MOMM* along with criticism addressing hybridity and the transgressions of the body, I situate Butler's fiction in a discourse invested in the transformative possibilities of the body within literature.

PARABLES AND *MOMM*

On Saturday morning, July 20 in the year 2024, Lauren Oya Olamina begins her fifteenth birthday with a brief journal entry describing a prophetic recurring dream. The dream reminds Lauren that the security that she and her community depend on is false and fleeting. Lauren's dream foreshadows the destruction of her neighborhood community and the changes she will have to adapt to if she is to survive.

> The neighborhood wall is a massive, looming presence nearby. I see it as a crouching animal, perhaps about to spring, more threatening than protective. But my stepmother is there, and she isn't afraid. I stay with her. I'm seven years old (*Parable of the Sower* 5).

In Lauren's dream about the wall that surrounds her small neighborhood in Robledo, California, "20 miles from Los Angeles" (10), the wall is compared to an animal preparing to strike out and devour all that Lauren calls her home. In the first three short chapters of *Sower*, we learn that the wall is supposed to protect the members of the Robledo community from its surrounding environment infested with "poor-squatters, winos, junkies, and homeless people in general" (10). Instead, in Lauren's dream, the wall is a symbol that threatens to unleash an inevitable change. The personification of the wall as an edifice constructed to protect and define the people within its boundaries suggests a symbiotic relationship between land and people. Such relationships between land and people are ancient and widespread, especially on the North American continent. Leslie Marmon Silko speaks of how Laguna Indians propagated the importance of such relationships in their oral traditions and general cosmology.

> It begins with the land; think of the land, the earth, as the center of a spider's web. Human identity, imagination, and storytelling were inextricably linked to the land, to Mother Earth, just as the strands of the spider's web radiate from the center of the web (Silko 21).

Silko's claim that the human identity and land are woven together with a web further complicates the meaning and significance of Lauren's prophetic dream.

> Landscape has similarities with dreams. Both have the power to seize terrifying feelings and deep instincts and translate them into images—visual, aural, tactile—and into the concrete, where human beings may more readily confront and channel the terrifying instincts or powerful emotions into rituals and narratives that reassure the individual while reaffirming cherished values of a group. The identity of the individual as a part of a group and the greater Whole is strengthened, and the terror of facing the world alone is extinguished (38).

Lauren's dream of the wall might be interpreted as a connection with the landscape that surrounds Lauren's community. Furthermore, Lauren's ominous feeling about the impending arrival of disaster might be the landscapes attempt to seize Lauren's subconscious fears of change and translate them into a warning powerful enough to move her toward a new beginning for a community of unique individuals.

Silko's web metaphor also speaks to some very important components of the *MOMM* novel with regards to the web-like pattern that is constructed by the protagonist, Mary. It is Mary's pattern/telepathic web that calls other hybrid "actives" and "latents"[2] together in Forsyth, California, to form the first family of Patternists. The *MOMM* narrative is the sequel to a creation story of a race of hybrid people created by Doro and Anyanwu, the patriarch and matriarch, of the *Wildseed* narrative. Mary is the daughter of Doro and granddaughter of Anyanwu and the product of centuries of eugenic experimentation. She is a telepath who Doro hopes will lead him to the evolution of a race of people more like himself. Thus, Mary represents the matriarch of the *MOMM* narrative who calls for the migration and transformation of hybrid bodies.

Throughout the Patternist series Butler consistently suggests that the family structure of Doro's people or "wildseed" is volatile and subject to dysfunction despite the need for close proximity among its members. In the prologue of *MOMM* Doro tells Mary that despite her very conscious desire to run away from her alcoholic mother and general family, she also possesses an unconscious "need to be close to them"(5). The need to be near bodies that are similar in appearance and ability to one's own is a key factor in understanding the patterns' involved with the migration of hybrid bodies in Butler's fiction and the real world. Doro, for example, has always been drawn to bodies that housed special abilities regardless of location or socially constructed identity written upon a body. Doro explains his attraction to the hybrid body in the following passage:

"I was able by then to recognize the people . . . the kinds of people that I would get the most pleasure from if I took them. I guess you could say, the kinds of people who tasted best" (90).

Despite Doro's need to feed on his offspring, it is important to keep in mind that Doro is himself tragically hybrid in identity.

For all but the first few centuries of his four-thousand-year life, he had been struggling to build a race around himself. He existed apparently as a result of a mutation millennia past. His people existed as result of less wildly divergent mutations and as a result of nearly four thousand years of controlled breeding (9).

Doro's cannibalistic tendencies might be representative of a basic need to congregate and ultimately exist among bodies that affirm his own existence. Consequently, *MOMM* can be interpreted as a narrative invested in the development and refiguration of a family of hybrid bodies with hybrid identities. Despite its mundane foundations, such a notion is potentially insightful with regards to understanding the perspective of the marginalized. According to *MOMM*, hybrid bodies migrate toward other hybrid bodies in an attempt to establish a state of normality. Mary's pattern and "proprietary feelings" (58) creates a situation where hybridity is equated with normative and a sort of racial purity which is oddly antithetical to most notions of hybridity.[3]

I couldn't help the feeling of rightness that I had about the pattern—about the people of the pattern being my people. I felt even more strongly than I had felt Doro's mental keep-out sign. But it didn't matter (58).

The body as capital is made evident by Mary's feelings about the people she has inadvertently collected in her transition. Of course, issues of power and propriety play significant roles in understanding the transformation of marginal to normative, but what is unavoidable is the acknowledgement of the temporality of either term. The locations of this transformation occur in the body, in Forsyth (a plantation city), and in the minds of both characters and readers of the narrative. But more important than the location and the boundaries that define it, is the medium of the transformation, which is the discourse of familial bonds and household.

Lauren's household in Robledo consists of her father, stepmother, and two younger brothers. Lauren's father is the community preacher and is in many ways the community patriarch. As the church leader, he holds the community together by providing direction and moral support in times of hardship. Lauren's father is also responsible for training the community youth in the use of fire arms.

It's my father's fault that we pay so much attention to guns and shooting. He
carries a nine millimeter automatic pistol whenever he leaves the neighborhood. He carries it on his hip where people can see it. He says that discour-
ages mistakes. Armed people go get killed—most often in cross fires or by
snipers—but unarmed people get killed a lot more often (*Parable* 37).

The not-so-futurist world that Lauren and her family exists in is something short of the old west, but reminiscent of a present day inner city Los
Angeles, or any contemporary urban ghetto. Besides the side-arm that
Lauren's father carries with him, the Olamina family has access to several
guns in their household with the purpose of protection. The environment
that Lauren and the Robledo community exist in presents considerable
danger to the body.

Lauren is the central character in *Parable* for several reasons. It is
through her journal entries that we are allowed to participate in the narrative. Even at the age of fifteen, Lauren's perspective on the events that
take place in and around her community present a frighteningly vivid
picture of how her world is changing and how our world may change.
Fear is used throughout the *Parable* narrative as motivation for change
and survival. Lauren ability to face fear marks her as a heroine in the narrative. Claire Curtis makes the observation that Butler's fiction writes fear
"as both a fact of human life and a motivation for human action" (Curtis
411). Lauren's seemingly mature outlook toward the world around her
is largely due to a condition known as *hyper-empathy*. Lauren's hyper
empathy makes her body sensitive to the feelings of those around her.
Much like the abilities possessed by characters in Butler's Patternist series, Lauren's hyper empathy marks her body as unusual and potentially
powerful. Butler consistently marks the bodies of her central characters
with difference. Butler's writing seems to imply that to be different or on
the margins of several identities at once is a potentially powerful position
to exist in, if one is aware of the transformative possibilities of his/her difference. Lauren goes through a transition-like process over the four years
of the narrative. Although Lauren initially views her ability as a disease,
she does learn to appreciate her difference and uses it to help her become
a more efficient leader and matriarch by the end of the narrative.

Lauren's hyper-empathy is a particularly difficult difference to carry
around because she exists in a space that places very little value on the
physical body. After a field trip to a neighboring church Lauren explains
why she tries not to take in too many of the horrific sights that are common on the streets outside of her Robledo neighborhood.

If I don't look too long at old injuries, they don't hurt me too much. There
was a naked little boy whose skin was a mass of big red sores; a man with a
huge scab over the stump where his right hand used to be; a little girl, naked,

maybe seven years old with blood running down her bare thighs. A woman with a swollen, bloody, beaten face . . . (*Parable* 13).

In the first section of *Parable*, entitled "2024," we learn that America has developed new drugs, colonized Mars, and deteriorated into some kind of capitalistic byproduct, where "Politicians and big corporations get the bread" (20), and the proletariat gets close to nothing. Members of the middle class have been forced to surround themselves with protective walls, and the unskilled masses are left as scavengers on the streets of what was once a thriving metropolitan. It is through Lauren's observations and opinions about the state of her world and its gods that she begins to construct Earthseed: The Book of the Living. Earthseed is Lauren's formulation of parables that outline a religion that identifies God as change and seeks to propagate itself and humanity throughout the stars. The stars or space is Lauren's vision of the ultimate frontier. The idea that migration is inevitable for humanity, even beyond the boundaries of the planet Earth is central to Butler's writing. In "Bloodchild," Butler's tells of a colony of humans (Terrans) that escape Earth to arrive on a planet inhabited by the T'Lic (Caterpillar People). The humans are forced into a symbiotic relationship that entails becoming hosts for T'lic larvae in order that both the humans and the T'lic might continue to survive.

Because your people arrived, we are relearning what it means to be a healthy, thriving people. And your ancestors, fleeing from their homeworld, from their own kind who would have killed or enslaved them—they survived because of us. We saw them as people and gave them the Preserve when they still tried to kill us as worms ("Bloodchild" 25).

The Terrans like the people of Robledo are marked by the land/planet they live on. The Preserve is a "protected" area of space that identifies those who live within its boundaries as people willing to adapt to living with aliens in hopes of surviving. The metaphorical walls of the Preserve act as a class divide among an "upper" and "lower classes" of humanity. Those willing to embrace difference and hybridity have a "better" ("prolonged life and prolonged vigor") quality of life than those unwilling to move beyond the stagnant and inevitable detriment associated with notions of racial purity and homogeneity. Ultimately, the borders of the Preserve, or Reserve, or Plantation, or Concentration Camp are relative and largely imaginary.

In this way the walls of Robledo are ineffective. The bodies within the community are not protected from their primary fears, fire and rape. The wall is more of a filter than the impenetrable fortress that the community members would have it embody.

Someone shot Amy right through the metal gate. It had to be an accidental
hit because you can't see through our gate from the outside. The shooter
either fired at someone who was in front of the gate or fired at the gate itself,
at the neighborhood, at us and our supposed wealth and privilege. Most bul-
lets wouldn't have gotten through the gate. It's supposed to be bullet proof.
But it's been penetrated a couple of times before, high up, near the top. Now
we have six new bullet holes in the lower portion—six holes and a seventh
dent, along, smooth gouge where a bullet had glanced off without breaking
(*Parable* 48).

Lauren's observations about the unpleasant things that did not seep in,
but were already within, seem to act as foreshadow to the inevitable
doom of the Robledo wall and community.

The wall that surrounds Robledo is literally a socially constructed border that serves as a marker of economic difference. Outsiders would toss
gifts of envy and hate over the Robledo wall: "A maggoty, dead animal,
a bag of shit, even an occasional severed human body limb or a dead
child" (47). Much like the borders of a nation within a nation, the walls
of Robledo are more abstract in function than a solid brick wall. The wall
is a symbol of false and temporary security for the bodies in the Robledo
community.

Lauren becomes the heroine of the narrative primarily because she
acknowledges the facts of her environment and prepares herself for the
change that will come. In other words, she listens to the landscape. Lauren understands at a very early stage in her life that the differences of
class that act as borders between the Robledo community and everyone
outside its walls are deadly fabrications. Beyond the walls is where Lauren must go if she is to survive. Beth McCoy alludes to this observation
in the following passage:

. . . common to many African American texts is an extraordinary critical
ambivalence about the concrete and abstract terrain that black people must
travel. Though the land is neutral, its topography can shelter—and betray—
even as political discourse and history transform that land into property,
violence, mystical experience, or slate upon which to inscribe meaning (223).

The political narratives written on and around the land/neighborhood
is what causes most, if not all, of the conflict in the *Parable* narrative. The
value placed on the land and the people inhabiting the land is a function
of capitalistic rational. Because the land is defined by a seemingly privi-
leged few, the land defines those few as "haves" and everybody outside
of its walled boundaries as "have-nots." Ironically, the premise of value
and capital within the walls is a fabrication grounded on the mythologies of a capitalistic mentality. Along with her lessons about the outside

world surrounding Robledo and its many dangers, the primary function of the second section of *Parable* is to account for the internal destruction of the community and its families, the Robledo body. In other words, there is a clear assertion that if the boundaries of the landscape are in jeopardy, the family is also in danger.

MIDDLE PASSAGES AND THE HOUSEHOLD

The final section of the *Parable* narrative begins with Laurens' account of the destruction of the Robledo community at the hands of pyro-addicts with painted faces and other street scavengers. It is not until Lauren returns to the ruins that she finds out that everything and everyone she understood to be her home and family were lost. It is at this moment that Lauren realizes that the survival training and preparation she had been putting herself through was finally going to serve its purpose. Lauren then begins a middle passage along with a small group of surviving neighbors.

As in all of Butler's previous narratives, special attention is given to the image of the female body as it travels. Lauren chooses to disguise herself as a man by cutting her hair short and wearing men's clothing. Lauren feels that by making her body appear male she will decrease the possibility of being an easy target for rape or worse. One of her more experienced companions, Zahra, is quick to inform Lauren that racial coupling should also be considered when traveling through the city. "Mixed couples catch hell whether people think they're gay or straight" (*Parable* 157). Despite the fact that racial difference should have little significance in a world on the verge of destruction, it still has its place among humanity.

As Lauren's group travels up the coast of California on Highway 101 toward Canada, Lauren continues to develop her Earthseed religion and begins to teach it to the members of her traveling congregation. Lauren proves herself as the leader of her small group when she takes the life of an already unconscious assailant. Zahra and Harry watched in shock as Lauren flicked open a sharp knife and cut the throat of a man she had just moments earlier brained with a small granite boulder from the fire pit (*Parable* 176). Killing the man served both as an act of protection for the congregation as well as a show of maternal power. Taking the man's life might also been interpreted as a demonstration of Lauren's proprietary feelings about the congregation and what they symbolize within the context of Earthseed. As Lauren, Zahra, and Harry, travel they encounter other travelers and allow some of them to join their group. Lauren takes on the role of a sort of shepherd guiding a flock of sheep to an unknown better place. Just as her father had once guided the people in the Robledo community, Lauren was now learning to lead her own congregation of Earthseed.

Lauren lives in a not so distant future where capitalism and its materialistic mentality have transformed America into a third world nation eating itself from the inside. A mysterious company enslaves people desperate for work and protection from deteriorating neighborhoods with promises of security and a normal life. The company uses entire families as slave labor and experimentation with the sole objective of making a profit. Lauren's philosophy/religion counters the company as well as much of the Christian doctrines that her father preaches in his neighborhood church. Earthseed advocates the acceptance of difference and change as the omnipotent forces of the world. The notion of property is devalued considerably by the mere fact that material is temporary and perishable in times of crisis and change. Lauren and her congregation of followers rethink materialism and the promises of the company and choose community values over individual prosperity.

Lauren's character is in many ways analogous to her father and Christ or Moses figures because she is clearly the leader in the narrative as well as the sympathetic and gifted philosopher behind the Earthseed doctrine. Lauren's hyper-empathy allows her to value life and its pleasures in a way that is both profound and prophetic. She is able to feel the pleasure and pain of anyone who is in her presence and therefore becomes attached and physically responsible for the bodies of her followers and enemies. As her father's child, Lauren takes up the role of leader, but chooses a different path that will lead her followers to a promised land that exists in outer space or the literal heavens. Lauren and the Earthseed doctrine both have biblical references with which they can be identified. For example, Lauren is clearly a prophet. Jesus was a holy prophet and the embodiment of God or the Father. Similarly, Lauren's father was in many ways a god in the Roblando community and is mysteriously represented through the body of Lauren. Lauren's role as an active community leader and shaper of a god who is omnipotent marks her body as being Jesus-like. Lauren is the voice that will lead her followers out of a west coast wilderness to a place of change and growth.

What is interesting about this move or migration that Lauren is participating in is that it is taking place in the midst of one of the most terrifying calamities that could ever happen in a nation. As Lauren travels up the west coast with her followers, binary racial illusions are in the process of being dismantled. The racial make up of Lauren's congregation is easily described as "motley" as is the marauding bands that they encounter during their travels. America as a nation is quickly falling apart along with its national identity as is the racial identities and prejudices in Lauren's congregation. As the racial, gender, and class identity boundaries fall by the wayside, so does the national identity. This seems only logical, as class, sex, gender, and racial identity all help to construct a national identity and the images of a nation. Bodies define and constitute a nation and national identities just as easily as they can deconstruct and reinvent nations and national boundaries.

In *MOMM* Mary is well on her way to creating a nation of her own, beginning in Forsyth. Like Lauren, Mary acts as the leader of a pilgrimage or middle passage for her own congregation. During her transition Mary's telepathic abilities forms a web-like pattern that inextricably links her to six other active and relatively powerful telepaths. Unlike Lauren's experience, Mary has no need to travel with her congregation as they are telepathically drawn to Mary's location in Forsyth, California. The other major distinction between the two narratives is that Mary's people are not voluntary members, but have been drafted by what appears to be a random process. The distances that Mary draws her new family from vary and span from as close as Arizona to as far away as New York and Pennsylvania.

The pattern took Seth Dana and his latent brother Clay Dana[4] from a desert home in Arizona. More importantly the pattern rescued the two brothers from lives that were not productive or healthy.

> Clay was slowly deciding to kill himself. It was slow because, in spite of everything, Clay did not want to die. He was just becoming less and less able to tolerate the pain of living (63).

As the guardian of his older brother, Seth was growing weary of his duties as his brother's keeper. He was becoming concerned that his need to use his telepathic abilities to manipulate Clay was jeopardizing the humanity of he and his brother. Ultimately, Mary's "one-word command that left him [Seth] no opportunity for argument or disobedience," was the best thing for both Seth and Clay. Mary's call was an invitation to family, guidance, and a new beginning. The same can be said for the other telepathic recruits of Mary's pattern.

Rachel Davidson posed as a religious healer who fed off of the life force of her congregation.

> By the time the service was half over, they would have cut their own throats for her. They fed her, strengthened her, and drove out her sickness, which was, after all, no more than a need for them, for their adoration (70).

In the case of Rachel, the body as capital is equated to sustenance. Like Doro and Mary, Rachel's abilities require that she nurture and possess the bodies in her congregation. This is a common scenario addressed in Butler's fiction which suggests discussions of symbiotic relationships rather than parasitic interactions. Rachel rewards her congregation by healing them of disease and injury. Without the congregation Rachel has no sustenance for survival. Mary's command to migrate releases Rachel from the confines of her congregation and introduces her to a much more resourceful symbiotic relationship with the telepathic pattern.

Jesse Bernarr, Ada Dragan, and Jan Sholto also benefit from Mary's newly constructed pattern. As all of the telepaths who were linked to the pattern were actives and fairly successful in the employment of their abilities, the actual trek to Forsyth, is hardly noteworthy. In other words, the middle passage does not begin for Mary's new family until they arrive in Forsyth, California. More specifically, the rights of passage take place in the household of the first recruit of the Patternist, Karl Larkin, Mary's newlywed husband. The middle passage for the Patternists entails testing the strength of Mary as their matriarch, expanding the pattern, and overthrowing the patriarch, Doro.

The middle passage motif is the most resonant structure in the architecture of the novel. The slave related middle passage is a commonly reoccurring motif in Butler's work. Butler reuses the middle passage motif in *Pattern Master* and the Xenogenesis series, and *Parable* is almost completely dependent upon the events that take place on a trek up the west coast of North America. As in *Kindred* the notion of transporting the body over time and space is an important tool employed by Butler in developing her main characters and story line. In *MOMM* bodies are moved from place to place as well, but it is the movement or employment of minds that make the most compelling statements in the narrative about bodies. The battle royal of Mary and Doro is one of the most illuminating moments in the narrative pertaining to the identity of Doro.

> At once, Doro was housed with her in her body. But she was no quick, easy kill. She would take a few moments. She was like a living creature of fire. Not human. No more human than he. He had lied to her about that once—lied to calm her—when she was a child. And her major weakness, her vulnerable, irreplaceable human body, had made the lie seem true. But that body, like his own series of bodies, was only a mask, a shell. He saw her now as she really was, and she might have been his twin (212).

In this climactic battle it is made evident that Doro has succeeded in creating a family that truly reflects who and what he is and is not. In his last moments Doro understands that Mary is a "complete version of him" (213). Where Doro lost his original body in transition and was doomed to borrow the bodies of others in order to construct a hybrid identity visible in the material world, Mary has mastered the ability to exist in the realms of the material and immaterial simultaneously without the sacrifice of her material body. Where Doro was forced to live as a parasite feeding off of the life force of his highly prized human livestock, Mary is able to siphon off only the energy required to sustain a productive symbiotic relationship with the members of her pattern. She was a symbiont, a being living in partnership with her people. She gave them unity, they fed her, and both thrived (213). Ultimately, Mary is shown to be a far better benefactor than Doro was ever capable of being because of the limitations of his body and his instinctive nature to kill. Mary is the product of centuries of eugenic experimentation/racial miscegenation and might be understood as the ultimate hybrid. What is interesting about this hypothesis is that Mary's hybridity has returned her to the beginnings and completion of another experiment, Doro. By animating a problematic of the body through these literary characters Butler makes a significant contribution to thinking about complicated bodies and the notion of hybridity and its function in defining the destination of human identity.

Lauren's direction toward the stars seems only natural given that after the boundaries of individual identity fall, nations and then world identities seek a broader field of inclusion, the stars. This sort of thinking clearly addresses some of the fears raised by scholars of hybridity and diaspora as it suggests that the notion of hybridity, if embraced, will "offer up festivals of difference in an equalization of cultures" (Hutnyk 95) where the value placed on one culture or body will depend on insignificant and individually constructed nuances. Butler's fiction seems to equate such fears with an inability to accept the inevitable. There is an implied suggestion that by embracing hybridity there will be a "flattening of difference" (96) as opposed to heightened since and valorizing of difference. In the fiction of Butler the latter is definitely the outcome of embracing change and all that naturally comes with it.

Both Lauren and Mary seek a space where they can exist without the boundaries placed on them by dominant societies. Lauren's move from Roblando and the urban walls that have literally began to crumble around her and her family. Mary moves from a position of submission toward a position similar to supreme authority, somewhere analogous to the feudal system of Doro's villages, but transcending Doro's Old Testament style of punishing and devouring those who would sin against their god. Neither heroine is running from one particular form of oppression; both are moving away from well developed societies that operate on the exploitation of difference and power or the lack thereof. Because the two are women, I am inclined to call their mobility and acts of survival, feminist and woman centered. To do this would limit the narrative because the heroines in the narrative do not struggle solely because of their gender. They struggle because of a system of thinking and oppression which threatens them as well as the entire social system. Their concerns are not limited to female characters nor do their problems stem solely from male individuals or collectives. Their struggle with power and mobility are results of oppression rooted in hierarchies of identity. The plots of the two narratives are then blue prints of how such environments might be dismantled and/or rebuilt. The dismantling of oppressive hierarchies is founded on the introduction and practice of new doctrines of social behavior and moorings. The term "womanist,"[5] as defined by Alice Walker, better captures the anti-oppression theme of Butler fiction.

Thus, in accepting the malleability of ones situation and embracing the inevitable fact that everything changes, the notions of difference, or at least the identities commonly associated with difference becomes less intimidating. If material gain is not the primary objective of human society scarcity becomes a less valuable notion. The struggle to compete for limited material resources such as land and minerals must necessarily diminish and methods of identifying the body for the purpose of constructing oppressive hierarchies must also necessarily cease. I do not wish to leap at the suggestion that capitalism is the root of all evil, nor do I want to suggest that without capitalism race, gender, and sexual difference and hatred will be eliminated because this is simply not the case. People will never love everything about "everybody." However the absence of material worship will undoubtedly affect how we as humans value the differences within the boundaries of the human race. Darkness of complexion may not continue to serve as a maker for certain stereotypical and false attributes such as laziness, sexual potency, or untrustworthy behavior. The female gender does not necessarily have to be associated with the physically weak and rationally sub-standard. In Lauren's story these differences may very well take on other negative connotations as a function of gaining the material.

Through Lauren's Earthseed community Butler outlines a particular behavior that advocates the end of oppression, but more importantly promotes the survival of a community despite oppression. A practical ideology is designed to fit any occasion. It is a way of thinking that will insure the survival of the thinker regardless of the environment. Such an ideology must be very malleable in application as well as form. It must thrive on changing systems and it must seek out diversity constantly shifting shape and definition with its one never changing objective, survival. The term "practical" holds significant weight in the *Parable* narrative because it accurately describes the behavior of the Earthseed followers. With each inductee and life threatening adventure that is faced, Lauren practices the theory of her parables by proving this ideology to be more than mere abstract theory. Each day Earthseed changes and each day the followers of Earthseed perceives the changes that occur and they adapt and adjust.

From her very first narrative to her most recent, there have been several recurring motifs, all centered around humanity's struggle with identity and power. At the center of these themes has been questions and a constant presence of different bodies; male, female, human, alien, gay, straight, and the like. In each case Butler's fiction seems to say the same thing—bodies and the identities placed on them change as they move toward a state of hybridity. Changes can result in a bodies survival, death, or rise to power.

NOTES

1. Rieder also discusses the hybrid-cyborg and its presence in the novels of H.G. Wells. Rieder asserts that the notion of a hybrid-cyborg has been employed to discuss issues of race. "I want to propose that racial ideology provides the point of departure for the pattern of repetition that constitutes the genetic convention, or in other words, that the hybrid-cyborg pair is a hyperbolic extrapolation of racial division. This does not mean that cyborgs represent white people and hybrids represent non-whites, but that the exaggerated separation between anatomies and the evolutionary status of the two figures plays upon the imaginary differences produced by racist ideology to buttress racist practices" (Rieder 112).

2. "Actives" are characters who have active/functional abilities that can be controlled and which are usually acquired after "transition," a period of metamorphosis that occurs in mid to late adolescents. "Latents" are individuals who have the potential to become actives but have not yet reached or completed a transition period.

3. In his explanation of body horror Roger Luchhurst asserts that in Butler's fiction "The process of cultural hybridity gives rise to something different, something new and unrecognizable, a new area of negotiation of meaning and representation" (Luckhurst 219).

4. Clay Dana's psychokinesis ability becomes the basis of the space travel technology used in *Clay's Ark* (1984) and *Survivor* (1978).

5. Womanist 1. From Womanish. (Opp. Of "girlish," i.e., frivolous, irresponsible, not serious.) A black feminist or feminist of color. From the black folk expression of mothers to female children, "You acting womanish," i.e., like a woman. Usually referring to outrageous, audacious, courageous or *willful* behavior. Wanting to know more and in greater depth than is considered "good" for one. Interested in grown-up doings. Acting grown up. Being grown up. Interchangeable with another black folk expression: "You trying to be grown." Responsible. In Charge. *Serious.* (Walker xi)

7

Vampires and Utopia: Reading Racial and Gender Politics in the Fiction of Octavia Butler

Political commentary (whether it is about religion, race, gender, the environment, or poverty) is a staple in Octavia Butler's prose. As a writer of speculative fiction Butler is easily identifiable as a concerned politician of sorts. Butler's writing is very much invested in the art of governing and influencing those who might be competing for power and leadership in one way or another. Her dystopian-cautionary tales reveal the frightening reality of today and sketches individuals' lives and relationships at local, state, and (to some extent) international levels (Stillman 15). Issues of global warming, economic and social disenfranchisement, or good old fashioned American racism all suggest that Butler is invested in the discourse of the political.

Classic Science Fiction (SF) has always been a forum for political commentary because it has always been an investigation of the Other. Allegory has often been the veil that politics has stood behind in order not to frighten away the genre's white adolescent male audience. SF ranging from J. R. R. Tolkien's *Lord of the Rings* to Kurt Vonnegut's *Slaughterhouse Five* have critiqued cold wars and world wars with a veil so thin that the authors themselves have denied a particular political agenda so as not to distract readers from the story on the page. As a matter of fact, many critics considered it a problem that *Lord of the Rings* provided so many of its readers with an "extraliterary" experience. So powerfully did Tolkien evoke the sense of wonder in his fiction that one could almost forget that it was only fiction (Attebery 154). The ability to transform an entire genre and its political value is the same sort of work that is being done by Butler's fiction. She has mastered the work of weaving the political with good storytelling, and there is no fear of distracting her audience with politics because all of her stories are about everything that is overtly and quintessentially political, race, class, sex, and identity.

Parable of the Sower is a cautionary tale of what might happen to America if its political institutions do not change their direction. There is no veil other than the SF itself and the general public's (mis)conceptions about the fantastic elements of the genre. Critics such as Hoda Zaki, Peter Stillman, and Claire Curtis have cogently analyzed the utopian and dystopian content of Butler's writing. They all seem to agree that Butler's fiction, utopian or dystopian, encourages its audience to consider how the political shifts of today will affect tomorrow. *Parable of the Talents* ends with a mixture of pessimism and hope as the eighty-one year old Lauren Olamina watches the first supply ships leave Earth to discover the new frontier of space. *Talents* recounts the life and struggles of the adult Lauren and the deterioration of the American Empire. If Parable of the Sower is a warning for tomorrow, *Talents* represents a likely outcome which appears very distant from any notion of utopia.

Among scholars who have followed the work of Butler and the critical discourse that has slowly been developing around her brand of speculative fiction, it is generally agreed upon that her writing has shifted the gender and racial politics of the genre of SF (Govan 14). Despite this fact, there has been no attempt made to quantify the significance of the shift that has been made. Quite frankly, Butler has changed the color and cultural complexity of the future. For a genre that was once considered to be white and green in its complexion, Butler has expanded humanity's future of white heroes and green aliens to include people of color as heroines, villains, and survivors.

Butler's entrance and great success (demonstrated by her numerous awards in the SF genre) necessarily changed the perceptions of black women as SF writers as well as SF characters. Although Butler's tactic of placing gender at the center of her narratives is not completely original—consider for example the contributions of Ursula Le Guin (*The Left Hand of Darkness*), Joanna Russ (*The Female Man*), and Margaret Atwood (*The Handmaid's Tale*)—Butler's combination of race and gender must be viewed as an overtly political change in the SF genre. As for contemporary African American fiction, Butler's influences are evident. Although writers like Toni Morrison and Alice Walker have not yet been classified as SF, their location of race and gender at the forefront of very successful novels enabled Butler to sell her work to publishers in a different genre. Furthermore, while Butler readily admits to the fact that many of the pioneer SF writers influenced her understanding of the genre, it must not be over looked that Butler's writing has both influenced writers who have been in the business of producing SF longer than her as well as paved a way for new African American men and women writers exploring the possibilities of SF. For example, Tananarive Due's novels *My Soul to Keep* (1997), *The Living Blood* (2001) and *Blood Colony* (2008) (Dedicated to Octavia Butler); Nalo Hopkinson's *Brown Girl in the Ring* (1998), *The Salt Roads* (2003) and *The New Moon's Arm* (2007); and the detective story writer Walter Mosley's *Blue Light* (1998), and *The Wave* (2006) are all examples of works of an African American SF tradition spearheaded by Butler's writing. Her writing of the black female body in the genre of SF fits into a political discourse of struggle for ascendancy among groups having different priorities and power relations from the classic heroic white male. In an assertion made about film critique Frances Gateward, Ali Brox suggests that Butler's writing attempts to disrupt several dominant ideologies of power.

> ... [V]ampires and vampire films are often dismissed or assigned cult status, "they have the potential to directly challenge the dominant ideologies of sexism, white supremacy, homophobia, and capitalism upon which highbrow aesthetics rest" (para. 18). The vampire figure symbolizes the potential subversion of dominant ideology. (Brox 391)

The primary goal in this chapter is to consider Butler's fiction as a location of political discourse. By examining racial and gender politics in conjunction with the political value of dystopian elements present in Butler's Parable series and in her last novel, *Fledgling*, I would like to begin quantifying the change that is evoked by complicated black female bodies in her fiction. The characters of Shori Matthews and Lauren Olamina are employed as heroines in politically volatile situations. Both women are put in positions that challenge the white male dominant power structure in place. Where Shori faces the threat of assassination and Lauren must guard against the horrors of a weak central government and a tyrannical president, both black women survive. Butler's fiction suggests that the black female body not only survives in dystopian environments, but thrives. The abilities of Shori and Lauren to navigate their way to success and survival in a space that is constantly on the edge of violent chaos via shape-shifting, adaptation, and extraordinary leadership abilities begs a refiguring of the politics that surround the black female body. In this chapter I assert that Butler's fiction suggests that the black female body is best qualified to navigate the politics of dystopian environments. By being the antithesis of the white male body or at least the furthest away from it in terms of social status, the black female body is by nature qualified to evoke the most radical change in a political system of advantage based on race and gender.

FLEDGLING

Despite its seemingly drastic departure from the Patternist, Xenogenesis, and Parable series, the vampire novel *Fledgling* fits quite nicely in Butler's canon of politically charged fiction. As Sandra Govan notes,

> The Ina have distinctive family structures; they have a legal system; they have codes of conduct and behavior, admirable methods of conflict resolution that have evolved to allow them to settle major differences of opinion or potential conflicts between families in a thoughtful, judicious, considered manner consistent with their customs (43).

The novel's protagonist, Shori Matthews, demonstrates that the politics of race and gender can easily make their way into the lives of alien vampires. The conflict that acts as the engine for *Fledgling* is racial discrimination. The melanin in Shori's skin has caused political factions and a feud among elite vampire families. As the melanin in Shori's skin allows her to survive in the light of day, it threatens the purity of the Ina/vampire race as well as presents the possibility of racial evolution. Shori threatens the utopian society of the Ina because she is half human and because her human identity is compounded with a racial difference.

Shori's blackness disrupts the homogeneity of the tall, slender, and pale Ina people. Consequently, her predicament in the narrative makes the suggestion that the social constructs of race and racism have the ability to evolve even among a race of alien vampires. The Ina society is hierarchical, some of the Ina people have fallen victim to the irrational quest of racial purity despite the blatantly obvious detriments to the race as a whole. Shori is a genetic experiment that was designed to improve the quality of life for the Ina people by helping them move beyond a completely nocturnal existence. The pigment of Shori's skin represents a relatively boundless existence for a people held hostage by the darkness of night. To borrow images from Plato and the Wachowski brothers, Shori may be the "One" to lead the Ina into the light of a new reality. As in most of Butler's fiction the truth is usually packaged with inevitable change that requires flexibility and imagination from those most directly affected by its bright light. "Education is not putting sight into blind eyes; rather it is a matter turning the soul around so it can behold the truth for itself" (Lawrence 4). In other words, Shori's task in the novel is not to convince the Ina Elders that being immune to daylight is a good thing. The obstacle that she faces is to persuade conservative thinking old vampires that the change that such immunity would bring would not necessarily equate to their individual physical and political demise. Where Butler has consistently asked the question of what part of your humanity would you be willing to sacrifice in order to survive, in *Fledgling* the same question is put to the Ina people.

Ina mythology suggests that a goddess who sent them to Earth wanted them to grow strong and wise and then prove themselves by finding their way back home to her (*Fledgling* 193). Perhaps the strong and wise element of the myth entailed becoming impervious to sunlight and moving beyond the desire to preserve racial purity or other social constructs associated with homogeneity and utopia. The Oankali or gene traders of Butler's Xenogenesis series have clearly established the fact that homogeneity is not a concept associated with her fiction's notion of utopia. In fact, heterogeneity and miscegenation seem to consistently be coupled with any and all races with the desire to survive.

A faction of Ina, the Matthews family, has developed a way to make a white race yield a black one. Such a feat can only be a product of advanced alien technology, as it seems to reject the terrestrial laws of dominant and recessive genetics. Reminiscent of the eugenic experiments of Doro (from *Wildseed*) and the Oankali (from *Dawn*), a group of Ina scientists utilizes miscegenation as a tool to cross human and Ina DNA. As the hard-science of the experiment is left to the imagination, it appears that after human and Ina are made somewhat compatible with regards to reproduction, pigmentation was the final goal. Consequently, Shori's skin pigment and eventual reproductive capacity translate into the potential longevity and mutation of the Ina people. More importantly, Shori's hybrid existence marks female black bodies as more valuable than other human and Ina bodies in the narrative. Shori's black female body is stronger and more resilient than any of the pale white male bodies in the narrative. Shori's ability to move in spaces that are out of the bounds of mobility for Ina male bodies should translate into immediate power and respect, but does not because it deviates from images of Ina homogeneity and utopia.

Isaiah Berlin, a popular voice in discourse that rejects utopianism, believes that utopias always posit a static idea of human nature and that they are attempts to make humans agree with one set of values or universal ideals (qtd in Curtis 149). As it appears to be human nature to deviate from universal ideals, the quest for utopias usually yields violent behavior against those who do not accept that which has been defined as universal. This is the case in the *Parable* novels and *Fledgling* and most of Butler's fiction. The term "politics" comes into play because any quest for a universal ideal requires a process of negotiation in order to quail the inevitable violence that will occur. In Butler's fiction politics is ideally a process of problem solving within a society. The Earthseed community has several problems that it wishes to solve in the way of establishing social order. Likewise, the Matthews and Silk families of the Ina people disagree on the problem solving path their people should follow, and violence ensues.

The political agendas of conservative Ina get in the way of rational thought and Shori is forced to prove herself through violent self-defense. The fear that Shori's hybridity will translate into a change of color and cultural complexity among the Ina people threatens an Ina aesthetic that the elders equate with stability and order in Ina society. In this way Butler's pseudo-vampire narrative critiques the relationships of sexual and gender politics to cultural aesthetics and cosmology. The vampire motif is expanded far beyond a sexual metaphor in Butler's fiction.

Jewelle Gomez's *The Gilda Stories* (1991) seems a likely source of research for Butler's creation of Shori's narrative. For Gomez's vampires drinking blood is tender, compassionate, erotic, and above all, "a fair exchange" (Gomez 25, Johnson 72). Although a symbiotic relationship seems to be central in both Gomez's and Butler's narratives, Shori's story differs from Gilda's in that it is not primarily about vampires. "Where Gilda's 'exchange' of blood is an obvious metaphor for a particular kind of economy of the erotic, in which both partners must be satisfied, and in which neither may be bought or sold" (Johnson 73), Shori's taking of blood is more proprietary. Shori's relationships are indeed symbiotic, but they are compounded by the fact that her body is black without a remembered history and prepubescent yet more than half a century old. According to Govan, "where *Fledgling* differs from the norm in vampire lore is that it does not depend upon horror, the supernatural, or the gothic for effect" (40). Butler's narrative resists more traditional vampire narratives in its critical attention to race, sex, and gender politics along with its concern with the construction and destruction of utopian spaces. As Govan notes, "Butler goes her own way, as she customarily does, and entirely credible community with individuals motivated by some of those universal human attributes that drive us all—love, hate, fear, family, hunger, pride, and prejudice" (42). Ultimately, it is Butler's ability to make Shori's story believable that sets it apart from most, if not, all other vampire stories in print or on the silver screen. *Blade Trinity* by Natasha Rhodes and *Underworld Evolution* by Greg Cox are examples of contemporary vampire stories that make an effort to engage issues of family, love, hate, and even the construction of humanity but fail pitifully at being believable or anything reminiscent of speculative or utopian fiction.

To be clear, Butler's fiction is dystopian, not utopian. Instead of the goals of perfection and homogeneity, Butler's fiction negotiates violence and difference. However, "dystopia aims us in the same direction as utopia, and if it does not posit a direction in which we should go, it surely points out the dangers of certain possible paths" (Curtis 153). If the term "realist utopia" can be applied to Butler's fiction, as Curtis suggests, then the political value of her fiction might be quantified by its ability to identify or locate an equilibrium of social order. It is evident in both Parable novels and *Fledgling* that humans and Ina will not agree upon one ideal. Therefore, finding the point that signifies a compromise in the mist of imperfection is the trait that moves Butler's fiction toward and away from the universal. The mantra "God is change" leaves much more room for individual perception than any fundamentalist vision (155). Allowing the Matthews family to create Shori may not be the solution for other Ina families, but the possibilities that her existence may yield a useful change good for Ina and humans.

The body politics that play out in *Fledgling* is both complicated and intriguing. Shori's body is complicated and difficult to imagine because the narratives written on it are so eclectic. Shori appears to be prepubescent "super jailbait" (*Fledgling* 18), yet she is a 53 year old child. She is unmistakably African American, and as evidenced by her proclivity to drink blood, she is also a vampire. One of Shori's vampire abilities is to heal her damaged body by devouring the flesh and blood of other people or large game animals. This ability is intriguing because it suggests that the narratives written upon her body in the form of scars and other memorable injuries are temporary. At the beginning of Shori's narrative she finds herself covered with narratives of violence and death.

> I stopped and looked at myself. My skin was scarred, badly scarred over every part of my body that I could see. The scars were broad, creased, shiny patches of mottled red-brown skin. I wondered how I looked. I felt my head and discovered that I had almost no hair. My head, like the rest of me, was healing (10).

What is most interesting about Shori's body is that it has no memory of itself because it erases all that has been written upon it, all except its racial narrative that only gains meaning when it is placed in a context of difference, that is—the presence of her very white, tall, and slender vampire relatives. Shoris's body is largely dependent upon familial bonds that transcend race, sexuality, gender, and species. Beyond its juvenile appearance and its loss of memory, Shori's body is child-like because of, not despite, its 53 years of age. Her father informs her that she can play sexually with her symbionts, but is too young to mate. For now, she is unable to conceive a child, and she has not yet grown as large or as strong as she will (86). Shori's Ina eldermothers were both over 350 years old, which suggests that she should potentially live a great deal longer than 53.

In addition to having a significantly different life span, the Ina also employ gender differently from humans. The family structure is divided by gender. Ina females live in separate locations from Ina males. Shori lives with her female family members, and her brother Stefan lives with his father, Iosif. The destruction of all of Shori's female family members defines her as a lone matriarch. As in most female centered narratives, familial bonds are threatened and even broken, but are quickly rewritten via community support and sacrifice. Shori rebuilds her family and consistently survives the attempts made on her life primarily because she is black and female. Shori's ability to be aware and mobile during daylight hours in addition to possessing superhuman speed and strength has saved her life and the lives of her symbionts on several occasions. Butler politicizes Shori's body via gender and race in the narrative by making it visible to those Ina that would otherwise marginalize and minimize its potential for power and change. By writing Shori as a force that cannot be easily manipulated or erased, Butler makes the suggestion that black female bodies can and should be sources of political power.

PARABLES

Sower ends with an 18 year old Lauren Olamina and her 57 year old husband Taylor Bankole burying friends and relatives and naming their mountain community "Acorn." An acorn is a small seed that has fallen from a healthy and robust tree that will one day grow into something much larger and much more significant. Lauren's Acorn community is a symbol of hope that their small community will soon grow into the image of a once strong and United States of America, "changed, but still itself" (*Sower* 298). In his discussion of future utopias Jerry Phillips notes that,

> *Parable* seeks to reinvent the utopian vision at a time when utopia allegedly has been rendered impossible. The novel adumbrates the paradoxical aestheticism of which Fredric Jameson identifies as characteristically postmodern: the project of "Utopianism after the end of utopia" (154). (Phillips 300)

Talents is a reading of the memoirs of Lauren by her daughter, Asha Vere (or Larkin). Christian fundamentalists have taken over the government with the help of a born-again Christian politician from Texas. President Jarret, the leader of the Church of Christian America "engages in foreign adventures and wars to mobilize and pacify the population, ignores environmental problems, encourages faith-based organizations as the chief means of aiding the poor, and imposes his ideas and policies by tolerating Christian activists even when they are outside the law"(Stillman 16). In his attempt to reestablish a Christian sense of morality, Jerret advocates and participates in witch burnings along with the burning of accused prostitutes, drug dealers, and junkies"(*Talents* 354). This is an excellent example of how one man's utopia is another woman's dystopia. Stillman agrues:

Sower and *Talents* are rich in their insights into American dystopias of evis-cerated government or aggressive and intrusive religious fundamentalism. But there are utopian potentials also. Earthseed's destiny of traveling to the stars has high risks, as Olamina's recognizes even as she hopes for and expects some success (*Talents* 405); and Butler presents with strength and sympathy Vere's doubts about Olamina leadership and Vere's arguments favoring Acorn. Butler does not present a single utopian answer, but she does propose utopian possibilities: whether working towards Acorn or Earthseed or both, human beings act with others to change themselves and their world (32).

Stillman's assessment of the presence of utopian possibilities in Butler's dystopian fiction supports my assertion that in Butler's fiction black female bodies are better equiped to navigate the complicated politics of ambiguity. Both Acorn and "Earthseed: The Book of the Living" yield solutions that are flexible and at least potentially universal or "realisti-cally utopian." Jarret's Christian fundamentalists approach is rigid and founded on the existence of an unchanging god.

Surely one of the most overt struggles in the Parable series is the struggle between Christianity's unchanging God and Lauren's constantly changing God. This is a struggle that is symbolic of the tension that exists throughout Butler's fiction—a struggle between utopia and chaos. A par-able from "Earthseed" suggests that although chaos is dangerous it can be both malleable, and manageable.

Chaos
Is God's most dangerous face—
Amorphous, roiling, hungry.
Shape Chaos—
Shape God.
Act.
Alter the speed
Or the direction of Change.
Vary the scope of Change.
Recombine the seeds of Change.
Transemute the impact of Change.
Seize Change
Use it.
Adapt and Grow (*Talents* 26).

The above parable suggests that the presence of chaos can exist in a state of realistic utopia. Disorder and destruction can yield advantageous situ-ations and opportunities for a society willing to utilize change. Stepping outside of a strictly binary perspective of good or bad to consider the causes and effects of change might yield a valuable outcome. The parable assumes that chaos like God is a social construct that can be shaped and directed by careful negotiation and preparation. Consequently, the parable disarms and demystifies the dooming connotations attached to chaos through a political approach that is also spiritual and philosophical in nature. Both Shori and Lauren represent advantageous opportunities for change as a result of their black female bodies.

Asha Vere acknowledges the importance of politics in her mother's life as well as the influences that politics and politicians had of the image of Lauren and the Acorn community.

> Politics and war mattered very much. Science and technology mattered. Fashions in crime as drug use and in racial, ethnic, religious, and class tolerance mattered. She did see these fashions, by the way—as behaviors that went in and out of favor for reasons that ran the gamut from the practical to the emotional to the biological. We human beings seem always to have found it comforting to have someone to look down on—a bottom level of fellow creatures who are very vulnerable, but who can somehow be blamed and punished for all or any troubles . . . My mother was always noticing and mentioning things like that. Sometimes she managed to work her observations into Earthseed verses (77).

I would like to suggest that all of the verses found in "Earthseed" are politically charged as are most religious text. The divide between state and church has always been blurred because most societies exist in a constant struggle with the real and the ideal. Religion acts as a social construct which assists in the maintenance of a particular social order via providing answers to the difficult or unanswerable questions of daily existence. Such answers yield the foundation of a society's mythology, truth, and history. In a conversation with her brother Marcus, Lauren defines Earthseed as a "collection of truths" (117) that are not necessarily complete or absolute. It is the absences of absolutes that make Lauren's insights appear to be flawed and unsafe to the "Christian thinking" critics of "Earthseed." The absence of absolute laws or universal truths suggests the presence of ambiguous space, unanswered question, and chaos; the very things that Christianity often associates with sin and tends to combat.

Despite the persistence of religious themes and the politics that surround them, *Talents* is also very invested in issues of sex and gender politics. Since the disappearance of Lauren's father in Sower, she has been the matriarch of her community. Lauren is the dominant force in the Acorn community as her official title, "Shaper," suggests. Butler writes Lauren as the mother of the Acorn family. Lauren's family is very analogous to the families of slaves depicted in feminine slave narratives or histories of families in Maroon villages.

So many members of our community have come to us alone or with only little children that it seems best for me to do what I can to create family bonds that take in more than the usual godparent-godchild relationship (65).

Lauren or Olamina (her father's surname) as she is called by her husband and the other members of Acorn (122), refigures what is meant by a female headed household. Lauren's family, like families of the traditional feminine slave narrative, escapes oppression together by way of familial bonds and sacrifice. There is no individual solution to the oppression of the group. There are no Frederick Douglasses making independent escapes from slavery, leaving behind siblings or loved ones. According to Lauren, "We're used to depending on one another"(65). Marcus assumes that Acorn belongs to Bankole—"that this was Bankole's place and that he'd taken you [Lauren] in" (116). Lauren confidently informs her younger brother that "its our place, but I've shaped it. And I've given them a belief system to help them deal with the world as it is and the world as it can be . . ." (116). Although Lauren carries the name and power of a man, her style of leadership is distinctly feminine in nature. Lauren is the ideal leader for Acorn because of her body and its hybridity.

Lauren's body is marked by a condition called hyper empathy. The condition allows her body to feel and experience the pain and pleasure of other bodies.

Sharers who survive learn to take the pain and keep quiet. We keep our vulnerability as secret as we can. Sometimes we manage not to move or give any sign at all. It is incomprehensible to me that some people think of sharing as an ability or a power—as something desirable (37).

Although Lauren may not appreciate her hyper empathy, it undoubtedly gives her a potential advantage. As a sharer Lauren is able to read the narratives written on bodies that may not otherwise be readable. Clearly, there are disadvantages to Lauren's ability, but it definitely marks her as powerful. The ability to read the language of the body suggests a mode of communication that transcends the limits of the written and spoken language. An example of this is given when Lauren is able to obtain possession of her brother Marcus from a slave trader.

. . . Cougar did want to get rid of Marcus. What he said just didn't jibe with his body language. I think being a sharer makes me extra sensitive to body language. Most of the time, this is a disadvantage. It forces me to feel things that I don't want to feel. Psychotics and competent actors can cause me a lot of trouble. This time, though, my sensitivity was a help (96).

Beyond the advantages of Lauren's hyper empathy, it is important to note that Marcus was taken out of harms way because of his sister's abilities.

Despite Marcus's gender identity his male body was in danger until Lauren intervened. After Lauren gets Marcus safely back to Acorn she comments that, "He's still one of the best looking people I've ever seen" (99). Bankole responds to the observation with a very provocative question. "I wonder whether his looks have saved him or destroyed him" (99). Butler engages the problematic of gender construction by placing male bodies in dangerous situations traditionally reserved for female bodies. Because Marcus possesses an attractive body, his gender is made irrelevant or invisible. In *Talents'* chaotic setting, Marcus' male body is emasculated and made subject to brutal beatings, forced prostitution, and rape. The treatment of Marcus's body suggests that gender does not insure the safety or visibility of a body. Marcus explains some of the details of his torture to Lauren;

> They didn't just beat the hell out of me and rape me and let me go. They kept me so they could do it over and over again. And when they got tired of me, they sold me to a pimp (119).

While Marcus's treatment is nothing short of horrible, it explains why the thought of embracing a political ideology like Earthseed frightens him so much. Marcus views his experience as a product of chaos. Chaos is a system of life that has no absolute laws that are stable or unbreakable. Race, class, sex, and gender identity have no stock in a chaotic environment. Fortunately for Lauren, Earthseed promotes the idea that navigating the fluctuations and blurring of identity is dependent upon the strength and foresight of the person or people engaged in political struggle.

THE POLITICS OF SEX AND CHAOS

Butler's manipulation of sexuality and gender identity constructs a dialectic that employs an involved interrogation and restructuring of how the "sexual" is posited in American and African American literary imaginations. More specifically, Butler's fiction disrupts the etiquette of the "sexual" that has been under construction by Western culture and media since the age of Victorianism. Such fiction attempts to dismantle the *logos* of what is acceptable and what is taboo with regards to sex as an act and / sex as a noun or body part (anatomy). Discussions of homosexuality, heterosexuality, bisexuality, interspecies, and incest are all common, and integral elements found in the project to define the body as being more than sexual and limited by its flesh.

Barbara Christian, Deborah McDowell, Hazel Carby, and other scholars of black women's literature agree that contemporary African American women write within a tradition of black struggles to represent the self in reaction and relation to external conceptualization (the Black Woman's literary Renaissance); Butler's use of the SF genre furthers this legacy. In fact, Samuel Delaney (the most prolific African American male writer in the genre) believes that "science fiction may be the ideal genre through which to challenge traditional representations of subjectivity" (qdt in Helford 259). Because Butler presents her identity in the highly metaphoric genre of SF, her narratives are able to address some of the tropes and gaps in traditional philosophy and popular culture, while dissolving boundaries between theoretical and literary discourse.

The appeal of SF lies in its subject: the Other—the alien world, the stuff of dreams, raw material from the unconscious is both the selling point and the key to longevity for the genre. Placed in a book with a subheading of "science fiction" or on the silver screen with special effects and imaginative costumes, the terror of crossing, constructing, and deconstructing, identity boundaries are manageable for most. However, facing the very real results of such phenomena has proven to be overwhelming in terms of praxis and theory. When examining the "other," questions of the self necessarily arise. Scholarship involving slave narratives and Other/African American literature, for example, have constantly shed light on the imaginations of not only the African American "self" but of the entire American culture. The politics of chaos and sex in Butler's *Parable* series and *Fledging* novel suggest that the identity of America and the American imagination is in the process of changing. Butler's fiction is not utopian but Butler was a utopian thinker. What was once normative with respect to labeling bodies with limited boundaries and destructive histories and futures has become unacceptable. Butler's fiction advocates the embrace of ambiguity and difference as devices for survival.

Afterword:
Vast Frontiers

This examination of Octavia Butler's writing has engaged several very important questions about the notion of the body and how it is imagined and employed inside and outside the genre of SF. It has been my goal to begin exposing some of the theoretical and practical values of Butler's earlier works. In this meditation I have taken a body of writing that has been considered as juvenile literature, by too many, and exposed it as theoretically rich and unbounded with regards to discourses surrounding the identities marking the body. In this work I have focused my attention on the problems of the body found in most of Butler's novels. I have argued that in Butler's fiction the body is largely constructed in our imaginations by way of historical narratives. Our ability to identify and place value on bodies in our society is dependent upon the values placed on them in the past. Markers such as race and gender, for example, change along with the movement of time, but the way a body is identified in the present necessarily speaks to its identity in the past. In the case of Kindred, what this means is that to be a black woman today is necessarily contingent upon what "black woman" meant yesterday. And until that understanding is reached with all of its ambiguities and contradictions there can be no body clearly marked as black woman in a present narrative.

The term body is ambiguous and subject to a great deal of intuitive abstraction. Butler's narrative suggests that an individual's body does not necessarily depend upon the flesh and bone or material element of an individual. Although the flesh is a large part of ones identity, the essence or non-physical elements mark the performance and agency of an individual's identity. Corporeal consciousness then becomes the only necessary criterion to connote an identifiable body. In thinking about Butler's characters the idea of having an identity without a physical body becomes a plausible and realistic notion. Ultimately, the body can be thought of as a collection of consciousness and agency which helps begin a re-figuration of the self.

This book in part has attempted to render rudimentary narrative chronology of Butler's Patternist and Xenogenesis series in an effort to examine how identity is written upon the body. Ultimately, our understanding of the body is challenged by all of Butler's fiction. Notions of ambiguity and hybridity saturate Butler's narratives suggesting that that which is defined as marginal is potentially empowering. Butler's fiction posits marginal bodies in the past, present, and near future with two main strategies "survival as resistance and the recreation of myths" (Melzer 54). Both of these strategies facilitate an attempt to critique and rewrite methods of imagining marginalized bodies.

The significance of this project is rooted in the fact that it demonstrates beyond a shadow of a doubt that SF is a genre that is prime for more African-American involvement. It is a genre without theoretical limitations, especially with regards to marginalized people. Butler's writing is evidence that the marginalized body, with or without form, can be tested in ways that traditional American and African-American literature will not allow. In Butler's speculative world the impossible does not exist. There does not seem to be anything that cannot be considered in the vacuum created by one of Butler's novels. Shedding bodies, changing race, defying the laws of physics, and traveling through time and space at the blink of and eye are all phenomena which constitute the technology of Butler's writing.

I am convinced that the trajectory of this technology is rooted in an attempt to refigure the body and the values around it by presenting alternative examples of thinking the body in an environment analogous to real world situations. The narratives of Butler suggest a social commentary that is both apocalyptic and pessimistic. However, it is the glimmer of hope in each of her works that stands out and has the most weight in the imagination of her readers. In the works that I have examined in the preceding chapters hope has predominantly been embodied in the form of exceptional women who all manage to survive extreme circumstances. Thus, the employment of identifiable, marginalized characters in familiar situations allows each of Butler's narratives to speak to one another in a fashion that presents continuity throughout all of her writing.

The continuity of narrative found in Butler's fiction is particularly interesting when the time line of publication dates is brought to light. For example, although Butler's first novel, *Patternmaster*, is published in 1976, it is the fourth narrative chronologically in the Patternist series. The first narrative in the series, *Wildseed*, is not published until 1980. *Mind of My Mind* (1977), the second book in the narrative, precedes Wildseed by three years. Butler's disregard of chronological publication of the Patternist series suggests an extremely complicated writing process that may have thematic or developmental intents. Furthermore, it is interesting to note that in the mist of Butler's development of the Patternist series, she published *Kindred* in 1979. The publication of *Kindred* falls between the last book in the Patternist series, *Survivor* (1978), and *Wildseed* (1980). This is significant because *Kindred* is a significantly different narrative with regards to its thematic focus and content in comparison to the other two novels. *Kindred* is independent of the Patternist series, yet it still demonstrates moments of artistic and critical continuity.

The engagement of race, sex, and gender issues in Butler's fiction seems to elevate its category far beyond that of juvenile literature. Although adolescents would clearly benefit from pondering the ideas that are suggested in Butler's fiction, her work is long over due for philosophical and critical engagement by the academy. The race and gender theory present in Butler's fiction is both progressive and imaginative in its delivery. It successfully reflects/projects women and people of color into a future where identity becomes extremely pliant. This act is something far beyond "common" in any genre of literature. Where SF once said the colors of the future will be green and white (green Martians and white men), Butler's fiction suggests something much more colorful and realistic.

The pleasure that I experience from Butler's fiction is largely based on the fact that I believe her fiction is proposing an ideology that has been pieced together through each of her narratives. Butler's fiction suggests an alternative route to moving into the future which is based on the values placed on our bodies. In each of her narratives, especially those found in her most recent series, *Parable of the Sower* (1993) and *Parable of the Talents* (1998), the body is seen as an empty canvas or a container for social values and historical narratives. It is essential to understand that such a view of the body could not have been developed without all of the preceding narratives before the Parable series. What I am suggesting here is that without the Patternist series, *Kindred*, the short stories found in the Bloodchild collection (1995), and the three books of the Xenogenesis series [*Dawn* (1987), *Adulthood Rites* (1988), and *Imago* (1989)] Parable of the Sower (1993) would not have been possible. That is to say, Lauren Olamina and her Earthseed religion are the product of the adaptability of Anyanwu and the Oankali people.

As such, Butler's fiction suggests that "the world might be a better place" if we valued the body as a function of change and difference as opposed the material that a body might represent. That is to say, Butler's fiction suggests that human society would benefit greatly if it would focus less on the material and more on the meanings behind the abstract. According to the first Parable in Butler's Parable of the Sower, "all that you touch you change, all that you change changes you" (3). This bit of wisdom might simply suggest that everything that an individual experiences influences him/her to some degree. Butler's writing as a whole suggests something a bit more complicated and much more significant with regards to her contribution to American literature and her affect on the genre of SF. Because Butler was the first successful African-American woman writer in SF to win the Hugo and the Nebula Awards; because Butler's fiction constantly complicates notions of gender with race in each of her narratives; and because her presence and work has and still is influencing and encouraging others (marginalized or not) to consider SF as an accessible media of expression, Butler has more than influenced or touched the genre. Butler has reshaped the genre of SF and perhaps the notion of genre itself by writing a frontier which seems to be boundless.

Octavia E. Butler died on February 24, 2006, in Seattle, Washington. Her short story "Speech Sounds," won a Hugo award as best short story of 1984. The story "Bloodchild," won both the 1985 Hugo and the 1984 Nebula awards as best novelette. Butler was awarded her second Nebula award for Parable of the Sower (best novel 2000). In the summer of 1995, she received a MacArthur Fellowship from the John D. and Catherine T. MacArthur Foundation (MacArthur Genius Award). In October 2000, Ms. Butler received a lifetime achievement award in writing from PEN. The genre of writing that has claimed Octavia Butler's art is science fiction, but the audiences that will benefit from her artistry are as unbounded and limitless as the identities of the characters in her writing. It is a sad thing to see an artist leave when there is so much promise for even greater signs of genius (Hampton 248).

On the Phone with Octavia Butler (October 2002)

*T*his *phone interview was done in October of 2002, five months before Octavia Butler attended the "New Frontier: Blacks in Science Fiction Conference" at Howard University in March of 2003. The purpose of the interview was to determine what might be good discussion topics at the conference. As Butler had agreed to be the keynote speaker for the conference, my intentions were to get her to talk about the genre of Science Fiction (SF) and its audience as well as how she defined herself as a writer. Although I was not able to fit all of my questions into the brief interview, I was able to get some interesting discussion about one of the two new short stories that were added to the new edition of* Bloodchild and Other Stories *in 2005.*

*As the author of 12 novels (*Patternmaster *(1976),* Mind of My Mind *(1977),* Survivor *(1978),* Kindred *(1979),* Wild Seed *(1980),* Clay's Ark *(1984),* Dawn *(1987),* Adulthood Rites *(1988),* Imago *(1989),* Parable of the Sower *(1993),* Parable of the Talents *(1998), and* Fledgling *(2005); and a book of shorts stories* Bloodchild and Other Stories *(1995, 2005), Butler says she never really fell in love with literature. The frown that this comment might cause dissipates quickly when one comes to understand that it is reading and writing that held Butler's heart. She acquired her first library card at the age of six and discovered that she enjoyed writing at the age of ten, a few years later in 1995, she received the MacArthur "genius" Award. Born on June 22, 1947 in Pasadena, California, Butler resided in Pasadena for most of her life and later relocated to Seattle, Washington, until her untimely death in February of 2006. She said she enjoyed the Seattle weather and that she had just completed two new short stories. Ms. Butler did not want to talk about the third book in the Parable Series, "it was still in the oven."*

The back-story of "Amnesty" that Butler renders in this interview is both in-formative and intriguing. Although several elements are reminiscent of a number of her previously published narratives, there is an originality that is unique to Butler's style of storytelling present. I had originally planned to publish this in-terview with the proceedings of the "Blacks in Science Fiction Conference" held at Howard University in the spring of 2003. As that publication never came to fruition, I present the interview now with the hope that it will reproduce a com-monly shared memory of anticipating the next Butler creation.

Greg Hampton: How do you distinguish the difference between SF and fan-tasy, if you do at all?

Octavia Butler: I really wish people would [stop asking that question], but it keeps turning up as though it mattered. As far as I'm concerned a good story is a good story no matter what genre label gets stuck on it. If you want differences, I can give them to you, but they don't mean anything except in the sense that people like to make divisions by placing things in categories.

GH: I understand that, but I think people who are not familiar with your literature, might need some sort of reference point. Definitions might help them understand and appreciate the differences.

OB: But that's what I mean.

GH: You don't think they need to know or should know?

OB: I realize that people want to know, because it seems to them like impor-tant knowledge. "Oh, now I can quote differences to you so it must mean something." If a book or a story is good . . . it's good.

GH: How do you feel about being acknowledged as one of the authors who opened the door of SF to black readers and writers?

OB: I hope you're keeping in mind that [Samuel] Delaney was there a long time before me.

GH: Yes, I am, but others and myself, have perceived your writing as be-ing more accessible and approachable than the literary criticism or literary theory that might be present in Delaney's more recent works.

OB: It's the college professor in him. (Laughs) Oh, dear. If it's true, I'm glad. There's never been any reason to not be drawn in [by the genre]. The thing that I love most about what tends to get called science fiction and fantasy is the openness of it. There are no closed doors, except of course, bad writing.

GH: Has bad writing been the plague of the genre?

OB: Yes, unfortunately people don't know this and assume that it's a very narrow little place confined by *Star Wars* and *Star Trek*.

GH: Over the past few years many Americans have been experiencing feelings of insecurity due to questionable elections, Sept. 11th, threats of war, snipers here in the Maryland/DC area . . . etc. As a writer of what has been referred to as speculative literature, literature that speaks to the reality of today and tomorrow, what are some of your thoughts on the state of things? Is the Parable series coming to pass?

OB: I certainly hope not. I was not trying to write prophecy. I was trying to draw out a few warnings. Now as for the sorry state of things today, things have always been sorry. When I was growing up I wasn't sure that I would grow up because of the cold war and the nuclear threat. I was around and aware for the Cuban Missile crisis. There was a very real feeling of maybe we weren't going to make it. I remember being a little kid and having drop drills and war drills where you go in into the hallway and kneel on the floor and put your hands over your head with your head against the wall. And I remember asking the teacher what good it was going to do to if the bombs were falling to put your hands over your head. And she said you'd rather hurt your hands than your neck wouldn't you. And even as a kid that didn't really, make much sense to me. I mean hands, neck, body, school, you know, hey. (Laughs)

GH: I guess it was like the Pledge of Allegiance. Children have to recite it whether it makes sense of not.

OB: Oh yes, but that was relatively harmless and this was preparing for something that couldn't really be prepared for. We were soothing ourselves. It's like having someone break the file off your fingernail clippers now when you go into the airport. You know, unless you maliciously give someone a manicure or something. (Laughs) It has nothing to do with security; it has nothing to do with safety. It's just people nullifying themselves; people trying to feel that their doing something. It's annoying too, [but a part of who we are].

GH: For some reason it brings peace to some people.

OB: We need to do something. And if they're doing something then they feel that it must be positive.

GH: Unfortunately, that positive action has developed into profiling and putting people into categories to divide them.

OB: The act of putting things into categories makes you feel like you're smart. It makes you feel safe. And you never have been.

GH: Is there anything you purposely avoid/ encourage with each literary undertaking.

OB: Not really, because if I really felt that strongly then I would have to go into it and find out why, and there might be a story in that. I've just done a couple of short stories, they are not out yet, but in one of them... well in both of them, I actually looked into things that I didn't believe in to see what it might be like if they were true. And they had to be things that hit some kind of emotional note with me. In [the development of] one of them, the one I believe is being bought by Asimov's SF magazine, I can remember having read an argument somewhere that there were black troops on the Confederate side [of the Civil War] and not just people who dug ditches and looked out for their master's clothing or whatever, but who actually fought. There is a Julius Lester book called *To Be a Slave*, I think it was done for kids, but anybody can read it. It's a lot of quotations from slaves. And one of the quotations is [made by] a guy who is clearly not too well off mentally. He's been [legally] freed from slavery, but he's been a slave all his life and his parents were slaves, and it's really all he knows and every now and then he goes back to his master and asks what he should do and his old master kindly gives him a few orders. I thought, my God! What can I do with that? I came up with a story in which the aliens have arrived and colonized. They're not interested in ruling over us or the places that we value. They live in hot deserts. It's where they choose to live and they have their dwellings there which are, pretty much, places where no one can get in unless they're let in. One of the things they need to do when they get here is to find out what sort of creatures we are, so they collect a number of us. And a number of the people collected don't survive because they don't really know what we can stand or what we can't stand or in effect how to look after us. So they kill a lot of people, Not deliberately and not out of cruelty, but they do. One of the characters, my main character is captured by them. She is 11 when she's taken and she's twenty-something when they finally let her go. She's been through a lot of seriously bad stuff and what she has done while she was a captive was learn to communicate with them. They [the aliens] have no hearing at all so of course they have no spoken language and they have no limbs in common with us, so communication is a real trial. Between the humans who have been captured and the aliens who look after them, a kind of language is established. Even though they have no limbs in common they manage. And finally they let her go, they have no intention of keeping her forever, they learn what they can and they let her go. Unfortunately, she is immediately picked up by government officials who treat her just about as badly as the aliens because they are sure she knows stuff and of course she doesn't. I mean, why would they teach her about their technology? Why would they teach her anything useful and then let her go? But anyway, because they [government officials] have no other source of information they hang onto her and treat her rather badly and finally when she is about to die, they let her go and her family gathers her up. They [characters family] actually fought to get her free when they found out she was in captivity. Her family saw to it that she got the medical attention she needed to heal. She [the main character] goes to school and she looks around and thinks what should I do with myself and what she winds up doing is going back to the aliens as a translator and trying to be an intermediary that keeps the two species from wiping each other out.

GH: Wow, where are you taking the reader with this narrative?

OB: It's a short story; most of what I told you is back-story. It's all done in the shape of an employment interview kind of situation during a worldwide depression. When human beings are confronted by aliens who won't move; who have no intent to harm; but who are acting as though they are there [visible and intelligent subjects], things go badly. The economies of Earth are down but the one group that's hiring happens to be the aliens. One of the things she's doing [in the narrative] is helping the new employees [humans] and the new employers [aliens] get along.

GH: Is the relationship symbiotic?

OB: If you consider getting a job a symbiotic relationship, sure. I mean, you have a symbiosis with Howard [University]. (Laughs)

GH: The notion of survival seems to be a crucial theme in most, if not all, of your writing. What is it about survival that makes for such mind twisting stories?

OB: (Laughs). We all want to survive. There's not really much to say about that, that's worth anything. People struggle for different things, but if they weren't struggling, there'd be no story.

GH: In the preface to *Bloodchild and Other Stories* you mention how your college-writing teachers didn't offer you a great deal a assistance with their "polite and lukewarm" commentary about the "science fiction and fantasy you kept turning out." It sounds as though there was something natural about your production of science fiction and fantasy; something unavoidable.

OB: Of course for me it is.

GH: Does your experience as an African American woman lend to the production of the fantastic?

OB: I think that's an unfair question because what else have I ever been.

GH: True, but we all have to negotiate several identities at once.

OB: Not really. I've been black and female all my life.

GH: Okay. Some people might say that gender and race, although they are inextricably linked, have to be dealt with individually on occasion.

OB: A lot of people would say that it doesn't. When I began writing back in the 60s, my writing of anything but utter reality was considered some kind of, almost a betrayal, a waste of time at best. I was supposed to, according to some people, be contributing to the struggle and not writing things that weren't real.

GH: Are you referring to the Black Aesthetic dogma of the Black Arts/Black Power movement?

OB: They really didn't know what they meant. They just didn't think what I was doing was worthwhile. One thing you learn very quickly as a fiction writer is that if you try to write what other people are telling you to write; try to tell someone else's story that they want told, it just doesn't work out.

Phone Interview Oct 2002

New Frontier Panel Discussion: Butler, Barnes, Due, and Hopkinson

The following panel discussion included four of the most prominent and well respected African American Science Fiction/Fantasy writers in the genre of SF. Octavia Butler, Steven Barnes, TananariveDue, and Nalo Hopkinson were guest speakers at the "New Frontier: Blacks in Science Fiction Conference," on March 27–28, 2003, at Howard University. After Octavia Butler's keynote address the panel was asked to participate in a non-formal discussion about who they were and how they imagined and crafted their art. In this brief and revealing discussion the writes share pieces of personal stories of struggle, perseverance, and success as Black writers bending the boundaries of a traditionally white male dominated genre.

Greg Hampton: How does your writing speak to and mold the tradition of SF?

Octavia Butler: I think SF has been wide open from the beginning, although it hasn't always lived up to what it should. It was called the literature of ideas. And sometimes it was, especially if those ideas didn't involve people as much as machines. But our coming in, the coming in of women, the coming in of black people, has opened it up a lot more. And we now have more Asian writers, there are Hispanic writers coming in. It's more a literature of ideas and the people than it ever was before, and it's a good thing.

Stephen Barnes: SF grew out of a tradition of adventure literature that promoted an image of the heterosexual white male as being a powerful figure. All groups of people create mythologies that reinforce themselves and their feelings about themselves, that's completely natural. Black Americans were cut off from this in some ways because we were never isolated enough to create our own mythologies in the same way as other cultures that were isolated for hundreds of years. We came to that a little bit later and we're not necessarily welcomed at the party. Editors like John Campbell would write letters and essays saying that he felt that no technological civilization could develop in sub-Saharan Africa because we just weren't genetically up to it. And ideas like that existed sub-textually even if they weren't addressed directly. In a literary tradition that spans seventy years and that entails many stories dealing with the future, I never saw [read of] a single mention of a consumer product produced in Africa no matter how far in the future I went. This suggested to me that the writers of SF universally believed that black people deserved to be where they were. They really didn't have more than that, there was no sense. And I think that trying to create works in which we were a part of that future and were functioning technologically and artistically [suggests that] we are moving against that cultural rhythm that was there. It might have been subtly, it might not have been talked about. I think a lot of people in SF didn't want to believe that it was there. They [SF writers] have this belief that because they deal with aliens and robots that they are more open to the other. They are actually just more open to variations within their own group. If you come from outside the group there is that resistance. But they have this belief about themselves. Does the percentage of black SF writers match the percentage of black writers in the mystery field or general fiction? No. How about the percentage in fans? No. How about the percentage in characters? No. Yet they [SF writers] still held onto this mythology even though it's absolutely not testable in the real world. So, I think that over the last 30 years writers like Chip [Samuel Delaney], and like Octavia, and Nalo, were strong enough writers. What I want to say is that black writers who have been able to survive in the field are far better than the average writers in the field. It suggested that you had to be much better just to get into the game and stay in the game. I think that opens doors for more people. I think that the average SF reader is a good and decent person, who like all human beings has a limit to how flexible their concepts of the world can be. You guys are helping to make those concepts more flexible. I think that we're all trying to add our dialogue to this so that SF is mythology of the twentieth century; that century of trying to create sense out of the universe that often seems senseless. Where are we? Who are we? Where do we come from? Where are we going? We have to participate in that dialogue.

Nalo Hopkinson: Yes, I think it was John W. Campbell. I could be wrong, but I think it was Campbell who said to Chip, to Samuel Delaney in the '60s, that he didn't think the world was ready for a SF novel with the black hero. That has clearly changed. And so I had sort of a double reaction from the SF community. For one thing, it is this openness in new ideas. When my books and my stories got published I had almost nothing but welcome. On the other hand, there is the fact that we are almost the sum total of the [Black] novelists the field right here. There are many more short story writers, thank heavens, and many more people working to get novel's published [by SF writers of color] and they are our allies. Yes, there is a fair amount of ignorance out there. When I started writing I couldn't think about that, I couldn't let it be a barrier. I just wrote what I wanted to see and threw it out there and put my faith in the will of the SF readers and SF editors to see something they hadn't seen before. And I was lucky that that worked.

Tananarive Due: I really had no concept, when I started writing, that there was such an organized SF and fantasy community in existence. For example, I understand from my husband, there is a different convention for SF and fantasy every weekend somewhere in the country all over the country. And I don't mean *Star Trek* conventions per se; just conventions where people get together to discuss the literature of the genre. It's only since the publication of my novels that I have been exposed to that world in the slightest. It is an overwhelmingly white world and I certainly never considered when I started writing that I would write for that audience, because I had no knowledge of that audience. I knew there was SF but I did not understand to the degree with which it was taken seriously. Who was our writing for? I was writing for myself, in all honesty. I didn't have any concepts that there was a huge black readership interested in SF or *dark fantasy/horror*. I hate to use that word, because it brings slasher movies to mind, and that's not what I write. Before, Octavia mentioned in the past that in the 1960s she received criticism at the height of the black power movement because of the kinds of stories she wrote. There was a feeling that there should be a much more literal discussion of the issues at hand. This is also an era where my husband has told me, he's had black students tell him in college, "You shouldn't drink white milk, you should only drink chocolate milk."

NH: We had issues. (*Laughter*)

TD: The struggle to find self empowerment and self-identity is difficult. There's a lot to cast off in that process and some of what you have to do to get back to sanity is to go insane for a little while. I did grow up in a civil rights household. I was raised by activist parents and spent my childhood on the picket lines and heard the phone ringing and during the riots wondered if my father would come home. Not because he was out there rioting, but because he worked for the county and he was trying to calm the rioters. Although I'm sure deep in his heart sometimes he wondered if he shouldn't be throwing some bricks too. My father has a four-hundred page FBI file, but both of my parents have FBI files, I'm proud to say. Even though I didn't received the criticism and my parents were always supportive of everything I wrote, I definitely internalized the sense that even if I wasn't the person out organizing the meetings and holding signs and going to jail, that if writing was my gift and writing was my voice then what ever I did should be threw my writing. And yet at the same time I was not drawn to protest writing. At the same time I was not drawn to what I thought traditionally [considered to be] the African American cannon that I admired so much. In fact, Stephen King was speaking to me at some pretty deep levels. There was a time when I felt very torn by all that. As I mentioned at signing last night, when I was in college taking workshop courses learning how to refine the poetics of language and that sort of thing, I was writing epiphany stories of characters who were having life changing realizations and who were invariably white. And if I wanted to write about blacks it was about kids from the hood who were not necessarily from my experience either. I really did have an identity problem. The first major piece of fiction I started to write that actually had primarily black protagonists, who were like me, and similar to my own background, was *The Between*. And I had no concept if there was a readership for a fantasy/horror novel about a primarily middle-class black family. I had no idea, but I started writing that story for myself. I had no idea that it would sell.

NH: I forgot to tell you. I was walking past a bookstore many years ago. I saw the cover of *The Between* and something said go check that book out. I had a feeling that book was written by black woman. (*Laughter*) It looked like fantasy and I gravitated to it and said there are people out there [in the SF genre] like me.

TD: And I owe a great deal to Terry McMillan frankly, because even though I don't write anything like what she writes; it was Terry McMillan who demonstrated to publishers that black folks do read commercial fiction; commercial fiction that is not necessarily Toni Morrison.

OB: Several years ago around 1980. Martin Greenberg and I tried to put together an anthology of black SF; SF by and about black people. Martin Greenberg is very well-known in the field. If anybody can sell an anthology he can. He couldn't sell this one, because everybody knew blacks didn't read SF. The other side of that coin, since we were just mentioning how few of us there are, I went to Michigan State University to speak and when I finished speaking a young woman came up to me and said, "You know I've always loved science fiction, I've always read it, and I wanted to write it but I didn't try because I didn't think we did that." I think that's why there are so few of us up here; a lot of self-limiting behavior unfortunately, people afraid to try because maybe they might not be let in.

SB: I think there's an additional factor and I'm hoping that there might be somebody out there to help ameliorate this, but there are obviously more women writers than black male writers. This is partially because I think women are more willing to identify with the struggles and concerns of other women than men are to identify with the concerns of men of other groups. I think that this is a factor in coming out of the closet about being a black SF writer. The first half of my career I stayed away from issues that dealt with that as much as possible. Frankly, I was trying to survive; I was trying to keep a roof over my family's head. Whether that was the better part of valor or whether I was right or wrong about that I don't know. I do think that I may be wrong about that, but I do have an informed opinion; it's not an uninformed opinion. So, I made the decision that the reason there are so few black writers in SF and in some ways why black men do not read as much fiction as they might, is because there hasn't been anything for them to read.

What is there for them to read in that sense? There was one black male writers conference and every single other guy there was writing girlfriend books. To me, it was nauseating. There was nothing there for young men who wanted to read stories about men doing "manly stuff." You know, beating their chest, acting like idiots; seducing women; boxing; strangling guerrillas, you know, that stuff. Where is that? Because that stuff, I think is important because all of the stories we have as human beings are stories of adventure. Hairy-chested-thunderers, that testosterone flush stuff, I'm not ashamed of that stuff, I love that stuff. There wasn't anything like that for me in the white SF community. I had to read a huge amount of truly negative, vile stuff about people who looked like me and it damaged me psychologically. I was so desperate to see anything like that I was willing to wade through that's emotional filth, "black people have no imagination," "and they smell this way," "and they're stupid in this way." I would actually have to disassociate from my melanin in order to be able to associate with my testosterone. Let me write that down. (Laughter) So what I'm doing is, I'm praying that there is a huge mass of potential black readers who will rally around me if I start writing stuff that specifically speaks to them while not alienating the white audience who's been paying my bills all this time. But it does exist out there and I know that there are some risks on one side and potential benefits on the other. If I don't write about black people as black people I feel as though I am betraying myself. I'm losing some aspect of myself and I feel that I have lost enough in my lifetime, and I don't want to hurt my family either. A friend looked at me and said, "Steve, eventually someone is going to have to start writing adventure stories for black people; If not you, then who? If not now, then when? And why would you want to write books for the pleasure of people you wouldn't even want to have in your house?" And I said, "Damn!" So, I've trusted that the people who have loved my work up until now will not be turned off if I speak about ethnic issues and I have found in general for that to be true. I'm so grateful to the white readers who were the readers in the first half of my career. I always want to make sure that they understand that my point is always "human beings are just human beings," but at the same time I'm hoping that I'll be able to open that door to younger writers who might take the risk, who might be willing to try this. If I can survive in this field I'll show others how to go beyond anything that I've ever done.

NH: Yes, what's been interesting to me is the number of white readers who said, "Thank God, there is someone to fill this gap of emptiness."

TD: And also the number of black readers too, I find. I'm so thrilled even though young writers often need to do more work. They may not be quite ready, but I am always so thrilled when I see other writers who want to go into writing supernatural suspense. Because it's a world of possibilities and with good reason, very often we've been a little hesitant to distance ourselves from the herd because there is safety in numbers. We do claim everybody we can claim and we're going to claim Vin Diesel too. (Laughter) We do have an historical tradition of self-loathing, and people who try to distance themselves, and who will actually sell you out; who would tell on you if you went to a meeting, because it might further them. But we have to realize that all of us as thinking individuals and growing individuals in a multicultural society will have the freedom to make decisions, which will not mean that we forget were we came from, that does not mean we will turn our backs on people less fortunate, but we have more of a freedom of expression than we have ever had and I'm very grateful for that. Whether or not my books crossover to that so-called "mainstream readership," I'd say right now that my readership is about 75 percent black women. I could be wrong about that, maybe it's seventy percent black women and 5 or 10 percent black men. But it's a slow process to crossover, the reasons for that we could list from day to night. Even if that doesn't happen it really doesn't matter to me, I'm writing the stories that I love; the stories that I have always wanted to write. And I'm hoping that the young writer will have an idea that they can do something that never occurred to me to do until fairly late in my career as a writer. Or you can start out knowing I want to write this kind of book.

GH: Panelists, what are you learning from each other and what have you learned from writers who have come before you?

SB: I was fortunate enough to live around the corner from Octavia for a while. I was living in my mom's house and we would get together sometimes. What was always going on in the back of my mind was that I felt like a dilatants in comparison to Octavia. In her presence I was dealing with the real writer who had bonded her soul to that journey on a level that I had not been courageous enough or single-minded enough to embark. Just knowing that here is somebody who is in one sense closer to what it is that I am, who was also doing this thing, and has had this kind of success in this way, and is excellent in these ways. It wasn't her writing which I always considered to be superlative as much as it was simply her heart.

NH: I've told bits of this story before. Where I have been lucky is that I grew up in a creative and literary environment. My father was a writer, poet, playwright, and actor. And an English teacher at the upper high school level. My mother was a library technician, and our house was always full of books. Our house was always filled with artists and writers. My dad said to me at one point, "If you want to become a writer you have to be prepared to suffer." Don't tell your children this but I decided I didn't want to become a writer. Despite my childhood decision I have always known that it was possible to become a writer. A lot of my colleagues and peers did not grow up thinking this way. What I did not have was anybody else who knew or who read SF. I was the only one. I didn't think to keep it closeted or hidden; I just didn't know anybody else I could talk to about it. There was a man whose work I found; it was Chip, Samuel Delaney. Reading *Dhalgren* broke my brain apart and remade it. When I finished that book I was a different person from when I had started. I understood a third of it; I had to go back and try again, but I knew there was something there I wanted. At that point I did not know the Chip was a person of color. I was reading *Stars in My Pockets Like Grains of Sand*, and I opened the back inside cover and there was a picture of the man, which was the first time I realized he was a black man. I cried for half an hour and I couldn't figure out why I was crying. It took me a while to figure out that my universe had just doubled in size. And then I started thinking, where are the others. So I started doing interlibrary loan searches. I found Steve's work; I found Octavia's work; I found Charles Saunders who is the first Canadian black SF novelist. I devoured their work in the course of about three months. I could feel my brain changing. I saw what Steve was doing, with taking the action/adventure hero and transferring it into a black character. I saw the appeal of that. I looked at the concepts that Octavia was wrestling with, and I started looking for the others, which is how I found Tananarive. I cleared off three bookshelves for all the work I could find that was fantastical or speculative that was by black writers. Now that's not enough anymore. I need more shelves. But to know that these people have been out here is precious beyond belief, because it tells you that your universe is bigger than you think and it tells you that you have company.

OB: I think there is something interesting about the four of us sitting here. Okay, we're all black writers, three of us are female, but I think if you gave all four of us a single topic, you'd come up with four very, very different books. I think it's neat the way we bounce off of each other when we're talking, and it might be the same when we're writing. I'm not trying to write like Steve, or he like me or whatever, but somehow it helps that they're there. When I was offered a chance to go to Clarion, it was back in 1970. Clarion had only been around for a couple of years before that. It was in Clarion, Pennsylvania, about 80 miles from Pittsburgh and 80 miles from anywhere else you can think of. It was one of those places where entertainment on Saturday night is driving your car up-and-down the street. I was afraid to go, didn't want to go, because it was a long way from home and it was in a little town with maybe three black people. I was afraid I was going to be the worst writer there. When Harlem offered me the chance to go, I think my very first question to him was, "Are there going to be any black people there?" He said, "Well, Chip." And at that point I did know who Chip was. Who? Samuel R Delaney . . . uh, he's black?" So that's how he became one of my teachers. It was an incredibly strange experience going because I thought I was going to the worst writer there. I was going to get there and I was going to be one of the few women. I was going to disgrace all women because I was going to be the worst writer there. I was going to get there and not have the scientific background that everybody else was sure to have. I was going to be the worst writer there and disgrace myself intellectually. You know, really set yourself up to succeed (laughter). I got there and I slept a lot. I wrote a letter to my mother detailing all the things that were wrong with Clarion, Pennsylvania. I walked down the street and a little child ran screaming from me because he'd never seen a black person. I finished this long letter of complaining and I nailed it the bottom of a drawer, which is what you should do with a letter like that, and I still had some energy. So I started to write. I wrote a story called *Crossover*, about a woman who is alone and frightened and doesn't know what to do. And where did I get an idea like that? That's part of the talk that I give sometimes called "From Woe to Wonder." I think it's a talk that Steve could give in his own way because he has all this background of frustration and need and desire that he can use to write great stories.

SB: I'd just like to piggyback on that for just a moment. Art, I believe, is self-expression. It's being able to take your own experience and communicate it honestly through whatever layers of skill and craft you have developed. I think that black people have had to sit on their actual emotions about how they felt for so long, because there was so much anger, so much pain. I remember talking to a white audience who couldn't understand what I had said to them. If we had ripped you away from your homes and for three-hundred years extracted labor at below its market value in order to enrich our own community and simultaneously sold away your children and raped your women. How badly would you want to kill us? (Laughter) And suddenly, it was like lights went on in their eyes . . . "Oh yes, why we would be angry too." Needless to say, if they were outnumbered by a factor of ten to one and there was no direct form of confrontation that was possible; they would be filled with repressed anger. And when you sit on your emotions it turns internal and devours your body like a cancer. Which is analogous to things we see going on in our community; we're not different from other people; we're the same as other people.

TD: It was a surreal experience to publish my first novel. Not only did I have no expectations that it would be published, the publisher had this fantasy that I would be admitted as the next Terry McMillan; never mind the fact that the subject matter is completely different. I was given a book tour and a nice advance. So here I am touring through all of these African American bookstores nationwide. It was a real eye opening experience to see that there were sections for mysteries, sections for romance books. I had no concept that they were so many writer of color writing so many different kinds of books. And that was wonderful. And then the Horror Writers Association discovered me and this was my first entry into that world of what is know as "fandom." Going to that Horror Writers Association meeting felt like going to a family reunion for the white side of your family that you've never met. It was estranged and thrilling. The crowning moment of the whole experience, and in fact the most surreal moment of the whole experience, was when Clark Atlanta University had a conference called "African American Fantastic Imagination: Explorations of Science-Fiction Fantasy and Horror." This was in 1997. Octavia was invited, Chip....I was lucky to be invited. I met all of them and I can't even tell you... I really don't have the words to tell you what it felt like. It was a group very similar to this one. It was filled with readers who have been somewhat more adventurous than many of their friends, and have embraced our writing. Mostly Octavia's writing, and Steve's writing, and Chip's writing and now me, but they were about to figure out who I was. It was a magical experience in every single way. And this reminds me that and I am very grateful, actually, to Greg for putting this together.

GH: Tananarive, reading *The Between, My Soul To Keep, The Living Blood*, and *The Black Rose*, caught me off guard. I was stunned by the way you were able to weave historical research with fiction so seamlessly. Panelists, please speak to the notion of research as it pertains to the development of your narratives.

TD: I try to be more diligent about research with ever book I write. *The Black Rose* came out of left field for you because it came out of field for me. I had just started writing full-time. I had just gotten married, and moved, and every single project I was working out was having trouble finding a home. I like telling the story because I want writers to understand that this is not an easy business. I had trouble selling *Freedom and Family*, the book I was working on with my mother. I had trouble selling *The Living Blood* in its first round. My editors had left the house and my cheerleaders were gone, and I had to start from scratch. So when Alex Haley estate approached me and asked me if I would be willing to look at this research and write this book I said, "Hell yes, I would!" Because I need the money and I had no faith I could pull it off. But just in case I could, I was willing to try. And I am grateful for that experience on many levels because I was able to take that feeling of accomplishing the impossible, which from beginning to end is what writing *The Black Rose* felt like, into the *Living Blood* because that also forced me to expand my idea of what I could do, what I could accomplish; without being able to visit all of those places I was writing about, no matter how desperately I wanted to. It helped me to transform the research of other people's experience into something that feels like walking through an experience. Research is vital and I have come to believe that anytime I have writers block, this was certainly true on *The Black Rose*, if I came to page and I couldn't write, it was because I had run out of my research. I literally could not envision the streets in 1906 because I had not looked in my file to see what would have been on the streets in 1906. Research has informed me in every project since. Every single detail is important and research should be used to bring whatever richness you can to the story to make it better.

NH: I just finished a novel last April. It has elements of the historical, magical, and realism. I tried to imagine how a god would think so I had to start dealing in fractals. I don't see gods linearly; I think they exist in time spherically. So, I found a wonderful book called *African Fractals*, which was exactly what I needed, because I failed sciences all through school. (Laughter) I had to go to eighteenth century Haiti before the revolutions; I had to go to nineteenth century France, into the world of Baudelaire and his Black Mistress Shantel. I had to go to fourth century Egypt, where Constantine had just declared Christianity the official religion of the Roman Empire. I had to look at St. Mary at Egypt; the prostitute Saint. Uh, I hate to research! I love knowing stuff. I had just the barest glimpse of what I needed to know to pull this book off. It was three different cultures and three different time periods, and three different ways of looking at the world; three different sets of history.

It was overwhelming, but each new piece I collected was a bit of a triumph. Discovering the color and pattern of the wallpaper in Baudelaire's apartment was a bit of a triumph. Discovering how much you paid for a sexual act in a tavern in fourth century Alexandria was a triumph. (Laughter) Discovering when you would harvest cane and what the cane factory looked like and eighteenth century Haiti to make sugar was a triumph. It was a lot of work and the hard part was deciding when I could write, because I had a deadline. I sold the thing in May of 2000, and Warner [Books] said, "Good, can you have it to us by September?" I kept putting them off to get a more realistic deadline. I could still be researching that novel now because there is so much I still don't know. I could get a Ph.D. in each section that I wrote. My bookshelves are starting to look very different than they did because of the research material I bought, and sometimes could not get from the libraries. I paid $150 for a book specifically on the French slave trade written in the nineteenth century, so I could get as detailed as possible; as close to what actually happened as I could. I got in touch with people I didn't even know. I emailed people who were translators and said, "Okay, I have this bit of French Creole, I need to know what it says." I read and speak a little bit of French, but French Creole is something else entirely. It's something I have gone through with every book. This has been the most intensive, which is why I want to write a great fat fantasy that I make the hell up.

SB: Beyond a shadow of a doubt, what I call the Inshala Universe, which is comprised by *Lions Blood* and *Zulu Heart*, is where I've done the most research. I recognized that I was playing with social dynamite. What I wanted to do was create an alternate history in which Africa developed a technological civilization before Europe; colonizing the Americas first bringing white slaves here. So I could do some things attitudinally and place black readers in the position of being able to read a book in which their civilization was dominant and they were the ones with the power. And also give white readers both an adventure story and a way to understand some things about black experience that they have never been able to understand before. Because there was literally no language depended upon references. There has to be agreed upon meanings for words before the words can mean anything. And there was no emotional bridge there. So, I wanted to do that, but like I said the slave trade, as far as I was concerned, was a neutral thing. The usage of human beings as machinery in order to exploit a huge amount of arable land so you could create excess capital that could then be invested in your society. But because America is a Christian nation that believed in doing unto others as you would have them do unto you, they needed a methodology to explain what they were doing to these people. In other words, they had to believe that it was good for the slaves. Without this they would not have been able to justify what they were doing. That methodology that slaves were natural slaves outlived the actual institution itself. That's one of the biggest problems we've had for the last 150 years. So, in trying to write a book like this I recognized that I was playing with some of the most cherished mythologies of white America that some how slavery wasn't so bad; and of black America that's slavery was something unique to white people. What I was saying was, were the situation reversed, we would have screwed them over just as badly. At least I hope so. (Laughter) So, I needed an explanation, why did Africa submit to Europe; why was it that Europe took Africa and not the other way around? This was a very important question to ask. I needed an answer that was not Euro-centric or Afro-centric, but global. It dealt with terms of the universal. It was not that Africans were more spiritual than white people and therefore would not be … I thought what a crock! It was not that white people were smarter… what a crock! It was something else and the first thing I had to do was step backwards and find a theory of social development that explained the way societies have developed worldwide. For that I ultimately relied about 90 percent on Jared Diamond's wonderful book *Guns, Germs, and Steel*. I don't have to agree with everything in that book to see that it comes closer to that global explanation I was looking for than anything else I found. But then I needed to rewrite history because the game of alternate history is that you only get to change one single fact. You only get to change one thing, and everything else comes out of that. I couldn't pull the butterfly phenomena, yeah, in 18 billion B.C. a Tyrannosaurus sneezes out his left nostril instead of his right, and therefore everything turned out differently. That doesn't work. It couldn't go back that far because as a dramatic device it doesn't have the kind of resonance in the reader's minds that I needed. I needed one phenomenon that would both speed Africa up and slow Europe down. But it couldn't have been an event that took place in sub-Saharan Africa, because that would have no emotional association for Western readers. I needed an event that would allow me to appeal to both the political right and left. I had to become an historian; trying to find a critical moment in history. It took me about 2 1/2 years of research to find a moment in history when I felt like things could have gone both ways, and has centered on 400 B.C. The triggering event is that Socrates does not drink the hemlock. Instead of that he goes to Egypt and opens a school of philosophy. Everything else arises out of that, where the Egyptians stand together with Carthage and break Rome; Alexander the great has twin sons by an Abyssinian princess who was on the thrown of Egypt and on the thrown of Abyssinia. Generations later the Egyptians become too lazy to patrol their own empire and start exporting janissaries from sub-Saharan Africa to patrol the empire in Europe. And in 700 A.D. the question of a unifying religion arises. Why is a unifying religion so important? One of the most important things an army can have is a philosophy about what's going to happen if you die in combat. What do you tell your troops? Religion is a great unifying factor. Islam is a great religion because it had proven its ability to expand rapidly; it had literature and access to the knowledge of the Greeks, so Islam was ideal. It took a massive amount of research; it took years. There are five or six different languages in the book. I hired someone to write me Irish slave songs. I had to learn enough about Irish culture to be able to represent that well. I did research from tons of different directions, so by far this was the most difficult project I've encountered.

OB: I think the most research I did for a novel was for *Kindred*. And I didn't really know how to do it. I didn't have a clue because I had never done anything like that before. Going to the library wasn't enough. I read all the slave narratives I could find and I read some general history. I knew I had to go to Maryland and that scared me because I didn't know anything about traveling. I'd been to Clarion and I had traveled a little bit, but going to Maryland to do research sounded scary to me. So, I got on a Greyhound bus and went. I sold my novel *Survivor*, before its time, to get to money to go and I went off to Baltimore. It took 3 1/2 Days on the bus, if you ever think about doing it don't. (Laughter) I got to Maryland and didn't have a lot of money, so I went to Travelers Aid and asked if they could send me to a hotel that was inexpensive but not dangerous. It was a scary hotel. A lot of men were standing around. I whispered to the desk clerk if any women live here. And she said, "I live here." So, I went to the room and noticed that there were cigarette butts lying on the furniture. I noticed that they (the cigarette butts) had dust on them. So, from there on the hotel was, for me, "The Hotel Sleazy." They didn't even have the decency to dust their cigarette butts. (Laughter) That hotel was around the corner from the free library, and across the street from the Maryland Historical Society, which I really needed because they had period-rooms that I could go into. I didn't have a camera because I was poor; you wouldn't believe how poor. I would go in with a notebook small enough to fit in a bag. I would sketch the rooms and because I am a horrible artist, I would label things. I would also describe the rooms, which helped most. As a matter of fact, I found that taking a camera is sometimes a mistake for me because it's better for me to be able to look at something and describe it. Then I can come back and recreate. On the other hand when I went to Peru, to the Amazon, to research the Xenogenesis books, *Dawn, Adulthood Rites* and *Imago* I needed that camera. I was born in the desert, raised in the desert, didn't know anything but the desert of Southern California. It doesn't necessarily look like a desert because we steal water from everybody, but it's a desert. And to go to a rainforest where everything lives very happily, including any infection you might get was fantastic. I went around with a notebook and began scribbling down everything I saw. This is probably not what you meant by research [to Nalo Hopkinson], but this is what I did constantly. When I was doing the parable books I did three different kinds of research. I went over to my mother's house and volunteered to help her with the gardening, because my characters had to know how to tend a garden in order to live. My mother's garden was her other kid, she always said when she retired she wanted a big garden, and she got one. She knew plants; she could make a dead stick grow as far as I was concern. So, if I helped her with her gardening, she would answer my questions. That was another kind of research. All sorts of things turn into research even if they wouldn't normally be [considered as such].

Bibliography

Alaimo, Stacy. "Skin Dreaming: The Bodily Transgressions of Fielding Burke, Octavia Butler, and Linda Hogan." Found in *Ecofeminist Literary Criticism: Theory, Interpretation, Pedagogy*. Edited by Greta Claire Gaad and Patrick D. Murphy. Illinois: University of Illinois Press, 1998: 123–38.

Aldiss, Brian W. *Trillion Year Spree: The History of Science Fiction*. New York, NY: Avon Books, 1986.

Alford, C. Fred. *The Self in Social Theory*. New Haven: Yale University Press, 1991.

Althusser, Louis. *Positions*. Essentiel; 9. Paris: Iditions sociales, 1976.

Andreolle, Donna Spalding. "Utopias of Old, Solutions for the New Millennium: a Comparative Study of Christian Fundamentalism in M.K. Wren's *A Gift Upon the Shore* and Octavia Butler's *Parable of the Sower*," *Utopian Studies*; 2001, Vol. 12 Issue 2, 114.

Apter, Andrew. *Black Critics & Kings: The Hermeneutics of Power in Yoruba Society*. Chicago & London: University of Chicago Press, 1992.

Asimov, Isaac. *Foundation*. Garden City, NY: Doubleday. 1951.

——. *Nebula Award Stories 8*. New York, 1973, Preface.

Attebery, Brian. *The Fantasy Tradition in American Literature*. Bloomington: Indiana University Press, 1980.

Barr, Marleen S. *Future Females: A Critical Anthology*, (Bowling Green, Ohio: Bowling Green State University Popular Press, 1981).

Bidwell, Duane R. "Carl Jung's *Memories, Dreams, Reflections*: A Critique Informed by Postmodernism," *Pastoral Psychology*, Vol. 49, No. 1, 2000, 13–20.

Blassingame, John W. *The Slave Community; plantation life in the antebellum South*. New York: Oxford University Press, 1972.

Blum, Joanne. *Transcending Gender: The Male/Female Double in Women's Fiction*. Ann Arbor, MI: University of Microfilms Inc, 1988.

147

Beal, Frances. "Black Women and the Science Fiction Genre: Interview with Octavia Butler," found in *Black Scholar* 17 (March-April 1986):14–18.

Berry, Mary Frances. *Long Memory: the Black experience in America*. New York: Oxford University Press, 1982.

Blight, David. "A Psalm of Freedom," An introduction to the *Narrative of the Life of Frederick Douglass* (Boston: Bedford Books of ST. Martin's Press, 1993).

Bogle, Donald. *Toms, coons, mulattoes, mammies, and bucks; an interpretive history of Blacks in American films*. New York: Viking Press, 1973.

———. *Blacks in American films and Television: an encyclopedia*. New York: Garland Publications, 1988.

Brown, William W. *Clotel, or the Presidents Daughter*. North Stratford: Ayer Company Publishers Inc., 1969.

Brox, Ali, "Every age has the vampire it needs": Octavia Butler's Vampiric Vision in *Fledgling*." *Utopian Studies* 19.3 (2008): 391–409.

Butler, Judith. *Gender Trouble: feminism and the subversion of identity*. New York: Routledge, 1990.

———. *Bodies That Matter: On the Discursive Limits of "Sex."* New York and London: Routledge, 1993.

———. "Foucault and the Paradox of Bodily Inscriptions." *The Journal of Philosophy* 86, (Nov 1989): 601–7.

Butler, Octavia E. *Patternmaster*. New York, NY: Warner Books, 1976.

———. *Mind of My Mind*. Garden City, NY: Doubleday, 1977.

———. *Survivor*. New York: Doubleday & Company, Inc., 1978.

———. *Kindred*. Boston: Beacon Press. 1979.

———. *Wildseed*. New York, NY: Warner Books, 1980.

———. *Clay's Ark*. New York, NY: Warner Books, 1984.

———. *Dawn*. New York, NY: Warner Books, 1987.

———. *Adulthood Rites*. New York, NY: Warner Books, 1988.

———. *Imago*. New York, NY: Warner Books, 1989.

———. *Parable of the Sower*. New York: Four Walls Eight Windows, 1993.

———. *Parable of the Talents*. New York: Seven Stories Press, 1998

———. *Fledgling*. New York: Seven Stories Press, 2005.

———. *Bloodchild and Other Stories*. New York: Four Walls Eight Windows, 1995, 2005.

———. *Parable of the Talents*. New York: Seven Stories Press, 1998.

Burroughs Catherine B. and Ehrenreich, David. *Reading the Social Body*. Iowa City: University of Iowa Press, 1993.

Cameron, James. "Aliens." 20th Century Fox, 1986.

Carby, Hazel. *Reconstructing Womanhood: The Emergence of the Afro-American Women Novelist*. New York: Oxford University Press, 1987.

Chambers, Samuel A. "Sex and the Problem of the Body: Reconstructing Judith Butler's Theory of Sex/Gender." *Body & Society* 13:4 (2007): 47–75.

Christian, Barbara. "Somebody Forgot to Tell Somebody Something." in *Wild Women in the Worldwind*. edited by Joanne Braxton and Andree Nicola McLaughlin, New Jersey: Rutgers UniversityPress, 1990. 326–41.

———. "Trajectories of Self-Definition." in *Conjuring: Black Women, Fiction, and Literary Tradition*. edited by Marjorie Pryse and Hortense Spillers. Bloomington: Indiana University Press, 1985. 233–48.

Cobb, John B., Jr., and Griffin, David R. *Process Theology: An Introductory Exposition*: Philadelphia: The Westminster Press, 1976.

Conde, Maryse. *I, Tituba: Black Witch of Salem*. (North Carolina: U P of Virginia, 1992.

Cornelius, Janet Duitsman. *When I Can Read My Title Clear: Literacy, Slavery, and Religion in the Antebellum South*. South Carolina: University of South Carolina Press, 1991.

Cuniberti, John. *The Birth of a Nation: a formal shot-by-shot analysis together with microfiche*. Woodbridge, Conn: Research Publications, 1979.

Curtis, Claire P. "Rehabilitating Utopia: Feminist Science Fiction and Finding the Ideal." *Contemporary Justice Review*, Vol. 8, No. 2, June 2005, pp. 147–62.

———. "Theorizing Fear: Octavia Butler and the Realist Utopia," *Utopian Studies* 19.3 (2008): 411–31.

Davis, Angela Yvonne. *Women, Race, & Class*. New York: Random House, 1981.

Dean, Carolyn. "Productive Hypothesis: Foucault, gender, and the history of sexuality." in *History and Theory*. Oct. 1994,v33, 271 (26).

Dery, Mark. "Black to the Future: Interviews with Samual R. Delany, Greg Tate, and Tricia Rose." in *Flame Wars: The Discourse of Cyberculture*. ed. by Mark Deny. Durham, NC: Duke University Press, 1994. 180–87.

DiTommaso, Lorenzo. "History and Historical Effect in Dune." in *Science-Fiction-Studies*. Greencastle, IN. 1992 Nov, 19:3 (58), 311–25.

Dixon, Thomas. *The clansman; an historical romance of the Ku Klux Klan*. Ridgewood, NJ: Gregg Press, 1967.

Donadey, Anne. "African American and Francophone Postcolonial Memory: Octavia Butler's *Kindred* and Assia Djebar's *La feeme sans sepulture*," *Research in African Literatures*, vol 39, number 3, fall 2008, pgs. 65–81.

Douglass, Frederick. *Narrative of the Life of Frederick Douglass: An American Slave*. Boston: Bedford Books of St. Martin's Press, 1993.

Du Bois, W.E.B. *The Souls of Black Folk*. A Norton Critical Edition. Edited by Henry Louis Gates and Terri Hume Oliver. New York: W.W. Norton & Company, 1999.

———. "The Comet." (1920) in *Dark Matter: A Century of speculative Fiction From the African Diaspora*. Edited by Sheree R. Thomas. New York: Time Warner, 2000, 5–18.

Drusius, Joannes (1550–1616). *Alphabet of Ben Sira. Latin & Hebrew*. Franerae, excudebat Aegidius Radaeus, 1597.

Due, Tananarive. *The Between*. New York: Harper Perennial, 1995.

———. *My Soul to Keep*. New York: Harper Prism, 1997.

———. *The Living Blood*. New York: Washington Square Press, 2001.

———. *Blood Colony*. New York: Atria Books, 2008.

Ferguson, Moira. *History of Mary Prince, A West Indian Slave*. Ann Arbor: University of Michigan Press, 1997.

Fincher, David. "Alien 3." 20th Century Fox, 1992.

Fishkin, Shelley Fisher. *Was Huck Black?: Mark Twain and African-American voices*. New York: Oxford University Press, 1993.

Foucault, Michel. "Nietzsche, Genealogy, History." in *Language, Counter-Memory, Practice: Selected Essays and Interviews*. edited by Donald F. Bouchard. Trans. Donald Bouchard and Sherry Simon. Oxford: Basil Blackwell, 1977. 139–64.

——. *The History of Sexuality*. 1st American ed. New York: Pantheon Books, 1978.

——. *Discipline and Punish: The Birth of the Prison*. New York: Vintage Books, 1995.

Fox-Genovese, Elizabeth. *Within the plantation household: Black and White women of the old South*. Chapel Hill, NC: University of North Carolina Press, 1988.

Franklin, John Hope. *From Slavery to Freedom: A History of African Americans*, 5th edition, New York: Alfred A. Knopf, Inc., 1980.

Frazier, E. Franklin. *The Negro Church in America*. New York: Schocken Books, 1974.

Fry, Joan. "An Interview with Octavia Butler," *Poets and Writers Magazine*, 25:2, (March/April 1997): 58–69.

Gates, Henry Louis, Jr. *The Signifying Monkey: A Theory of African-American Literary Criticism*. New York: Oxford University Press, 1988. 3–124.

Gates, Henry Louis, Jr. *"Race," writing, and difference*. Chicago: University of Chicago Press, 1986.

Gateward, Frances. "Daywalkin' Night Stalkin' Bloodsuckas: Black Vampires in Contemporary Film." *Genders* 40 (2004): 38 paras. 1 Nov. 2007, www.genders.org/g40/g40/gateward.html

"Genius Author Takes Sci-Fi Approach to Earthly Issues." *Los Angeles Times*, July 22, 1995. Metro; Part B; Page 5.

Govan, Sandra Y. "*Fledgling* by Octavia Butler." Found in *Obsidian III: Literature in the African Diaspora*. Volume 6, No.2/volume 7, No. 1, Fall/Winter 2005–Spring/Summer 2006, pgs. 40–43.

——. "Going to See the Woman: A Visit with Octavia E Butler." Found in *Obsidian III: Literature in the African Diaspora*. Volume 6, No.2/volume 7, No. 1, Fall/Winter 2005–Spring/Summer 2006, pgs. 14–39.

Griffith, D.W., director. *The Birth of a Nation*. Majestic Motion Picture Company, 1915.

Grosz, Elizabeth. "Inscriptions and Body-Maps: Representations and the Corporeal." *Feminine, Masculine, and Representation*, ed. Terry Threadgold and Anne Cranny-Francis (Sydney, 1999).

——. *Volatile bodies: towards a new corporeal feminism*. Bloomington, IN: Indiana University Press, 1994.

Haley, Alex. *The Autobiography of Malcolm X*. New York: Ballantine Books, 1964. 164–168.

Hampton, Gregory J. "In Memoriam: Octavia E. Butler," *Callaloo* 29:2, (Spring) 2006.

——. "Migration and Capital of the Body: Octavia Butler's *Parable of the Sower*" *College Language Association Journal* 49.1 (Sep2005): 56–73.

——. "Vampires and Utopia: Reading Racial and Gender Politics in the Fiction of Octavia Butler" *College Language Association Journal* 52.1(Sep2008):74–91.

Haraway, Donna. *Primate Visions: Gender, Race, and Nature in the World of Modern Science*. New York: Routledge, 1989.

——. "A Cyborg Manifesto: Science, Technology, and Socialist-Feminism in the Late Twentieth Century." *Simians, Cyborgs, and Women: The Reinvention of Nature*. New York: Routledge, 1991.

Harper, Frances E. *Iola Leroy*. Boston: Beacon Press, 1987.

Harrison, Rosalie. "Sci-Fi Visions: an interview with Octavia Butler,"*Equal Opportunity Forum*, (Nov 1980): 34.

Heilbrun, Caroln G. *Toward a Recognition of Androgyny.* New York: W.W. Norton, 1964.

Heinlein, Robert A. *Stranger in a strange land.* New York: Putnam Press, 1961.

———. "Science Fiction; Its Nature, Faults and Virtues," found in *The Science Fiction Novel: Imagination and Social Criticism,* ed. B. Davenport. Chicago, 1969, pp. 21–30.

Helford, Elyce. "Would you really die than bear my young?:" the construction of gender, race, and species in Octavia E. Butler's "Bloodchild." *African-American Review.* Summer 1994, v28, 259 (13).

Herbert, Frank. *Dune.* Philadelphia: Chilton Books, 1965.

Hodge, Joanna. "A Small History of the Body." *Angelaki: Journal of the Theoretical Humanities* 3:3, (1998): 31–43.

Holloway, Karla F.C. *Mooring and Metaphors: Figures of Culture and Gender in Black Women's Literature.* New Brunswick: Rutgers University Press, 1992.

Holy Bible King James Version, The. Nashville: Holman Bible Publishers, 1989.

Hopkinson, Nalo. *Brown Girl in the Ring.* New York: Warner Books, 1998.

———. *The Salt Roads.* New York: Warner Books, 2003.

———. *The New Mooon's Arms.* New York: Warner Books, 2007.

Hopkins, Pauline E. *Contending Forces.* New York: Oxford University Press, 1988.

Hooks, Bell. *Talking Back: thinking feminist-thinking black.* Boston, MA: South End Press, 1989.

———. "Representing Whiteness in the Black Imagination." *Cultural Studies.* edited by Lawrence Grossberg, Cary Nelson, and Paula Treichler. New York: Routledge, 1992. pp. 338–46.

———. *Feminist theory from margin to center.* Boston, MA: South End Press, 1984.

Hufford, Don. "The Religious Thought of W.E.B. Du Bois." found in *Journal of Religious Thought,* 1997, vol. 53/54 Issue 2/1, p73, 22p.

Hutnyk, John. "Hybridity,"*Ethnic and Racial Studies,* Vol. 28 No. 1, January 2005 pp. 79–201.

Jacobs, Harriet A. *Incidents in the Life of a Slave Girl.* Cambridge, Mass: Harvard Univeristy Press, 1987.

Jameson, Fredric. *The Political Unconscious.* Ithaca, New York: Cornell University Press, 1981.

———. *Archaeologies of the Future: The Desire Called Utopia and Other Science Fictions.* London & New York: Verso, 2005.

———. *Postmodernism: Or the Cultural Logic of Late Capitalism.* Durham: Duke University Press, 1991.

Johnson, Charles. *Being and Race: Black Writing Since 1970.* London: Serpent's Tail, 1988.

Johnson, Judith. "Women and Vampires: Nightmare or Utopia?" *Kenyon Review;* Winter 1993, Vol. 15 Issue 1, 72–80.

Jones, Gayl. *Corregidora.* Boston: Beacon Press, 1975.

Ketterer, David. "*The Left Hand of Darkness:* Ursula K. LeGuin's Archetypal 'Winter-Journey.'" *Riverside Quarterly,* Gainsville, FL: 1973, n5, 288–97.

Krimmer, Elisabeth. "Mama's Baby, Papa's Maybe: Paternity and Bildung in Goethe's Wilhelm Meisters Lehrjahre." *The German Quarterly* 77.3 (Summer 2004) p. 257–77.

Lacan, Jacques. *Feminine sexuality: Jacques Lacan and the icole freudenne*. New York: Patheon Books, 1985.

———. *Feminine Sexuality*. New York: W.W. Norton & Company, 1982.

Lawrence, Matt. *Like a Splinter in Your Mind: The Philosophy behind the Matrix Trilogy*. Malden, MA: Blackwell Publishing, 2004.

Lefanu, Sarah. *In the Chinks of the World Machine: Feminism & Science Fiction*. London: The Women's Press, 1988.

LeGuin, Ursula K. *The Left Hand of Darkness*. New York: Walker Press, 1969.

Levine, Lawrence W. *Black Culture and Black Consciousness: Afro-American folk thought from slavery to freedom*. New York: Oxford University Press, 1977.

Luckhurst, Roger. *Science Fiction: Cultural History of Literature*. Cambridge: Polity Press, 2005.

McCaffery, Larry. "Interview with Octavia Butler." in *Across the Wounded Galaxies*. ed. Urbana and Chicago: University of Illinois Press, 1990.

McCoy, Beth A. "Walking the 5: Octavia Butler's *Parable of the Sower*." Found in *The Sonia Sanchez Literary Review*, Volume 9, Number 1, Fall 2003, Special Issue "Black Travel Writing," guest editor R. Victoria Arana, 223–36.

McDowell, Deborah. *The Changing Same: black women's literature, criticism, and theory*. Bloomington, IN: Indiana University Press, 1995.

———. "The Changing Same: Generational Connections and Black Women Novelists," in *Reading black, reading feminist*. New York: Penguin Books, 1990 pp. 91–115.

McKay, Nellie Y., Gates, Henry Louis Jr. *The Norton Anthology of African American Literature*. New York: W.W. Norton, 2003.

McLaurin, Melton A. *Celia, A Slave: A True Story*. New York: Avaon Books, 1993.

McKnight, Utz. "The African in America: Race and the Politics of Diaspora," *African Identities* vol. 6, no. 1, (Feb 2008):63–81.

Mehaffy, Marilyn and Keating AnaLouise. "'Radio Imagination:' Octavia Butler on the Poetics of Narrative Embodiment." *MELUS*, Volume 26, Number 1 (Spring 2001), pgs. 45–76.

Meier, August. *Negro Thought in America 1880–1915*. Michigan: University of Michigan Press, 1966.

Melzer, Patricia. *Alien Constructions: Science Fiction and Feminist Thought*. Austin: University of Texas Press, 2006.

Mitchell, Angelyn. "Not Enough of the Past: Octavia E. Butler's *Kindred*," found in *The Freedom to Remember: Narrative, Slavery, and Gender in Contemporary Black Women's Fiction*. By Mitchell. (New Brunswick, NJ: Rutgers University Press, 2002, 42–63).

Mixon, Veronica. "Futurist Woman." Essence. 9: 12, April 1979. 12–15.

Morrison, Toni. *Beloved*. New York: Signet Book, 1991.

———. *Playing in the Dark*. Cambridge, MA: Harvard University Press, 1992. v–xiii.

Morth, Ingo. "Elements of Religious Meaning in Science Fiction Literature." *Social Compass*; 1987, Vol.34 Issue 1, 87–122.

Nicholson, Marjorie. *Voyage to the Moon* (New York: Macmillan, 1948) pp. 1f; phonograph record of the broadcast published by Longines-Withaure Co.; found in *Science Fiction Handbook*, Revised by L. Sprague de Camp and Catherine Crook de Camp (New York: McGraw-Hill Book Company, 1975 pp. 1–2. Taken from the radio dramatization, *The War of the Worlds: the complete original radio broadcast*. New York, NY: M.F. Distribution Co., 1978. Two sound discs (CA. 60 min): 33 1/3 rpm; 12 in.

Phillips, Jerry. "The Intuition of the Future: Utopia and Catastrophe in Octavia Butler's *Parable of the Sower*." *Novel* Spring/Summer 2002: 299–311.

Probyn, Elspeth. *Sexing the Self: Gendered Positions in Cultural Studies*. London: Routledge, 1993.

Putzi, Jennifer. "Raising the Stigma": Black Womanhood and the Marked Body in Pauline Hopkin's *Contending Forces*." *College Literature* 31.2 (Spring 2004): 1–21.

Raffel, Burton. "Genre to the rear, race and gender to the fore: the novels of Octavia E. Butler." *The Literary Review*. Spring 1995, v38, 454 (8).

Rieder, John. *Colonialism and the Emergence of Science Fiction*. Connecticut: Wesleyan University Press, 2008.

Riggs, Don. "Future and 'Progress' in Foundation and Dune." in *Spectrum of the Fantastic*. Westport, CT: Greenwood, 1988. 113–17.

Roberts, Adam. *The History of Science Fiction*. New York: Palgrave Macmillan Press, 2005.

Rodney, Walter. *How Europe Underdeveloped* Africa. London: Bogle-L'Ouverture Publications, 1972.

Rubenstein, Roberta. *Boundaries of the Self: Gender, Culture, Fiction*. Chicago: University of Illinois, 1982.

Rushdy, Ashraf H.A. "Families of orphans: relation and disrelation in Octavia Butler's *Kindred. College English*. Feb 1993, v55, n2, p. 135 (23).

Scott, Ridley. "Alien." 20th Century Fox, 1979.

Sewdgwick, Eve Kosofsky. *Epistemology of the Closet*. Berkeley: University of California Press, 1990.

Shinn, Thelma J. "The Wise Witches: Black women mentors in the Fiction of Octavia E. Butler." in *Conjuring: Black Women, Fiction, and Literary Tradition*. edited by Marjorie Pryse and Hortence Spillers. Bloomington: Indiana University Press, 1985. 203–15.

Silko, Leslie Marmon. *Yellow Woman and a Beauty of the Spirit*. New York: Touchstone, 1996.

Soyinka, Wole. "The Fourth Stage: Through the Mysteries of Ogun to the Origin of Yoruba Tragedy." *Art, Dialogue & Outrage: essays on literature and culture*. New York: Pantheon Books, 1988.

Spaulding, A. Timothy. *Re-Forming the Past: History, The Fantastic, and the Postmodern Slave Narrative* (Ohio, Columbus: Ohio State University Press, 2005).

Spillers, Hortence. "Mama's Baby, Papa's Maybe," found in *Within the Circle*. edited by Angelyn Mitchell. Durham, NC: Duke University Press, 1994, pp. 454–81.

Stark, Rodney. "Physiology and Faith: Addressing the 'Universal' Gender Difference in Religious Commitment." *Journal of the Scientific Study of Religion*; Sep 2002, Vol. 41 Issue 3, 495–507.

Steinberg, Marc. "Inventing History in Octavia Butler's Postmodern Slave Narrative," *African American Review*, Volume 38, Number3, 2004, pp. 467–76.

Stevenson, Randall. *Modernist Fiction an Introduction*. New York: Harvester Wheatsheaf, 1992.

Stillman, Peter G. "Dystopian Critues, Utopian Possibilities, and Human Purposes in Octavia Butler's Parables." Utopian Studies, Vol. 14, 2003, pp. 15–35.

Sundquist, Eric J. *To Wake the Nations: race in the making of American literature.* Cambridge, Mass: Belknap Press of Havard University Press, 1993.

Synnott, Anthony. *The Body Social: Symbolism, Self and Society.* London and New York: Routledge, 1993.

Thomas, Sheree R. *Dark Matter: A Century of Speculative Fiction From The African Diaspora.* New York: Time Warner Company, 2000.

Thomson, Oliver. *A History of Sin.* Edinburgh: Canongate, 1993. *The Interpreter's dictionary of the Bible.* New York: Abington Press, 1962.

Toth, John F. "Power and Paradox in an African American Congregation," *Review of Religious Research*, Vol. 40, No. 3 (March, 1999).

Torjesen, Karen Jo. Genders, Book Review, *Bodies, Religion: Adjunct Proceedings of the XVIIth Congress for the History of Religions.* Edited by Sylvia Marcos. ALER Publications, 2000. Found in *Journal of the American Academy of Religion*, Dec 2001, Vol. 69, Number 4, 945–48.

Turner Bryan S. "The Body in Western Society: Social Theory and its Perspective." Found in *Religion and the Body.* Edited by Sarah Coakley. Cambridge University Press 2000. p. 15–41.

Vint, Sherryl. *Bodies of Tomorrow: Technology, Subjectivity, Science Fiction.* Toronto: University of Toronto Press, 2007.

———. "Only by Experience:" Embodiment and the Limitations of Realism in Neo-Slave Narratives." *Science-Fiction Studies*, Volume 34 pt2 J1 2007, pp. 241–61.

———. "Becoming Other: Animals, Kinship, and Butler's *Clay's Ark*," *Science Fiction Studies*, Vol. 32, No. 2 (July, 2005): 281–300.

Walker, Alice. *In Search of Our Mothers' Gardens.* New York: Harcourt Brace Jovanovich, Publishers, 1983.

Walker, Barbara G. *The Woman's Encyclopedia of Myths and Secrets* New York: HarperCollins, 1983.

West, Cornel. *Race Matters.* New York: Vintage Books, 1994.

White, Eric. "The Erotics of Becoming: Xenogenesis and *The Thing*." *Science Fiction Studies* Volume 20, Number 3. (1993): 394–408.

Zaki, Hoda M. "Future Tense." in *The Women's Review of Books*. Vol. xi, Nos. 10–11, July 1994. 37–38.

———. "Utopia, dystopia, and ideology in the science fiction of Octavia Butler." *Science Fiction Studies.* July 1990, v17, n2, p239 (13).

Zimmer, Marion. "Interview with Octavia Butler." *Marion Zimmer Bradley's Fantasy Magazine.* July 2005. www.adherents.com/people/pb/Octavia_Butler.html

Zindell, David. "Octavia Butler: Persistence." Locus Magazine. June 2000. www.locusmag.com/2000/issues/06/Butler.html

Index

resistance: passive,15, 23, 38, 45n5, 60

Rhodes, Natasha: Blade Trinity, 120

Sartre, Jean-Paul, 27, 45n3
seed village, 29, 37–39
serpent, 44
shape-shifter, xvi, xxiv, xxvii n8, 31
Shelley, Mary: Frankenstein, xxvi n6
Shinn, Thelma, 62
Silko, Leslie, 101–2
slave narrative: xviii, xxvii, 1–2, 6, 22–23, 28–29, 96n2, 97, 127; feminine, xx, 6–7, 21, 124–25; postmodern, 3, 8–9, 85
Sodom and Gomorra, 40
Soyinka, Wole: chthonic realm, 70; "Fourth Stage," 71–74, 79; The Strong Breed, 69–70; W.E.B. Du Bois, 80
space travel, 10, 113n4
Spaulding, Timothy, xviii, 1–3, 8–10
specter from the future, 16
Spillers, Hortense, 48, 50, 54, 64
subjectivity: xxii, 127; female, 48; male, 48; cyborg, xv
survival: xix, xxi, xxv, 14, 16, 20, 34, 41, 52, 58–59, 67, 71–72, 76–77, 80, 86, 88, 91, 96, 104, 107, 110–13, 117; mechanisms xxv, 127
symbiotic relationship, 17, 75, 101, 105, 110–11, 120

technology: xv; alien, 59, 119; fiction, 84; of identity, xxiv, 47–48; science, xx, 124; space travel, 113
teleportation: imagination, 10
third sex, 73, 78
Thomas, Sheree: Dark Matter, xii; dark matter, xii–xiii
Thompson, Robert Farris: Flash of the Spirit, 71
time machine: metaphysical, 9; time travel, 10
transformative possibilities, xxv, 100–101, 104

utopia, xix, xxi, 30, 67, 70, 83–84, 86, 88, 92, 96, 116, 118–20, 122–23, 127
Vint, Sherryl: xii, 18, 24n1; "Becoming Other: Animals, Kinship, and Butler's Clay's Ark," 35; Bodies of Tomorrow, xxii–xxv, 2, 31

Walker, Alice, xxvii n10, 112, 116
West, Cornel: Race Matters, xiii
Wheatley seed village, 37–39, 41–43, 45
Wheatley, Phillis, 96n2
womanism, xvii, xxvii, 77, 81n4, 112, 113n5

Yacub, 42–43
Yoruba: aesthetic, 70–72, 74; art, 72; deity, 79; sensibility, 45, 71, 79; tragedy, 71, 73